The Empire Triumphant

The Empire Triumphant

Race, Religion and Rebellion
in the Star Wars *Films*

KEVIN J. WETMORE, JR.

McFarland & Company, Inc., Publishers
Jefferson, North Carolina, and London

This book has not been prepared, approved, licensed or sponsored by Twentieth Century Fox, Lucasfilm, or any entity involved in creating or producing *Star Wars*.

LIBRARY OF CONGRESS CATALOGUING-IN-PUBLICATION DATA

Wetmore, Kevin J., 1969–
    The empire triumphant : race, religion and rebellion in the Star
wars films / Kevin J. Wetmore, Jr.
        p.   cm.
    Includes bibliographical references and index.

    ISBN 0-7864-2219-X (softcover : 50# alkaline paper) ∞

    1. Star Wars films—History and criticism.   2. Race in motion
pictures.   3. Motion pictures—Religious aspects.   I. Title.
PN1995.9.S695W48   2005
791.43'75 — dc22   2005020088

British Library cataloguing data are available

Cover images ©2005 PhotoSpin

Manufactured in the United States of America

McFarland & Company, Inc., Publishers
   Box 611, Jefferson, North Carolina 28640
      www.mcfarlandpub.com

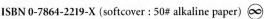

To Tom Quinn,
my childhood best friend with whom I watched the films,

to my father, Kevin Sr.,
with whom I watch them now,

and to my nephew Sean Fitzgerald,
one of the newest generation of fans—
I want a lightsaber, too, man.

Acknowledgments

A galaxy of individuals and institutions assisted in the development of this book:

Thanks to *Studies in Popular Culture*, Michael Dunne and Sara Lewis Dunne, its editors, and the Popular Culture Association in the South for publishing an early version of this research.

Thanks to the Department of Theatre, the College of Arts, Media, and Communication, and the administration and faculty of the California State University, Northridge, under whose generous auspices this work was researched and completed.

Thanks to the administration and faculty of Denison University and the Department of Theatre for their support of early research on this project.

Thanks to Erin Malone, Anthony Miller, Andrea Swangard, and Cynthia Turnbull for their insights, thoughts and observations. Thanks as well to Dr. Keiko McDonald who has opened my eyes to viewing Japanese cinema as more than just a fan but as a scholar.

Thanks to Dover Publications and the Special Collections and Archives of the Oviatt Library, California State University, Northridge, for their assistance in providing photographs for this book.

To paraphrase Sir Isaac Newton, if I can see these films differently, it is only because I am standing on the shoulders of giants, from Frantz Fanon and Edward Said to Ursula K. Le Guin to Henry A. Giroux to Patrick Brantlinger. One of my mentors in graduate school said that the role of the scholar is to make the connections that have not yet been seen. It is an honor to draw upon the work of so many fine individuals.

Thanks to my family: Kevin Sr., Eleanor, Lisa, John, Sean, Tom, Eileen, Toni, Mike, Faith, and Daniel, as well as my deepest gratitude to my wife, Maura, without whom none of this would be possible.

Thanks as well is due to George Lucas, Lucasfilm, and the thousands who have worked to create the phenomenon that is *Star Wars*. As much as I may critique their work, I also admire it and hold it dear and like many fans, find that it has filled my hours and given me purpose. Change whatever they may want, however, I know that Greedo did *not* fire first.

Contents

Of Fanon
and Fanboys

It is not rebellion itself which is noble but the demands it makes upon us.
— Albert Camus, *The Plague*

I hold it that a little rebellion, now and then, is a good thing, and as necessary in the political world as storms in the physical.
— Thomas Jefferson, 1787 letter to James Madison

The existence of an armed struggle shows that the people are decided to trust to violent methods only.
— Frantz Fanon, The Wretched of the Earth

Popular culture is a contradictory site of pleasure and ideological contest. We enjoy the films we seek out to watch. That is, after all, the primary purpose of most filmgoers: to enjoy themselves. And the *Star Wars* saga is indeed enjoyable. Yet behind it also lurks ideological assertions and assumptions and a complex interaction between the imaginative world of the films and the real world which it can and does reflect.

The growth of popular culture studies has made virtually every cultural product worthy of study. The popular culture represented most obviously by the *Star Wars* films needs to be read and considered using the same tools and methodologies which students use to read Conrad, Hemingway, Achebe, and other significant literary figures, or study such films as *Citizen Kane, The Grand Illusion, 8½,* or *The Bicycle Thief.*

Arthur Asa Berger reminds us to distinguish between "education"— the things that we learn, versus "instruction"—formal teaching.[1] One is almost always being educated in one manner or another, and the largest

1

source of the gaining of knowledge for college age Americans is via electronic media (television and the Internet). For the key demographic of males ages 18 to 34 and the large teen market, Benjamin Barber claims, "Disney does more than Duke; Spielberg outweighs Stanford."[2] Richard Simon Keller announces in *Trash Culture* that the narrative of the original *Star Wars* trilogy is "the only story that virtually all ... students know today."[3] My own experience as a college educator has borne this supposition out — students do not necessarily recognize references to the Bible, "masterpieces" of Western literature (such as Dickens, Dostoevsky, or even Twain), or even classic cinema (such as *Citizen Kane, High Noon,* or *The Seven Samurai*), but any mention of "Jedi," "The Force" or blowing up the "Death Star," and no explanation is necessary.

This book concerns itself with the application of the usual aspects of collegiate education — the interpretation and comparison of texts (even cinematic ones) via different methodologies (in this case, postcolonialism)— to this "only story that virtually all ... students know" and discover how American and non–American cultures are appropriated and represented.

Star Wars and American Culture

The world into which *Star Wars* emerged was a radically different one from the world of this writing. The outline for the saga was written during Nixon's presidency and the final days of the Vietnam War: "A very powerful and technological superpower trying to take over a little country of peasants was big on my mind," claims Lucas.[4] In 1977, Jimmy Carter was in the White House. It was the height of the Cold War. High inflation and spiraling oil prices were the norm, affecting the economy and the lives of the average American, and the television miniseries *Roots* dominated American popular culture. Egypt's Anwar Sadat went to Israel as part of an ongoing peace process in the Middle East.

The next two parts of the trilogy, released in 1980 and 1983, entered a world in which the Cold War had been kicked up a notch. President Reagan, using the language of *Star Wars*, cast the Soviet Union as an "evil empire" that had to be brought down. The Soviets had invaded Afghanistan, and small wars and rebellions were occurring with frequency all over the globe. Reagan had also engaged in numerous plans to make a nuclear war winnable, via such programs as the MX missile and the Strategic Defense Initiative. In 1983, the same year *Jedi* was released, one of the top television shows was *The Day After*, directed by Nicholas Meyer, already known for his science fiction work, in which a nuclear war between the Soviet Union and the United States and its aftereffects were demonstrated. In short, the original trilogy is reflective of the fight between "freedom-loving" people who are fighting an evil empire that has enough destructive power to destroy a planet. *The Day After* demonstrated that both the United States and the Soviet Union had that power as well.

The new trilogy, formulated and released between 1999 and 2005, is much more concerned with evil corporations (what else are "The Trade Federation" and "The Techno Union" if not stand-ins for contemporary corporations, especially foreign-owned ones), terrorists (what are the separatists of *Clones*, which begins with Amidala's ship being bombed just when all thought it had landed safely on Coruscant, if not terrorists?), and the corruption of the political process (the one person who seems to be a strong and good chancellor, Palpatine, is, in fact, the one orchestrating the violence and terrorism to consolidate his power). The second trilogy reflects a different world from the original one — the evil empire is replaced by more complex and difficult challenges, yet both trilogies reflect the eras that produced them.

Not only is the *Star Wars* series an embodiment of key American political and cultural concerns, the films themselves have become the embodiment of American culture. Will Brooker refers to the *Star Wars* saga as "one of the key cultural benchmarks of the last thirty years."[5] Its imagery, characters, terminology, concepts, and plots are almost universally recognizable, not because of the mythic structure, as Lucas and Joseph Campbell have argued, but simply because global marketing of the films have ensured that more people have encountered these movies than almost any other. As Nick Clooney notes, "It is a measure of the lasting impact of *Star Wars* that a number of its character names are now used as generic terms to describe a particular kind of personality."[6]

Will Brooker argues, correctly so, that *Star Wars* has also created a community, a culture, and a common ground for people. His book *Using the Force: Creativity, Community and Star Wars Fans* analyzes the role the films have played in not only the creation of individual fan identity, but also in the creation of entire communities, virtual and real.[7] *Star Wars* is community-creating. It has resulted in symbolic relational culture — the moment when a group of otherwise unconnected individuals' shared appreciation of an aspect of popular culture "fuses them in an intimate way."[8] Fans of the films have a shared language, concepts and codes.

Even beyond fan culture, the language of *Star Wars* has entered the popular lexicon: Jedi, "May the Force be with you," the "dark side," Luke Skywalker, Darth Vader, Wookiee, droid, and many other words and phrases are recognizable around the world. Not only in the United States, not only in the English-speaking world, but across cultures the films have found not only a following but a popular audience that has remained knowledgeable about the films long after their initial release.

The *Star Wars* series is also, however, an industry, a business, and, in the words of Brooker, a "multi-million dollar global franchise, a commercialized enterprise run by an increasingly stubborn and reclusive creative mastermind."[9] Although, truth be told — it is a multibillion dollar global franchise, "the most successful film franchise in history," according to a 2005 CNN report, in which it was noted that the combined income of the first five *Star Wars* films has outgrossed the combined income of the *twenty-one* James Bond movies.[10] As of May 2005, before the opening of *Revenge of the Sith*, the estimated worldwide theatrical gross of the first five films was $3.4 billion, with another $9 billion in merchandising.[11] The websites of Barnes and Noble and Amazon.com list more than 1,000 titles each based upon the series— novels, film tie-ins, graphic novels, scholarly analyses, biographies of Lucas, and others. Many of these are published by Lucas Books, the publishing wing of the Lucasfilm empire. Lucasfilm has not only copyrighted its intellectual property, it has trademarked it. Each year hundreds of businesses petition for marketing and licensing rights for *Star Wars*. The money generated by toys, books, food, games, clothing, and so forth linked to *Star Wars* is in the billions, more than that generated by any single film or group of films at the box office. Nick Clooney concludes, quite accurately, that "*Star Wars* changed the way we make movies."[12] It has also changed the way we market movies, understand culture, and do business.

Who the fans are is a key issue in the study of *Star Wars*, particularly as it relates to the marketing and "ownership" of the films. The slang term "fanboys" is often used to describe not only *Star Wars* fans, but also those of other subcultures, such as those who are fans of graphic novels, the *Star Trek* series, and/or other science fiction, science fantasy, and speculative fictions in a variety of medias. As the name suggests, these individuals are overwhelmingly male. They are also most likely white and middle class with disposable income that allows them to pursue (and collect items related to) their narrative of interest. Thus, the *Star Wars* marketing is often aimed at the young, white, male middle-class demographic. It might be argued that the films themselves are aimed at the same demographic as target audience — the main characters are white males, with women in subservient roles and people of color in minor roles or absent.[13] The films themselves are also aimed at youth. The sheer amount of merchandise related to the film needs a target audience with a substantial disposable income, but many of the items (toys, games, bed sheets, breakfast cereal, pajamas) are aimed at a young consumer. According to Lucas, in an interview with Stephen Zito, the target audience is "fourteen and maybe even younger than that."[14] The merchandise is to be purchased by middle-class parents to satisfy their children's desire for things linked to a film marketed to them.[15]

It's only a movie, right?

There are many arguments or defenses that fans, students, or others might make against a postcolonial critique of the films, and these opinions are often heard when teaching undergraduates and attempting to show them the ideologies and assumptions behind things they ordinarily engage uncritically. The first and most often heard defense is, "It's just a movie!" This argument is quite simply wrong. There is no such thing as "just a movie"; all films are the product of the culture and individuals who produced it, even if the implications in the film are unintentional. No culture is innocent.

The model for understanding how a popular product aimed at a youthful audience is read and understood in a radically different manner from what its creators intended is Dorfman and Mattelart's *How to Read Donald Duck*, which demonstrably shows that Disney comics denigrate foreigners, shows Americans as obsessed with the accumulation of money, and posits the Third World as primitive, savage, and filled with easily impressed, easily fooled, simple people. While the writers and artists may not have the intention of doing so, the fact that they do demonstrates assumptions and beliefs about foreigners and the Third World on the part of the creators. Such popular culture relies upon stereotypes and implied negativities that result in a continuation of a culture of exploitation and false representation.

Also of particular influence in my thinking in the writing of this book is Eric Greene's award-winning *Planet of the Apes as American Myth: Race, Politics, and Popular Culture*, in which it is argued that the *Planet of the Apes* films, when taken as a whole, form a liberal analysis of race relations and the Vietnam War. The original film is as much about power and violence as *Platoon, Born on the Fourth of July, The Manchurian Candidate*, and *The Deer Hunter*. Greene posits that out of the five *Apes* films, the first two allegorize Vietnam and the last three concern racial relations between blacks and whites.[16] As will be analyzed in the first chapter, science fiction has served as a distancing form, allowing analysis of and commentary on contemporary issues under the guise of the distant future or a fantasy world.

Star Wars is not "just a movie" in a larger sense as well. In late twentieth-century speculative cinema, The Last Starfighter was just a movie; Enemy Mine was just a movie; Battle Beyond the Stars was just a movie. The Star Wars series exerts a powerful cultural influence — it is a touchstone that has changed our culture and changed the way in which movies are made, marketed, and seen. Although every film has ideological assumptions, even the films that are "just a movie," Star Wars also carries a powerful international influence.

The Star Wars milieu has exerted powerful economic force around the world. By 1997, the year of release of the special edition of the original trilogy, the first three films earned almost $1.5 billion at the box office and more than $3 billion in licensing fees.[17] As noted, those numbers have significantly grown. Subsequently, Lucas was able to dictate how Phantom Menace was distributed. Theatres wanting to show the new Star Wars film had to guarantee lengthy runs and follow guidelines set by Lucas. No other filmmaker has been able to dictate such terms.

A second response to a postcolonial critique of the films is that they are anti-imperial. The Rebellion is good; the Empire is bad. How, therefore, are the films pro–Imperial, or at least encouraging of imperialism in the real world? The answer is that the fantasy world serves as a distancing device to hide the construction of the Rebellion as predominantly white (as opposed to most of the rebellions and revolutions of the twentieth century, which often featured people of color as the rebels). As will be analyzed in the following chapters, the films also appropriate Asian culture and offer it up as alien. The films engage in a kind of racial deconstruction in which non–Westerners are represented as aliens, particularly since there is a noticeable lack of non–European human characters. The films, therefore, while seeming to support rebellion against imperialism, actually invert the real world situation in which white characters with Asian names are attacked by Asian aliens with European names.

A third defense follows on the first one, that the target audience is people under 14 who arguably have no knowledge of the real world analogues and who have no real world power. Actually, this defense heightens the problem of the films— that they can shape the real world perceptions of young viewers by creating a world in which negative characters become associated with real world equivalencies. Films teach: Star Wars is education. As will be seen in Chapter 5, the films create a world in which Asians are evil and no humans of color are presented as either worthwhile role models or active role models for viewers. A ten-year-old white boy can focus on Luke or Han. A ten-year-old African-American boy must wait until *Empire* for Lando (a scoundrel and traitor). A generation later, white children can identify with Anakin, Obi-Wan, Qui-Gon, or Amidala. Children of color may identify with Mace Windu for the few minutes he is on the screen. Asians, Latinos, and others non–Western children may identify with nonspeaking extras or aliens but will more likely identify with the white heroes.

Star Wars is family entertainment. Its target audience, as stated by Lucas time and again, is children. It is accessible, inspirational, and offers a clear view of the world, unmuddled by complexity. Good is good, evil is evil. It is this very factor that is offered as another reason to view *Star Wars* as apolitical: the nostalgia for simpler times (and simpler entertainments)—Lucas sought to re-create the films of his boyhood.

Fredric Jameson observes, as others have, correctly so, that Lucas followed *American Graffiti*, one of the inaugural films in this new genre of nostalgia film, with *Star Wars*, itself another nostalgia film.[18] The *Star Wars* series is a nostalgia film in that it does not portray a real past but rather evokes a sense of cultural past — other mediatized experiences. But, notes Jameson, it is not a parody of Saturday afternoon serials; it is a pastiche of them. The key difference, according to Jameson, is that *Star Wars* "satisfies a deep (might I even say repressed?) longing to experience them again."[19]

Star Wars returns us to the serials of the '40s and '50s, evoking *Flash Gordon* and *Buck Rogers* and jungle adventures, Westerns, and space operas. The films return us to childhood, even if we never experienced the Saturday serial.

Not only is the *Star Wars* series rooted in nostalgia, the films originated in reactionary politics and cinema and reinforced both in its audience. Peter Biskind writes:

> *Star Wars* had a profound effect on the culture. It benefited from the retrenchment of the Carter years, the march to the center that followed the end of the Vietnam War. As Lucas was the first to notice, audiences were exhausted by the Sturm und Drang of the 60s.[20]

Audiences desired a return to a simpler time, with a less complex world. Lucas, relying on the models of movie serials before World War II, created and offered a simple, uncomplex world. An audience in search of reaffirmation of a more conservative, simpler world found their needs met in *A New Hope*.

We might even argue that *A New Hope* was a science fantasy version of *American Graffiti*, Lucas's previous film. In *Graffiti*, the Vietnam War will soon begin to dominate their lives (and, in fact, is at the center of *More American Graffiti*, in which Terry goes to fight in Vietnam and several characters are anti-war protesters), although it is only peripheral to the young characters in Modesto in 1962. *Graffiti* also concerns the desire of young people to leave what they see as a dead-end town, the main characters preparing to enter college. In *A New Hope*, the war between the Rebellion and the Empire has not yet reached Tatooine, a dead-end planet without much for its young people to do. Luke wants to go to the Academy (presumably the galactic equivalent of college) and tools around Tatooine in his speeder. By *Empire*, Luke, like Terry, is in the thick of the war.

This book will not engage the films that were not made. It seems incontrovertible, however, that the series could have been much more non-exploitive and more progressive. Lucas, who has revolutionized movies in so many ways—marketing, special effects, sound, story structure and awareness of and increase in "action beats," etc.—chooses to defend colonialist constructions rather than create a more positive and encompassing view of the future.

The Role of Lucas

This book is not a critique of George Lucas, nor do I posit that he is racist, sexist, or in favor of colonialism. No assumptions are made about Lucas, his personal beliefs, or his personal life, nor are any assumptions made about any of the people associated with the films, the philosophies of Lucasfilm and its employees, or even the fans who identify with and love the films.

However, we must also note that Lucas is identified as being not only very much the sole creator of the work but also as being inextricably linked with the films. Lucas himself claims the lion's share of credit for the films:

> In the case of the *Star Wars* films, not only am I the producer, but I wrote the stories, a lot of the casting decisions are made by me, and I pretty much oversee all the special effects.[21]

Even when others direct, such as in *Empire* and *Jedi*, even when others write the screenplay based on Lucas's story, such as in *Empire*, or when Lucas co-writes, as in *Jedi* or *Clones*, Lucas is considered the creator and sole master of the *Star Wars* universe.

Many of the books about the *Star Wars* films are also about Lucas, and conversely many biographies of Lucas cannot separate the man from the movies. The story of *Star Wars* is inextricably intertwined with the story of its creator and vice versa in these biographies. There is an element of hagiography in such books as *Mythmaker: The Life and Work of George Lucas, Skywalking: The Life and Film of George Lucas,* and *Empire Building: The Remarkable, Real-Life Story of Star Wars.*[22] Not only is *Star Wars* rooted in mythology, the making of the films is mythic and mythologized by those who write about it. For many biographers, the story of the Skywalker came from the hand of God to Lucas to us. Kevin Smith, among others, refers to the original films as "The Holy Trilogy."

Lucasfilm, of which Lucas is the sole stockholder and owner, has copyrighted and trademarked everything associated with the films and actively works to protect its intellectual property. Lucas went so far as to seek to control *Star Wars* fan publications, "seeing them as rivals to [his] officially sponsored and corporately run fan organization," as Henry Jenkins reports in his study of fan culture and how cultural consumers become cultural creators.[23] Lucas, as sole owner of the corporation that makes all things *Star Wars,* as the one who takes major, if not sole, credit for the films, and as the one who is linked by biographers (official and unofficial) directly with the material he has created, is thus the one responsible for the content of his films.

Lucas himself acknowledges the cinema's responsibility and culpability as educational. In an interview with Aljean Harmetz he remarked:

> Film and [other] visual entertainment are a pervasively important part of our culture, an extremely significant influence on the way our society operates.... People in the film industry don't want to accept the responsibility that they had a hand in the way the world is loused up. But, for better or worse, the influence of the church, which used to be all-powerful, has been usurped by film.[24]

Accepting Lucas's comments at face value, we must acknowledge three things for the purpose of this study. First, Lucas believes that film exerts a powerful influence on society. Second, Lucas believes that filmmakers are responsible for not only the films they create but also the influence those films have. Third, Lucas sees the cinema as having replaced traditional organized religion as a meaning-maker in audience's lives. For Lucas, film is religion.

Again, neither I nor this book posit the argument that Lucas is racist nor that he nor anyone else involved at any and all levels of the creation of any and all of the *Star Wars* films planned to create racist, exclusionary films. Yet, as Stuart Hall argues, "an ideological discourse does *not* depend on the conscious intentions of those who formulate statements within it."[25] In other words, while Lucas's (and the other filmmakers') announced intentions can and will be taken into account, that they might be counter to the messages and ideologies present in the final film does not discount those messages or ideologies. Or, to put it even simpler — it does not matter whether it matters if Lucas intended his films to be racist.

What Henry A. Giroux asks of Larry Clark, I ask of George Lucas: The "pertinent question" is not whether Lucas is racist, but rather "whether the effects of his cinematic representations perpetuate racist discourse and practices in the wider society."[26] The problem is not simply that there are few nonwhite performers in the *Star Wars* movies (as discussed in Chapter 4), or that non-whites seem to be represented as aliens (as discussed in Chapter 5), or even that elements of Asian culture are appropriated out of context to represent alien cultures (as discussed in Chapter 3), but that these elements are indicative of larger trends in American popular culture in which racist depictions of people of African and Asian descent are on the increase in American popular culture, while other cultures are mined for their novelty in American culture.

A further reason to critique the films (and to involve Lucas in that critique) comes from science fiction author Ursula K. Le Guin, writing in a 1987 essay, "Where Do You Get Your Ideas From?," later collected in *Dancing at the Edge of the World: Thoughts on Words, Women, Places*:

> If the writer is a socially privileged person — particularly a white or male or both — his imagination may have to make an intense and conscious effort to realize that people who don't share his privileged status may read his work and will not share with him many attitudes and opinions that he has been allowed to believe or pretend are shared by "everybody." ... The choice, then, would seem to be between collusion and subversion; but there's no use pretending that you can get away without making the choice. Not to choose, these days, is a choice made. All fiction has ethical, political, and social weight, and sometimes the works that weigh the heaviest are those apparently fluffy or escapist fictions whose authors declare themselves "above politics," "just entertainers" and so on.[27]

Le Guin, whose work is briefly considered in the first chapter, notes, like Lucas, that artists have a responsibility for the worlds they create. Over and above that, however, if the artist comes from a position of privilege there is an added responsibility to ensure that one's work does not, even inadvertently, employ and continue derogatory stereotypes, appropriate for selfish purposes elements of other's cultures, and present women and minorities as Other. The privileged artist must not assume that his (or her) perspective is the only one, or even the one that should be privileged, particularly in speculative fiction, in which the alien perspective is purposefully engaged.

Lucas does not see himself as an artist, although he recognizes both the cultural and economic clout of his work. Kenneth von Gunden quotes Lucas as saying that "art ... means pretension and bullshit" and that he prefers to be called "a craftsman."[28] Yet despite his disavowal of the term "artist," by definition Lucas is one. He has created an entire imaginative history and geography. He can call himself "craftsman," "filmmaker," "imaginer," or even "Jedi," if he wants, but it does not change the reality that he is the acknowledged creator and master of this world and its geography and history. In short, Lucas is linked thoroughly with his creation by his and others' accounts. When he is referenced in this work, nothing is assumed about the man Lucas, but the artist Lucas, who is the creator and maintainer of the imagined world as well as the real world corporation that controls and benefits from it, is the one who must take responsibility for its content, implications, and appropriations. When Lucas is referenced in this text, it is Lucas the artist that is referenced.

The Author

To site the two trilogies, I am obligated to also site myself. The author of this book is a Euro-American male of Anglo-Irish descent, originally from New England, but now teaching in a private university in Southern California in the geographic heart of the film industry. I first saw *Star Wars* upon its release in 1977 and saw it six more times that year alone and countless times since. I am a fan, perhaps even a Fan, or a fanboy. I grew up with the films. I can quote entire sections from the original trilogy from memory. I know that the odds of successfully navigating an asteroid field are 3,720 to one. I did not need to look that up. I know to let the Wookiee win. I know that the rebel fleet massing near Sullust is of no concern. I understand that one must do or do not, there is no try. I argued with friends at the lunch table at school between 1981 and 1983 whether Darth Vader was Anakin Skywalker, or if that was another Sith trick. I reference the films in my everyday life and in my teaching.

On the other hand, I have never dressed up in a costume (except for Halloween 1979, but as I was ten years old, that seems acceptable). I do not speak any of the languages in the films.[29] Any action figures I own are now part of the décor of my office, instead of an opportunity to create my own adventures. I have not read any of the novels, graphic novels, or most of the websites associated with the *Star Wars* series. Yet I fully acknowledge my position within the community of fans and as a knowledgeable fan. I find myself in agreement with Brooker when he says of himself, "I am inside the *Star Wars* culture, and I consider that a benefit, rather than a hindrance to academic research."[30]

Given my position within the fan community, I must also agree with the phenomenon described by Jeffrey H. Mills. What he writes in regard to *Star Trek*, I now cite about the two trilogies:

> It is a strange sensation to critique that which you love. Strange because it doesn't feel good, but you know you must do it anyway.... There's a certain sense of heightened responsibility that comes with being a fan of something: because the fan knows the object of his love so very well, he is able to identify standards of quality that the casual observer may not see.[31]

A "heightened sense of responsibility" comes from being a fan, but also from being a teacher, specifically of Asian and African theatre and culture, and a postcolonial scholar whose chief focus has been intercultural theatre and cinema, especially as they relate to Africa and Asia. I have published two books on African and African American adaptation of Greek tragedy and numerous articles on the theatres and cultures of Asia and Africa. The impetus for the present book, therefore, is derived from rewatching the original trilogy and the new films in the *Star Wars* series with the knowledge of a postcolonialist and postculturalist and the experience of teaching undergraduates and graduates who can read the texts of Wole Soyinka, Endo Shusaku, Ola Rotimi, Gao Xingjian, Athol Fugard, Ngugi wa Thiongo, Oh T'ae-sok and Chikamatsu Monzaemon, to note but a few, but whose viewing and reading of their own popular culture is unquestioning.

Robin Woods writes in *Hollywood from Vietnam to Reagan* that it is "unlikely" that people engage in multiple viewings of films such as the *Star Wars* series to "discover new meanings, new complexities, ambiguities, possibilities, and possibilities of interpretation" as they do with *Late Spring* or *Letter from an Unknown Woman*.[32] And yet students (and others), in fact, do watch these films over and over. With the advent of recording technologies (DVD, VCRs, etc.), one may watch the films multiple times in the comfort of one's own home. Furthermore, with the appearance of the films on cable television (where, for example, *Attack of the Clones* is presented on Home Box Office at least a dozen times a week as of this writing), audiences need not even engage the films in their entirety, choosing instead to channel surf and watch only particular parts or view only the beginning or only the end. Thus, individual moments and even single frames can have different readings and meanings from the film when taken as a whole.

With the advent of DVD technology, one can even see "deleted scenes" or alternative endings, as well as receive further background information never before available to the typical film viewer. As such the "text" of a film is now even less stable and defined. One can shape the viewing experience to one's individual taste, and therefore, for example, the *Lord of the Rings: Fellowship of the Ring* seen in the cinema is different from the *Lord of the Rings: Fellowship of the Ring* that one could watch when it was first released to home media, and both are different from the "special extended edition" of *Lord of the Rings: Fellowship of the Ring*. Which one is the actual film? Which one is the definitive canonical text? The answer is all and none. They are all *Lord of the Rings: Fellowship of the Ring*. The same holds true for *Star Wars: A New Hope*, for example, which was first released as *Star Wars*, then *Star Wars: A New Hope*, then *Star Wars: A New Hope Special Edition* (which, as of this writing, is now coming out on DVD). Any additional materials will continue to shape both the film and our reception of it.

After Henry A. Giroux, I submit that one of the roles of the educator is to reach beyond the academy and apply academic theories to the actual meaning-making texts of students' lives:

> The curriculum must analyze and deconstruct popular knowledges produced through television and culture industries, and be organized around texts and images that relate directly to the communities, cultures, and traditions that give students a historical sense of identity and place.[33]

When one considers Giroux's comments in light of Wood's accusation that popular culture is rewatched only for pleasure, not to discover new meanings, the need for educators familiar with the popular culture (dare I even suggest, are fans of that culture, as well) to reread the films and television programs and apply the same theories to Lucas and Spielberg that they do to Antonioni and Cocteau becomes apparent.

I can still enjoy these films—but I cannot ignore the larger cultural issues that have shaped them. As Le Guin has stated, coming from a position of privilege in the academy, in the world of *Star Wars* fanboys, and American society, I am obligated to "make an intense and conscious effort" to deconstruct these films and read them through a postcolonial framework.

Given that charge, however, I also must acknowledge the multiple and contradictory possible readings of these films, both individually and collectively. There is no guarantee that audiences experience and understand films in the same way. In fact, as anyone who has read more than two reviews of the same movie, films are often experienced, understood and evaluated in radically different ways by different individuals. We should note, therefore, that while this work critiques the *Star Wars* films and how Asian culture is appropriated by the makers of those films to make the narrative seem more remote from a Western center, and how ethnicity is represented in them, this postcolonial reading of the films does not cancel out my or anyone's love of the films or the positive messages contained therein that other scholars or fans have found.

The Reader

A dilemma faced in the writing of this book is that I am writing for numerous readers with a variety of backgrounds. You may have picked up this book because of your interest in *Star Wars*, or an interest in postcolonialism, or in popular culture in general. Both the general reader and the one with a specialization or localized interest must be engaged. A balance must be struck between appropriate levels of background information for the variety of materials covered. Too little background information and detail and too much background and detail are equally problematic situations. An attempt has been made to give the appropriate amount of information on all subjects engaged by this book.

This book has been written with an eye toward undergraduate students, graduate students, and scholars, with an eye toward *Star Wars* fans, postcolonialists, science fiction historians, and popular culture scholars and students. It draws upon history and theory of cinema, postcolonialism, popular culture, theatre, religion, philosophy, and science fiction. Those familiar with some of these areas may not have a background in the others, and the book attempts to keep all equally balanced.

The only assumption made is that the reader will have seen some or all of the *Star Wars* films but is not necessarily overly familiar with them. Upon completion of reading this book, I suggest reviewing the films again with an open mind.

The Canon

It is important to note that the world of *Star Wars* is not limited to a single film or even to a series of films. The six films that make up the two trilogies are only a small part of the much larger narrative that makes up the *Star Wars* universe, "official" and otherwise. The *Star Wars* films are not separate entities but one huge work, singularly directed (in all senses of the word) by George Lucas. As John Seabrook observes in his wonderful cultural analysis *Nobrow*, "*Star Wars* is a single story — 'a finite, expanding universe,' in the words of Tom Dupreer who edited Bantam's *Star Wars* novels."[34] There even exists "The Bible," as it is referred to in-house: "a burgeoning canonical document that [is] maintained by 'continuity editors.'"[35]

In addition to the films, the "official" parts of the world of *Star Wars* are comprised of elements from every media. National Public Radio broadcast an official radio adaptation in 1981. A variety of cartoons have been made based on the characters: the short-lived Saturday morning series *Droids*, featuring R2-D2 and C3PO and, many years later, *The Clone Wars* on the Cartoon Network. Holiday specials and made-for-television specials such as *Star Wars Holiday Special* (1978, which celebrated the Wookiee version of Christmas, "Life Day"), *The Ewok Adventure: Caravan of Courage* (1984, which brought back the small, furry species from *Jedi* but this time interacting with children), and *Ewoks: The Battle for Endor* (1985) added to the metahistory of the galaxy.

Immediately after the release of *A New Hope*, novels approved by Lucas began to appear — *Splinter of the Mind's Eye* by Alan Dean Foster and Brian Daley's Han Solo series. Since these initial efforts, comic books, a series of novels and anthologies, games and toys, and a set of official "Lucas Books" guides, encyclopedias, and technical manuals all add to the world of *Star Wars*. Timothy Zahn's Thrawn trilogy and Steve Perry's *Shadows of the Empire* series especially shaped the history of the world, introducing new characters which then were made into action figures and began appearing in video games, board games, and online sites. Though Prince Xizor and Dash Rendar have never appeared in a film, they share the same canonical status as Darth Vader and Han Solo.

Many of the new books continue the storyline after the end of the Empire in *Jedi*, forming the story of "The New Republic" and "The New Jedi Order," in which the children of the characters from the films are part of a return of the Jedi through training by Luke and Leia. Through such books, the larger narrative of the characters need not be confined to six films, but rather a limitless series of backstories and new adventures. Individual characters are given complete histories and further connected to the main narrative: Mace Windu, Lando Calrissian, Ki Adi Mundi, General Grievous, and even droid bounty hunter IG-88 each have their character and presence much more fully explicated in the official *Star Wars* fictions.

The master plot of the metanarrative is kept by Lucasfilm, and all major events and significant inventions or changes must be approved by Lucas himself. Thus while the *Star Wars* universe is now the work of many hands, anything canonical must be approved by Lucas, who, like the pope, is the sole authority of the Force on Earth. His blessing is needed for any major contribution to the growing narrative.

With each addition, new ways of reading and understanding the larger narrative of the *Star Wars* world develop. The new trilogy, for example, has moved the center, so to speak. Previously, the story was seemingly about Luke and his rise as a Jedi. Now, the series is about the fall and redemption of Anakin Skywalker. Anakin is seduced by the dark side, becomes an agent of the Emperor, destroys the Jedi, and yet in his son he finds not only a worthy opponent but a savior. The Jedi who now returns in *Return of the Jedi* is not Luke, but his father, redeemed from the dark side and returned to the fold of Obi-Wan Kenobi and Yoda, rendered literally and visually at the end of that film.

For the purposes of this study, focus is solely on the films, for the primary reason that the films are the form in which most people engage the *Star Wars* universe. These other media, other narratives, other characters are primarily engaged by fans, but remain unknown in the larger culture. It is also the films that are widely disseminated to different nations, and the other forms are only present in these cultures to a far lesser extent. Other "official" sources from Lucasfilm are occasionally cited in this text as further evidence of things present in the films. The focus, however, will remain on the visual and narrative elements of the two trilogies on film.

Methodologies, Ideologies, and Outlines

This volume focuses on the six films that make up *Star Wars*. It is a postcolonialist reading of the two trilogies that focuses on the representation of rebellion, the representation of religion (and the concordant appropriation of Asian culture), and the representation of race and ethnicity. Given that all film is intertextual and that Lucas has admitted to multiple cinematic influences on his work, much of this study also considers similarities between the *Star Wars* films and other films. Such comparison is not to argue in favor of direct influence, which can be difficult to prove at best. Rather, we will look for "echoes" of earlier films and cinematic representations of rebellion, race, and religion. *Star Wars* echoes earlier films and is itself echoed by later films. The themes, imagery, structure, characterization, and presentation of the Other as seen in the two trilogies echoes a variety of other films—*The Hidden Fortress, Yojimbo, Bridge on the River Kwai*, adventure and jungle serials, the Flash Gordon movies, the Fu Manchu movies, to note a few. Throughout the course of this study, the echoes of these films in the *Star Wars* films will be examined, both for what they indicate about *Star Wars* and its perpetuation of stereotypes and ways of viewing and thinking and for what they indicate about cultural appropriation by American cinema. In addition, each chapter will also engage in a survey of existing critical responses to these various aspects of the *Star Wars* films.

In chapter one, the series is analyzed using postcolonial methodologies, considering especially the history of the use of imperialism and colonialism in science fiction and science fantasy. Of particular interest is also the trilogies' use of archetypal language of colonialism: "The" Rebellion, "The" Empire, and the use of the word "Force" as a guiding principle.

In the second chapter, religion and myth are considered. Though Lucas and Joseph Campbell cite numerous Western sources for religion and myth in *Star Wars*, this chapter considers the numerous Asian influences on the concept of the Force, particularly Taoism and Buddhism. Also considered in this chapter is how the ideology of myth allows the films to ignore other ideologies present in the film.

Continuing the exploration of the influence of Asian cultures on the *Star Wars* series, the third chapter examines the variety of ways in which the series appropriates elements of Asian culture, particularly the influence of the films of Kurosawa Akira and other Asian cinemas.

Turning from culture to ethnicity and the representation of race, the fourth chapter, taking its title from Kevin Smith's *Chasing Amy*, in which an African American graphic novelist objects to the "holy trilogy" in profane terms, considers the representation, or lack thereof, of people of color in the *Star Wars* universe. In five films less than a dozen people of color occupy key roles. Those who are present are presented in less than positive lights: Lando is "a scoundrel" and a traitor who redeems himself by blowing up the second death star; Mace Windu is the underling of a puppet who is slowly losing his ability to use the Force; the voice of Darth Vader, James Earl Jones himself, is the only black presence in the original film. Thus chapter four provides an Afrocentric reading of the two trilogies.

Lastly, returning to the Asian presence in the films, the fifth chapter considers the representation of Asians and other ethnicities particularly through the literalization of the metaphor of "aliens." Given the lack of people of other ethnicities in the *Star Wars* films, it naturally follows that the Other is represented not by Asian, or African, or Arab, but by the truly alien — monstrous beings from other planets. This chapter considers how Lucas follows a long cultural tradition in the West of viewing the East as home of the monstrous and non–Westerners as nonhuman.

Within popular culture there has been a newfound interest in imperialism and empire, both classical (as represented by the film *Gladiator* and made-for-television movies based on the life of Caesar and a remake of *Spartacus*, to note but a few examples) and modern, given the war in Iraq and the concern for the seeming growth of American imperialism. It is the role of the scholar to engage this interest in imperialism, at the very least for the purpose of somehow moving us beyond imperial desire, imperial perspective, and imperial designs.

One final note on names—in the text and photo captions, Japanese names are given Japanese style, with family name first and given name second. Western names are given in Western order, with given name first and family name second. Names from the *Star Wars* films follow the example of Lucasfilm's official publications. Every effort has been made to ensure the correct spelling of all names and titles. I follow Lucasfilm's model in referring to the first film, still identified in the VHS Special Edition collection as *Star Wars*, as *A New Hope*. I have also abbreviated the titles in the text using the following model:

Star Wars: Episode 1: The Phantom Menace	*Phantom*
Star Wars: Episode 2: Attack of the Clones	*Clones*
Star Wars: Episode 3: Revenge of the Sith	*Sith*
Star Wars: Episode 4: A New Hope	*A New Hope*
Star Wars: Episode 5: The Empire Strikes Back	*Empire*
Star Wars: Episode 6: Return of the Jedi	*Jedi*

CHAPTER 1

Frantz Fanon in a Galaxy Far, Far Away, or What Is an Empire Without Colonies?

For de little stealin' dey gits you in jail soon or late.
For de big stealin' dey makes you emperor....
— Eugene O'Neill, *The Emperor Jones*

The cinema does not exist in a sublime state of innocence, untouched by the world; it also has a political content, whether conscious or unconscious, hidden or overt.
— Leif Furhammar and Folke Isaksson, *Politics and Film*

Cinema ... is a contest of phantoms.
— Jacques Derrida

In one of his last writings before he died, Edward Said commented that "The great modern empires have never been held together only by military power."[1] What is necessary over and above force is "imperial perspective," defined as "that way of looking at a distant foreign reality by subordinating it in one's gaze, constructing its history from one's own point of view...."[2] Historically speaking, science fiction and science fantasy allow for "imperial perspective," in fact may be the best vehicle for conveying it by literally alienating the "distant foreign reality." The history, politics, races, species, and religions of a science fiction or science fantasy are literally constructed, even though they may carry real world echoes. The audience can see in the created work things analogous to real world politics, situations, ethnicities, cultures, and even individuals.

In the case of the two trilogies of the *Star Wars* films, "imperial perspective" is front and center, not least of which because the original trilogy concerns a rebellion against an empire and the new trilogy concerns the creation of that empire. The six films taken together are a meta-narrative that matches two stories: the fall and redemption of Anakin Skywalker and the rise and fall of the Galactic Empire. The two stories are interrelated, as Anakin becomes Darth Vader as the Republic is manipulated into becoming an Empire, then, through the efforts of his son Luke, Vader once more becomes Anakin as the Empire is destroyed.

Yet present in these films are the cultures, religions, clothing, languages, ethnicities, and martial cultures of Earth. Though the films are clearly anti–Empire, pro–Rebellion, the films invert the real world equivalencies. The films use the language of empire and imperialism, all the while subverting the reality of history. The six films involve domination and subjugation by the Empire, and resistance to it by the Rebellion. The films visually and through narrative are lengthy ruminations on violence and power — even the "good guys," the Jedi, are trained warriors who do not hesitate to use violence in order to achieve their ends, when necessary.

The Empire itself, apparently rooted at least in part in Roman history, in which a republic became an empire, does not necessarily directly follow the model of nineteenth century Europe. In other words, the Empire, as such, does not call the worlds it dominates "colonies," as all of them were, at one time, member states of a collective. In that sense, the model of the Empire can also be seen as Athenian, in which ancient Athens organized the Delian League, but slowly converted it to the Athenian Empire. As Martin Green posits, an empire does not merely involve having colonies, it also entails a power relationship in which "one group is dominant over others whom it regards as alien and inferior."[3] That description certainly mirrors the *Star Wars* film. A case can also be made, however, for evidence of direct colonization in the films as well. What is the invasion of Naboo by the Trade Federation in *Phantom* if not direct colonization? What is the slowly changing presence of the Empire on Bespin in *Empire*, in which Lando first makes deals with Vader, who then leaves a garrison, and who threatens much more violence to control the city, if not direct colonization? What is the imperial presence on Tatooine, or for that matter, the human presence on Tatooine, a planet whose only indigenous sentient species are Jawas and Tusken Raiders, if not direct colonization through settlers? What is the transformation of the Supreme Chancellor into an emperor (in fact,

"The" Emperor) by declaring himself such and declaring the Republic an Empire, to be ruled and policed by the Great Clone Army, if not the seizure of power without limits and the threat of violence without limits? The *Star Wars* films are dominated by a discourse on imperialism and colonization.

As in real history, the Empire represents the assertion of absolute power by a small group over a number of cultures through a combination of technology, capitalism, imperialism and imperial perspective. We see in the *Star Wars* films the use of technology: transportation technology, communication technology, and martial technology — up to and including the ability to destroy a planet — that echo nineteenth century Europe's use of transportation technology (steam ships), communication technology (the invention of telegraph, radio, and telephone), and martial technology (firearms, bayonets, machine guns, cannon, etc.) to dominate and subjugate parts of Africa, Asia, the Middle East, and Latin and South America. Also present, both in the films and historically, is an entire imperial organization dedicated to the direct administration of other peoples and cultures for the benefit of the center.

It is easy to miss what you are not looking for. Science fantasy is a deceptive form — one may use the literal distances of time, space and alien species to comment upon or reflect the realities of this world. If one does not look to the two trilogies from a postcolonial perspective, but rather merely considers them from their own perspective, one may not consider the implications and appropriations present in the saga. It is the purpose of this study to interrogate the assumptions behind the films, the implications of the films' representations, and the appropriation of real world languages and cultures.

As in Ariel Dorfman and Armand Mattelart's classic work *How to Read Donald Duck: Imperialist Ideology in the Disney Comic* (1971), what may seem at first to be a simple narrative to entertain and delight children of all ages actually carries with it an ideology full of unquestioned assumptions. This text, like Dorfman and Mattelart's, questions those assumptions, after pointing them out to the reader. *How to Read Donald Duck* demonstrates how Disney comics privilege the first world and whites over the third world and non-whites. Non-westerners are demonstrated in Disney comics as childlike, simple, easily-fooled and inferior. Money is the sole thing of value, and others may be trampled by any means to gain more. A Chilean sociologist and a Belgian sociologist living in Chile, Dorfman and Mattelart consider how Disney is read in the third world. They argue that Disney is "arguably the country's most important figure in bourgeois popular culture."[4] I would argue that the *Star Wars* films have surpassed the Disney influence, which means that Lucas has surpassed Disney in importance in popular culture, and in terms of American culture exported to other cultures that demonstrate how other worlds are viewed from the first.

Colonies and Conflict: Science Fiction and Imperial Literature

Science fiction has routinely dealt with colonization, imperialism and empire, whether in literature, such as Issac Asimov's *Foundation* novels or the *Lensman* series of E.E. "Doc" Smith (one of Lucas's acknowledged influences and inspirations), in television, such as the various incarnations of *Star Trek* or *Babylon 5*, or in cinema, such as the *Alien* films, or *Independence Day*, in which the horror comes from aliens treating the earth in the same manner as Europeans treated Africa and Asia (a society with greater technology exploits the natural resources and peoples of a society with lesser technology until they are destroyed or used up).

Science fiction usually deals with settler colonies, although occasionally with administrative colonies. Settler colonies involve the sending of people from the colonizing culture to the colonized land, settling there and taking over the land through a literal presence and perhaps even viewing the colonized land as the new homeland, certainly so by the second or third generation of settlers. Kenya, the United States, Canada, and South Africa are all examples of former settler colonies. Administrative colonies have a much smaller, but not less intrusive, presence in the colonized land. Rather than settling, a rotating colonial administrative presence is kept. After a finite period, the administrators return to their homeland and new administrators are sent. Rather than viewing the colonized land as a place to settle, it is run as a business in which profits flow to the colonizer by importing to the colony manufactured goods and exporting back to the colonizer raw materials.

In science fantasy and science fiction, distant planets are seen as places to which human beings can go and recreate the society of their homeland, as well as exploit the natural resources of that world. These worlds are often seen as empty until the arrival of the colonists, mirroring the European attitude towards the colonization of the third world. Basil Davidson writes, for example, that Sir Charles Eliot, Britain's first High Commissioner to East Africa, "believed that the African continent was a tabula rasa for the European to deal with as he pleased."[5] Much speculative fiction echoes this view of newly discovered planets as tabula rasa, upon which humankind can settle and exploit the resources. Much of the conflict of science fantasy and science fiction arises from the juxtaposition of the belief of the planet as tabula rasa and the presence of indigenous species that resist the human presence. *Aliens* contains an example of a colony of humans that discovers another species present on the planet which leads to direct conflict and the elimination of the humans. Likewise, in *Empire*, the Rebels treat Hoth as a tabula rasa, with unfortunate results when Luke Skywalker then runs into an indigenous species, the Wampa.

In terms of the representation of imperialism and colonialism, especially for the purposes of making imperial practices palatable to the colonizing people, Edward Said writes, narrative is the key to representing both imperialism and the colonized culture back in the home country:

> Stories are at heart what explorers and novelists say about strange regions of the world; they also become the method colonized people use to assert their own identity and the existence of their own history.[6]

The colonizers define themselves and know who they are by defining themselves in opposition to the colonized. The colonized are automatically (and must be) Othered to establish the Self of the colonizer, who believes he not only is right to colonize and has the right to colonize, but must colonize in order to assert his superior culture over the inferior culture of the colonized.

These stories of which Said writes often share common narrative elements with science fiction. Said writes:

> In all of these instances the facts of empire are associated with sustained possession, with far-flung and sometimes unknown spaces, with eccentric or unacceptable human beings, with fortune enhancing or fantasized activities like emigration, money making, and sexual adventure.... The colonial territories are realms of possibility.... [7]

Science fiction, or speculative fiction as some call it, is also about "realms of possibility" and "far-flung and sometimes unknown spaces." What are aliens other than "eccentric or unacceptable human beings?"

In his seminal book *Orientalism*, Said also discusses the idea of "imaginative geography and history," in which the West rewrites the geography and history of the East:

> Imaginative geography and history help the mind to intensify its own sense of itself by dramatizing the distance and difference between what is close to it and what is far away.[8]

As well as what is far, far away. Science fiction and science fantasy entail a projection of the Other through imaginative, or speculative, if you will, history and geography. In the case of *Star Wars*, for example, there exist entire chronologies of the "history" of that galaxy, entire analyses of cultures and societies, and entire guides to the technology. We the audience define ourselves in terms of *Star Wars*, by what is presented as being similar to us and what is presented as distant and different.

It is no coincidence that speculative fiction developed primarily in imperial Europe, specifically nineteenth-century France and Victorian England. In the 1930s, one quarter of the Earth's surface and one quarter of the Earth's population lived under the British Empire. During the height of the British Empire, and, for that matter, the French Empire, with the advent of the technologies of empire and the contact with and representation of other cultures, science fiction and science fantasy, alongside adventure stories and other speculative fiction, are created and developed. This period produces the writings of H.G. Wells, Jules Verne, Edgar Rice Burroughs, and H. Rider Haggard, as well as speculative horror that engages the foreign and alien, such as Bram Stoker's *Dracula* (1897), Robert Louis Stephenson's *The Strange Case of Dr. Jekyll and Mr. Hyde* (1887), and Oscar Wilde's *The Picture of Dorian Grey* (1891). This fiction then served as subject matter for adaptation, first for the stage and then for the screen. The same period also saw the development of cinema and the first genre films. In 1902, Georges Méliès produced, directed, and starred in *Le Voyage dans la Lune* (*A Trip to the Moon*), based loosely on moon-travel novels by Wells and Verne, in which a giant gun shoots a craft into the eye of the man in the moon. Upon disembarking onto the lunar surface, the first cinematic space travelers encounter "Selenites," who explode when touched with the hero's umbrella. *Le Voyage* is generally considered to be the first science fiction film. It encompasses all of the elements of colonial literature, including technology, travel over great distances, encounters with strange and different but human-like beings, and the defeat of monstrous enemies.

The two dominant streams in Victorian literature, argues Patrick Brantlinger, are imperialism and occultism, which he argues are practically accorded the status of "religions."[9] The meeting of cultures, the encounters with beings that appear different, speak different languages, and represent a possible threat to the Self that explores are common to both science fiction and imperial literature.

Much of science fiction represents a melding of scientific materialism with the transcendent faith of religion and spiritualism. In the *Star Wars* films, the Force is presented cheek by jowl with technology. The weapon of the Jedi is the lightsaber — the ultimate melding of science and technology with religion and spirituality. It is a weapon that requires years of training to master, has a limited range, and cannot kill from a safe distance, as can a blaster. Yet it is "an elegant weapon," states Obi-Wan, and it is a mark of a Jedi's completion of training when she or he can make her or his own. The Jedi use spacecraft and other technological apparatus, yet are also able to harness and use the Force, a field generated by all living things. Vader even informs the Imperial High Command that "The ability to destroy a planet is insignificant compared to the power of the Force." In this melding of religion and science, *Star Wars* echoes Victorian science fiction and speculative fiction.

Much imperial literature in Victorian England is what has been termed "Imperial Gothic"—a blending of the adventure novel and the occult gothic novel. Brantlinger, after Judith Wilt, argues that at the end of the nineteenth century, Victorian gothic became Victorian science fiction.[10] The principle themes of this literature as outlined by Brantlinger include: one, "individual regression or going native," two, "an invasion of civilization by the forces of barbarism or demonism," and three, "the diminution of opportunities for adventures and heroism in the modern world."[11] These themes might be applied to the *Star Wars* films as well: the galaxy is threatened in the original trilogy by the forces of the Empire, which, from the perspective of the Rebellion are the forces of demonism, although it can also be argued that from the Empire's perspective, the Rebellion is the forces of barbarism. Han Solo, it can be argued, "goes native." Like Hawkeye in *Last of the Mohicans*, who is accompanied by Uncas and Chingachgook, and who is seen by the white settlers as having "gone native," Han is accompanied by Chewbacca. They understand each other and Chewbacca is clearly dedicated to his human friend. Lastly, the original trilogy concerns the emergence of what might be termed the last Jedi. Once upon a time, thousands of Jedi served as the guardians of the Old Republic. The Empire has destroyed the Jedi order and established a military order. There are no opportunities for adventure or heroism unless one is willing to join the Rebellion. The Old Republic is romanticized in the original trilogy, in much the same way that Imperial literature romanticizes the colonial experience.

Imperialism and colonialism also offers a good deal of potential for conflict, much necessary for narrative: between colonizer and colonized, between colony and homeworld, between human and universe or natural world, and between human and Alien Other. It is this last that is so particularly potent and popular in early science fiction, partly, as noted above, because of its potential to define the identity of the culture that produced it. The (presumably colonizing as opposed to colonized) reader defines him or herself in opposition to that which is different. The same holds true for the viewer of speculative cinema. As Edward James writes in his own study of race and science fiction, latent xenophobia on Earth transfers from other humans to aliens in science fiction.[12] We fear that which is different, but feel that such fear is justified because of the clear danger and sheer Otherness of the alien.

Larger issues are also explored in the confrontation of human and alien in speculative fiction: genocide, slavery, economic exploitation, cultural oppression, a native population that resists colonialism, all of which figure rather largely as well in the *Star Wars* films. For example, H.G. Wells's *War of the Worlds* (1898), by its very title, suggests the conflict that results when one culture meets another. In that novel, invaders from the planet Mars arrive on Earth and, utilizing superior technology, devastate the people and cities of Great Britain and other major nations of the world. Finally, they are defeated by a virus—the common cold. The horror of this novel, of course, emerges from the idea that alien races with superior technology could do to Europe what Europe had done to Africa, Asia, and the Americas.

The Victorian era saw numerous writers use speculative fiction to create narratives that would explain the relationship between England and France and their colonies in distancing terms. Arthur Conan Doyle, H. Rider Haggard, and Edgar Rice Burroughs, in addition to Verne and Wells, wrote stories of Africa and the center of the Earth and other distant (from Europe at least) places that were "primitive," "savage," and dangerous, but full of opportunity and adventure. It is worth noting that Conan Doyle's *The Lost World* is Lucas's favorite book, according to John Baxter.[13] These adventure stories were "the energizing myth of English imperialism," states Walter James Miller, which posited the value and necessity of the English going into "darkest Africa" or the center of the Earth.[14]

Jules Verne, the father of modern science fiction, wrote his speculative novels during the height of the colonial period. His Captain Nemo, a major figure in two novels, *Vingt mille lieues sous les mers* (*Twenty Thousand Leagues Under the Sea*, 1870) and *L'Île mystérieuse* (*The Mysterious Island*, 1874-5), is an anarchist and a revolutionary. In some ways, Nemo is the original Luke Skywalker. According to Walter James Miller, Verne conceived of Nemo "as a role model of the freedom fighter persecuted by the oppressor."[15] Nemo helps the Greek independence movement, Indian divers, and other revolutionaries. Although originally planned as a Polish nobleman, in *L'Île mystérieuse* he is revealed to be the Indian Prince Dakkar of Bundekhand, who led the 1857 rebellion against the British who executed his family when the could not find him.

From Nemo's perspective (and for the purposes of the novels), the

British are the enemy. Miller explains that Verne could not make France the enemy in his novels and still get published, so, using the distance of geography as well as speculative fiction, he made the British, and especially the British navy, the antagonist in *Vingt mille lieues sous les mers.*[16] By critiquing the British colonial policies, Verne was indirectly critiquing the practices of France in Africa, Asia, and the "New World."

In the novel, Nemo fights the British, arguably one of the first examples of the colonist striking back against the empire being presented not only sympathetically, but heroically. Nemo is a model for *Star Wars*'s Rebels. Similarly, in the sequel (of sorts), the heroes of *L'Île mystérieuse* are Americans, Civil War soldiers, trapped on the island by circumstance and forced to live the life of Robinson Crusoe, only without Friday, though they have a black man with them who initially acts as servant until he is replaced by a trained Ape named "Jupiter." They maintain "civilization" and conquer all that not only nature but the local savages can throw at them. In the end, however, it is Nemo with whose help they could not have survived. He secretly assists them, aids in their battles against pirates, and gives life-saving medicine. It is only at the conclusion of the novel that Nemo and the Nautilus are revealed as being the presence felt by the islanders. Nemo tells his history and then, as he is dying, sinks his beloved submarine. To the very last, Nemo helps brave, honest men, but resists the British navy. Americans are acceptable to Nemo as they have not (yet) had any colonial adventures, nor has their military been used to oppress or suppress indigenous peoples. In Verne's world, America is to be admired for fighting a civil war over the rights of people of color while the British (and by implication the French) are busy still suppressing people of color in their homelands.

In the sense that it, too, celebrates freedom, adventure, and resistance to oppressive forces, the *Star Wars* films invoke the world of Victorian literature, or, at least, they are heir to its tensions of science versus religion, its concern for encountering the alien, and its interest in conflict, especially revolution, in the name of freedom.

Verne's novels were followed by other examples of speculative fiction engaging the issues of imperialism and colonialism, Andrew Blair's *Annals of the Twenty-Ninth Century* (1874), for example. Not all of these works were critical, as Verne's were, however. Robert W. Cole's *The Struggle for Empire* (1900), subtitled *A Story of the Year 2236*, envisions Great Britain conquering other planets and solar systems, even as it had the nations of Africa, Asia, and the Caribbean. The theme of the colonization of space became and remains a major theme in science fiction, science fantasy, and speculative fiction.

The colonization of Africa and the adventures which it presented were most vividly imagined in the work of Edgar Rice Burroughs (1875–1950), whose Tarzan novels, beginning with *Tarzan of the Apes* (1912), are an example of a poor boy discovering his aristocratic heritage, and an example of the white man being accepted by blacks, first as a member of the tribe and then as a superior or king. We might compare these to Luke Skywalker discovering he is not the son of a simple pilot but the son of the greatest Jedi and his heir, and Han Solo's acceptance by Chewbacca, the acceptance of the Rebels by the Ewoks, and the acceptance of the Naboo by the Gungun. The shaping influence and echo of Tarzan is seen most clearly in *Sith*, when, during the battle on Kashyyyk, a Wookiee, flying through the air on a vine like Tarzan, attacking a droid troop ship, clearly makes the Tarzan jungle cry, made famous by Johnny Weismuller. It is Lucas's tribute to the Tarzan films, but it also has the effect of connecting the Wookiees and the jungles of Kashyyyk to the jungles of Africa.

Burroughs also wrote speculative science fantasy, beginning with *Princess of Mars* (1912), which initiated the Barsoom series, set on Mars. Like the *Star Wars* films, which were influenced by them, Burrough's Barsoom novels featured the adventures of a white man, John Carter, among the aliens and monsters of Mars. Swordplay is used side by side with more potent weapons, including firearms, later echoed by the mixing of blasters and lightsabers. Only in science fantasy are swords actively used next to laser projectile weapons. Militarily speaking, the advent of firearms, which kill at a distance, render swords redundant and useless. The *Star Wars* films overcome this fact by showing how Jedi are so fast and well-trained, they can use their light sabers to defend against, deflect, and even return blaster fire.

In the Barsoom series, Burroughs also places white male John Carter side by side with a variety of monsters, aliens, and beasts. The people of Mars are a variety of different colors, including green, yellow, and red. Indigenous Martians have four arms. They employ strange and monstrous beasts, some of whom Carter must fight in order to achieve his objectives in each novel, including initially winning the hand of the Princess, Dejah Thoris. Likewise, in the Tarzan series, Tarzan must often, while in remote parts of the African jungle, face strange and monstrous men. In *Beasts of Tarzan* (1914), *Tarzan and the Ant Men* (1924), *Tarzan and the Lost Empire* (1929), *Tarzan and the Lion Man* (1934), and *Tarzan and the Leopard Men* (1935), as their very titles suggest, involve Tarzan, the white European male of aristocratic descent who has become "Lord of the Jungle," meeting strange and bizarre men who are part animal. Whether Mars, Africa, or a galaxy far, far away, much of science fiction is rooted in the idea of

Euromales meeting strange, monstrous men — sometimes fighting with them, sometimes fighting alongside them against a greater threat. But the alien is present and is different and is known for his (or her) difference.

In a third series of novels, set in Pellucidar, the center of the Earth, and a fourth series, set on Venus, and a fifth series, called *Eternal Savage*, the formula is repeated: an individual or team led by a white male enters into a strange environment that is unlike one "back home" and must contend with strange technology, alien landscapes, monsters and beast men, and then usually conquer or defeat some sort of despotic tribal ruler — a central enemy figure.

From its very origins in Victorian England (although, in fairness, though Burroughs wrote about England, he himself was American and served briefly in the United States Cavalry) science fiction literature is and has been part and parcel of imperialism. Early science fiction cinema also engages in real world political and colonial parallels. Fritz Lang's *Metropolis* (1926) deals with a worker's revolution led by a robot duplicate of a young woman who protects the workers' children in an oppressive future city ruled by elite industrialists. John J. Pierce reports on André Mas's *The Germans on Venus* (1913), in which "European powers divide up the solar system in a futuristic parallel to the then-current scramble for Africa."[17] Several other films, as noted above, engage the same themes of colonization and imperialism as speculative literature.

It is not until later in its development that authors begin writing socially responsible science fiction. After Verne the dominant stream was one of promoting imperialism through science fiction, and showing the foreign, the alien, the distant, as in need of conquest, colonization, and civilization. In the post World War II era, however, progressive science fiction came into vogue, including narratives about rebellion and revolution that portrayed such activities in a positive light, perhaps echoing the growing rebellious sentiment in colonies which had just fought for Europe's freedom but still lingered under imperialism themselves.

As Edward James analyzes in his study of revolution in science fiction, there are good revolutions: scientific revolution, industrial revolution, and the American revolution, for example.[18] There are also "bad" revolutions: the Russian, French, and colonial revolutions that were (and still are) represented negatively. The determining factor, argues James, is whether the revolution is determined to allow the people to escape a despotic and confining system or overthrow a system that works in order to replace the people in power with a new set of people who will also repress and oppress.[19] Ultimately, all revolution is about change — whether the change is for the better or not is what will determine the value of the revolution.

One of the most significant and influential examples of speculative fiction positing a successful rebellion at the same time that liberation struggles were occurring in Asia and Africa is Robert Heinlein's *The Moon Is a Harsh Mistress* (1966), about a successful revolution on the moon against Earth. In the Hugo Award–winning novel, the moon is (obviously) a settler colony which the Earth controls. The revolution against the home planet is meant to parallel the American Revolutionary War, and Heinlein's fiction is usually seen as right-wing, almost to the point of being fascist, as witnessed in such novels as *Starship Troopers* (1959), *Sixth Column* (1941), and *Glory Road* (1963), the last Heinlein's own contribution to the "swords and science" genre. *The Moon Is a Harsh Mistress*, however, would seem to suggest that instead of fascism, Heinlein embraces radical libertarianism. Regardless, the novel displays a revolution by a colony against its imperial "owner" and justifies that revolution as good, necessary, and successful, much as the first trilogy later will.

The writings of Ursula K. Le Guin, Philip K. Dick, D.C. Fontana, and Gene Roddenberry, to name but a few, demonstrates a promise of progress and a willingness to move past positive views of imperialism. Furthermore, such authors also often frequently question power, institutions, and the use of force, recognizing both the responsibility of science fiction to offer a non-exploitive vision of humankind as well as the power of narrative (both textual and visual) to shape our understanding of the world. Ursula K. Le Guin's *The Dispossessed* (1974) deals with two dystopian societies, one of which is a settler colony on the moon of the other. Le Guin's *The Word for World Is Forest* (1976) won Hugo and Nebula awards for its tale of humans settling "New Tahiti." One meter tall humanoids covered in green fur — "Creechies" — are turned into slaves as their forest is destroyed for human colonization. They are forced to learn English and the females are used as sex slaves for sexual pleasure. Eventually, a revolutionary figure emerges and the planet is the site of a colonial war which the humans lose. The whole novel is a metaphor for the independence movements of Africa and Asia.

At the same time that literary science fiction embraced progressive values, the same trend began to emerge in cinematic and televisual speculative fiction. *Star Trek*, for example, has recognized the multiracial nature of the exploration of space from the beginning, as well as recognizing the "inalienable" right to political and cultural sovereignty — the "prime directive" first states that Star Fleet and its officers (the military wing of the United Federation of Planets [itself echoing the United States of America]) may not interfere "in the normal development of any society, and that any Starfleet vessel or crew member is expendable to prevent violation of this rule."[20] Formulated in the original series and frequently invoked in *The Next Generation, Deep Space Nine, Voyager,* and *Enterprise,* the Prime Directive, also called "Starfleet General Order Number One," provides a useful plot device: many episodes revolve around the violation of the Prime Directive by key characters and the ramifications of doing so. The Prime Directive is so often violated, one wonders why it exists, but as explained several times in the series, the Prime Directive is an ideal — one the characters must attempt to live up to. When two cultures meet, there will always be an exchange of culture. Yet one culture may not impose itself over another. The Prime Directive moves to guarantee non-exploitive relations within the worlds of the *Star Trek* universe.[21]

In the original series of *Star Trek,* the episode "The Devil in the Dark" is set on the pergium mining colony on Janus VI, an administrative colony which humans from the Federation have established in order to mine its natural resources. No tabula rasa, the planet already has at least one intelligent indigenous species, a silicone-based life form called a "Horta," that is killing the miners because they, mistakenly, are destroying her eggs. When Mr. Spock performs a Vulcan mind-meld, the Horta and the miners are able to communicate and reach an agreement. This episode features a representation of cultural conflict occurring when two cultures meet. Rather than a vindictive and genocidal conflict that results in subjugation of one of the two conflicting cultures, mutual understanding and respect is reached. The audience is told that as a result of their cooperation, the miners are able to more efficiently get to the ore they need and the Horta benefit from the presence of the miners who are able to use their technology to aid, rather than suppress. It is an example of a potential colonial/imperial situation that instead results in a positive interaction between cultures as equals.

This is not to say that the imperial model of colonial science fiction is gone or not still dominant and popular. As noted above, *Aliens* (1986), James Cameron's sequel to *Alien* (1979), deals with a "shake and bake colony," in which human colonists from Earth, sent by "The Corporation," set up a colony on a world again believed to be a tabula rasa. When contact with the colony is lost, the previous reports of a violent alien species are taken seriously and "colonial marines" are sent in on a "bug hunt." The aliens, glistening black and driven by instinct, not intelligence, are parasitic, insect-like, with a queen and a hive and functional roles within the species. They are clever and cunning, but not sentient and intelligent. They must hitch a ride with, on, and sometimes literally inside, those who have technology. They must be eliminated to the last one. One might compare the approach to fighting the aliens in *Alien* with the fight against the

Africans in such films as *Zulu*. They embody fear of contact, fear of contamination—what are the colonists bringing back from the alien lands? Perhaps something that can kill us all in the nastiest of ways. Though the Marines themselves are multicultural and multiethnic, the only colonists that we see (Newt and a few trapped on the wall, presumably with larval aliens inside them, including the woman who begs to be killed right before her stomach "hatches") are white. The aliens themselves, all of whom are black, must be destroyed, even if the entire colony must be sacrificed. The film ends with the colony (and presumably all the aliens) being destroyed by a nuclear bomb and the queen, who has malevolently stolen on board the rescue ship, must be blown out into space. The only good alien is a dead alien, and, like the Zulu, they will not stop coming until we kill them all. If we cannot have the colony, the film says, then we will destroy it all.

Even today, the language of science fiction is the language of colonization and empire. The situations of science fiction, dealing with colonization and the meeting of cultures and species mirrors the intercultural and intersocietal relations of our world. Science fiction cinema continues to embrace and explore the meeting of cultures and the variety of violent and military responses to that meeting. This exploration echoes not only early speculative literature and cinema, it also echoes other films that deal with colonization.

As Mark Nash observes, "The trope of 100 years of cinema is also 100 years of cinema's relationship to colonialism and neocolonialism."[22] French film companies sent filmmakers "to collect images from the colonized countries—images of the other which would change the way the other is thought about and referenced today."[23] The audiences in the colonizing country can see the people they have colonized. "Imperial perspective" and the imperial gaze are part of colonization—the pleasure of looking at the people one has conquered and both defining and distancing them at the same time.

This practice can and will have an influence on modern filmmaking practice. Remote places are used in contemporary filmmaking to stand in for alien and remote places. For example, in *A New Hope*, *Jedi*, and the new trilogy, the Tatooine scenes were filmed in North Africa in Tunisia. For *A New Hope*, filming began in 26 March 1976, right near a village called Tatahouine.[24] While this fact may be serendipitous or coincidental, it still indicates how the North Africa desert is meant to represent a distant planet.

Garry Jenkins reports five main sites in Tunisia used to create the desert planet of Tatooine: Chotti el-Djerid was used for the farm exteriors, the Isle of Jerba for Mos Eisley, the town of Matama for the Lars family home, a canyon beyond Chotti el-Djerid for the Tusken Raider attack on Luke and the droids and the first meeting of Luke and Obi-Wan, and outside the city of Tozeur for the droids' arrival on Tatooine.[25] Jenkins further reports that Tunisia was chosen "because of its strikingly primitive architecture and the cooperative attitude of its government."[26]

These perceived "benefits" of filming in Tunisia are indicative of the alienization of North Africa by equating it with an alien planet and of the attitude of the filmmakers who perceive the structures of Tunisia as "strikingly primitive." Tatooine is a barren, dangerous, and "primitive" place. Tunisia, by extension, then, is a barren, dangerous, and primitive place. As will be argued below, Tatooine is also presented as being marginal and distanced from the center of the galaxy, which is Coruscant. As Tatooine is to Coruscant, Tunisia is to England, where the rest of *A New Hope* was filmed.

Interestingly, the filmmakers displayed sensitivity to the local culture and society in securing the location. The local government vetted the script to ensure that there was nothing offensive to the majority Muslim population. In the edited, finished film there is nothing offensive to Muslims. However, desert-dwellers are represented in the film in surprisingly negative and marginalized terms, as will be argued in Chapter 5.

Accounts of the filmmakers' presence in Tunisia both echo colonialist attitudes toward non-western people and are echoed in the *Star Wars* films themselves. For example, compare C3PO's "I can't abide those filthy Jawas" with the remark of Anthony Waye, the British assistant director who kept a diary of the *New Hope* shoot. An early entry, written in Tunisia, reads, "Cannot abide the filthy hotel."[27] C3PO echoes cinematic (and, arguably, real world) colonial administrators, with his British accent, his desire to serve and serve well, and his concern with protocol and propriety. He is also represented as being utterly useless in most situations, in contrast to the more rugged and action-oriented heroes. His echoing of colonial administration and colonial attitudes is made manifest behind the scenes in comments like Waye's.

Subsequently, the role that it played in *Star Wars* was used to draw attention to Tunisia. Arnold reports that by 1980 a sign was placed in the center of the village of Matmara proudly proclaiming, "*Star Wars* was filmed here."[28] While huge flocks of tourists did not descend upon rural Tunisia, it is interesting to note the attempt to engage tourism by associating the location with the film shot there. "Tunisia" is not present in *Star Wars*, "Tatooine" is. But because Tatooine does not exist, and Tunisia represents the planet in the filmmakers' imaginations, the converse occurs as well and Tatooine represents Tunisia as well. Matmara's sign proclaims an identification with the film created there, and claims ownership of the representations contained therein. Tunisia now defines itself in terms of its presence in *Star Wars*. The American culture that appropriates the visual appearance of Tunisia is then the granter of authority and authenticity that allows Tunisia to define itself in terms of its own appropriated image.

In another sense, however, Lucas and company use Africa to represent another world in the same manner that movie serials used studio sets and stock footage to represent Africa. This substitution of real geography for an imaginary one carries real world repercussions. The Saturday morning serial connection also indicates the myriad shaping influences on the series, not all of which can be considered as positive models of foreign societies and ethnicities or cross-cultural encounter.

Lucas and his collaborators have admitted numerous influences on the development of the *Star Wars* saga, including: the *Flash Gordon* serials, the writings of Edgar Rice Burroughs, Edwin Arnold, Joseph Campbell, Carlos Castaneda, Frank Herbert's *Dune* books, E.E. "Doc" Smith's *Lensmen* books, Isaac Asimov's *Foundation* series, C.S. Lewis's *Chronicles of Narnia*, J.R.R. Tolkien's *The Lord of the Rings* — in other words, numerous Victorian adventure and speculative fictions, epic fantasies, and works that focus on interplanetary political organizations. Lucas's films are also strongly influence by other films not necessarily in the science fiction or science fantasy genres — John Ford's *The Searchers* and other westerns, Leni Reifenstahl's *Triumph of the Will*, and war films.[29] Lucas himself describes the aesthetic of the original trilogy as "1940s style storytelling and acting, which verges on the operatic — and something that's contemporary and has weight to it."[30] Kenneth von Gunden sees Lucas as belonging to a generation of filmmakers inspired and influenced not by theatre, literature, history or politics, but rather by film, television, and popular culture.[31] He may have a point, inasmuch as the list above cites more films than other narratives in other media, as well as the fact that ideas and narrative are not the only presence in cinema, but there is a visual aspect to it as well. Films can and do "quote" visually from other films, as well as echoing lines, characters, situations, and themes. One might even argue that a cinematic legacy, far more than a mythic heritage that so many claim for the saga, lies beneath its familiarity and popularity. It is even called a "saga" in order to demonstrate how "mythic" it is. But even its most ardent fans acknowledge that the *Star Wars* series is rooted in movies.

For example, Robin Wood locates the origins of *Star Wars* not in science fiction or science fantasy but in the war movie, not only because of the martial content, but because of the ethnic constructions in both:

> The war movie gave us various ethnic types (Jew, Pollack, etc.) under the leadership of a WASP American; the Lucas film substitutes fantasy

figures (robots, Chewbacca) fulfilling precisely the same roles, surreptitiously permitting the same indulgence in WASP superiority.[32]

The heroes of both trilogies— Luke, Han, Obi-Wan and Anakin — are all white males who achieve victory and dominance over their (often alien) adversaries with the assistance of subservient Others. At the center of the *Star Wars* universe is the white male.

"Imperial relations," Tiffin and Lawson remind us, are "maintained by textuality," or, in other words, by representing the people of the Empire, we control them.[33] Likewise, by representing the places of the Empire, we control them. The series makes definitive distinctions between the cosmopolitan and technologically advanced urban areas which are predominantly populated by white humans (Coruscant, Theed, Bespin, etc.) and the distant, backwards, primitive undeveloped areas, which are primarily populated by non-humans who read as non-westerners (Dagobah, Tatooine, Endor, Otoh Gunga, etc.). The center is white, technologically advanced, and urban. The margins are alien, primitive, and undeveloped.

Imperial discourse contains— it inscribes and limits. Present in the series is a pair of imperial discourses. The first is the surface one, the one that posits a Galactic Empire, ruled by evil men, who are opposed by a small but valiant Rebellion. The original trilogy indicates a pro–Rebellion, anti–Empire perspective. The audience is intended to side with the Rebellion. There is a subsurface imperial discourse that shapes the film as well, however. Even within the Rebellion, power remains in the hands of the few and the privileged. The Jedi are an elite order with tremendous power. The Rebellion is led by a princess/senator and the son of a queen and the most powerful Jedi of all. The Rebellion appears to have limitless resources. Over the course of three films the audience is forced to assume the existence of no less than a half dozen Rebel bases, including the moon of Yavin, Hoth, Dantooine, Ord Mantell, and Sullust. Despite huge losses at Yavin and Hoth, the Rebel fleet never appears to be significantly depleted or devastated. This revolution is certainly very well funded and very well armed. It is also led by an all-white, all-human officer corps, as is the Empire as well. People of color are absent, although their culture(s), as will be argued in chapters 2 and 3, are present, having been appropriated to make the entire enterprise seem "alien." This subsurface imperial discourse limits the presence and power of non-humans and non-whites. It serves to contain and define real world equivalencies. Tatooine is all Tunisia ever can be. Westerners remain in the center.

Peter Lev calls the science fiction film "a privileged vehicle for the presentation of ideology."[34] He is correct. Through the guise of science fiction or science fantasy, a privileged ideology asserts itself but can always claim to be "just a story," with no real world correlations. Nevertheless, as the *Star Wars* films engage in a discourse of imperialism and revolution against it, the message of Eurodominance, privilege and power is also asserted. In order to understand the imperialist ideology present in the films and shaping our understanding of the world, we must consider the theories of Frantz Fanon, who actually participated in a rebellion against an Empire and whose ideas have given shape to the postcolonial movement.

Frantz Fanon: Hero of the Rebellion

Frantz Fanon was born on 20 July 1925 in Martinique to a black bourgeois family. After completing secondary education, he was mentored by Aimé Césaire. He fought for France during the Second World War, and then studied medicine and psychology in France. Moving to Algeria, he practiced psychology in that colonial setting. As a result of his experiences in Algeria, he became a revolutionary theorist. In 1953 he was made Medical Chief of Blida-Joinville Psychiatric Hospital, the largest in Algeria. The hospital was segregated — French colonials were privileged over indigenous Arabs and received the best care. The following year the war of liberation began, in which rebels fought against the imperial power of France, and Fanon provided medical supplies to the FLN (National Liberation Front). It was during this period that he formulated and disseminated his theories on the colonial experience from the perspective of the colonized rather than the colonizer. He died on 6 December 1961 in Washington, D.C., and his body was surreptitiously returned to Algeria for burial.

Fanon wrote several significant volumes on colonialism, imperialism, and race relations: *Black Skin White Masks* (1952), a "sociodiagnostic" of black people in a white-dominated world; *A Dying Colonialism* (1959), a history of the Algerian revolution; *Toward the African Revolution* (1961); and his final, and arguably best known work, *The Wretched of the Earth*, written in 1961 and published in 1963.[35] In these books he analyzes not only the relationship between imperial powers and their subjugated colonies, but what this subjugation does to the subjugated people psychologically. He observes, for example, in *Black Skin White Masks* that popular culture, such as cinema, constructs the image of the colonized for the colonizer *and* for the colonized as well: "Insofar as he conceives of European culture as a means of stripping himself of his race, he becomes alienated."[36] The representation of blackness in Euroculture as Other alienates the black viewer, not from the film or book or play, but from himself or herself.

Jean-Paul Sartre, in his preface to *The Wretched of the Earth*, sees "the Third World find[ing] itself and speak[ing] to itself through [Fanon's] voice."[37] Fanon asserts many things, two of which in particular are useful for the present study. First, he argues that violence is the only natural response to colonialism, as colonialism itself is violence — violence against the culture, society, and psychology of the colonized, but also often with attendant violence in the form of physical suppression — rape, beatings, killings, etc.— to maintain colonial domination. Furthermore, violence proves to effect social and historical change, and is respected by those who have first employed it. Violent rebellion, asserts Fanon, is the natural and proper response to the violence of imperialism. The technological superiority of the colonizer is no excuse. Fanon argues in *Wretched of the Earth* that guerrilla warfare can defeat advanced weaponry.[38] History has proven him right, as have the *Star Wars* films.

Second, colonial culture and the colonial condition, as noted above, alienate the colonized from his or her own history, culture, and even self. Colonialism works to refute identity and create a new identity from the colonizer's perspective. This results, says Fanon, in a kind of schizophrenia in the colonized, who learns to hate him or herself, his/her identity, and what he/she represents. Again, the only possible healthy response to this is a violent decolonization, not just of society, but of the mind. The colonized must learn not to think of her or himself in the colonizer's terms. The colonial world is centered on the white male. Fanon asserts that the colonized culture must shift its center away from that model. The so-called "margins" of society must become the center of focus for a decolonized, postcolonial world.

Star Wars is a world in which the center is continually embedded in white maleness — Luke Skywalker, Han Solo, Obi-Wan Kenobi, Qui-Gon Jinn, and Anakin Skywalker, as well as the villains: Darth Vader, Chancellor Palpatine, and Grand Moff Tarkin — are all white males, despite non-westerns names and cultural heritages, as discussed in the following chapters. The people of color of the *Star Wars* universe are literally alienated — they are represented as aliens, as complete and utterly non-human. For the most part in the two trilogies, non-white means non-human. They are alienated from human psychology by literally being aliens.

The original trilogy is not in the center — it is set in the margins. Tatooine, Yavin, Hoth, Dagobah, Bespin, and Endor and its moon are not the center — many of the settings are rebel bases which are set far from the Galactic center. As Luke remarks to Threepio of Tatooine, "If there's a bright center to the universe, you're on the planet that it's farthest from." The Death Star(s) are mobile — they are free-moving space stations that can travel from one system to another. The first trilogy is about marginalized peoples and movable worlds. The second trilogy concerns the growth of power at the center — Coruscant is the center of the galaxy, both geographically and politically. Although most of the action takes place in the margins — Naboo, Tatooine, Geonosis, Kamino, Kashyyyk, Utapau, Mustafar, etc., Naboo is called "the provincial and little populated planet,"[39] Tatooine and Utapau are in the "outer rim," etc. — the new trilogy is much more focused in and on the center than the original — the centers of power, the centers of commerce, and the center of the galaxy. Coruscant is the galactic capital and the heart of the Republic, and eventually the heart of the Empire. The audience is shown how the consolidation of power at the center has an effect at the margins. Yet, even in the margins the focus remains on white males.

In short, *Star Wars* is rather contradictory and embraces a wide variety of different and differing ideologies. Nevertheless, it contains within it a narrative of the conquest of the galaxy and the eventual rebellion against the conquering power. While using the archetypal language of postcolonialism and asserting the value of rebellion, the center remains dominated by a white, male power structure. The people of color are still alienated. One must ask the larger question of who the Empire really is.

Bill Ashcroft, Gareth Griffith and Helen Tiffin have even written a book entitled *The Empire Writes Back*, which discusses postcolonial literature.[40] The title, an obvious pun on *The Empire Strikes Back*, forms an intertext with that work. Yet, the two texts have very different meanings for "empire." In *Star Wars*, "Empire" refers to the instruments, technology, and individuals who serve the purpose of imperialism. In *The Empire Writes Back*, however, the word "empire" is used to refer to the occupied lands, in opposition to the colonial power. The "empire" — the subjected peoples — write back to and back at the center, i.e., the colonizer.

In the case of the *Star Wars* films, the Empire remains at the center, as do white males. The rebellion does not exist to achieve liberation for the oppressed indigenous peoples — it seeks to restore the previous privileged to power. There is no "empire" responding to the construction at the center. The disenfranchised of the galaxy remain so, regardless of which group is in power. The Empire uses violence to suppress and the Republic simply ignores the margins.

Fanon is a hero of the Rebellion because he asserts the right to violence in response to the multiple levels of violence that Empire engenders. Many of those levels of violence, such as the suppression of indigenous culture and language in favor of that of the colonizer, for example, are not visible in the films. Yet no one can assert that the Empire does not hold onto its power without resorting to violence and fear of every type. Fanon is a hero of the Rebellion because he asserts the psychological damage done to the colonized, and proposes shifting focus from the center to the margin to combat the decentering off the colonized in his or her own mind. Fanon, however, would not be a member of the Rebellion, ultimately, as it is not a true colonial revolution in the Fanonian sense, despite its use of archetypal language. Both the Rebellion and the Empire are fighting for the right of privileged white males to control the galaxy.

The Political History of the *Star Wars* Universe

Though the fourth film made, *The Phantom Menace* is the first in the series. The unnamed galaxy far, far away has been organized into a loose collective called "The Republic." Over a thousand worlds for over a thousand years have participated in this collective. The primary governing body is the Senate, in which each world or system has three representative members. No indication is given as to how Senators are selected. In *Clones* it is implied that Amidala is asked to be a Senator by the Queen of Naboo, which is an elected position with a finite term. No term or term limitations are implied in any of the films for Senators.

It also seems that each individual world is responsible for selecting its own Senators, and one might assume that the dominant group on each world or system does the selecting. For example, on Naboo there are at least two sentient species— the Naboo (after whom the planet is named, or vice versa) and the Gungun. Yet only Naboo are sent as Senators. Not until after the Battle of Naboo and a treaty between the two species is a Gungun sent as a representative, in this case, Senator Jar Jar Binks.

The Senate is headed by the Supreme Chancellor who presumably sets the agenda, runs the proceedings, and works to negotiate differences and conflicts between member planets. The first Supreme Chancellor the audience is introduced to is Valorum (Terence Stamp) who, the audience is informed, is corrupt and in the hands of "the bureaucrats," presumably the underlings who actually run the Senate and who may or may not be in the service of special interests.

In addition to the bureaucrats, who are responsible for the day to day running of the Republic, there are the Jedi, who serve as "the guardians of peace and justice" in the Republic. The Jedi are a warrior priesthood, a religious organization that trains its members in the use of the Force and in martial arts. The Jedi Council oversees the training and employment of the Jedi. Jedi can be trained collectively, in classes, by the masters on the

Council. Individual Jedi may also take a Padawan learner, an apprentice of sorts whom the Jedi trains one-on-one. When the Jedi and the Council believe a Padawan is ready, the Padawan is submitted to "the trials," presumably exams and tests in a variety of fields to determine whether or not the Padawan is ready to be a full Jedi. The only one of the trials made clear from the films is that the Padawan must make his or her own lightsaber. They are responsible to the Republic and the Supreme Chancellor, but it would seem the Supreme Chancellor must request their services. He cannot order them to do anything.

The Jedi serve as negotiators, peacekeepers, and law enforcement. It would seem that the Jedi are only employed for external conflict resolution. Planets that are members of the Republic have their own internal systems of governance, whether an elected monarchy as on Naboo, a loose organization of criminal syndicates as on Tatooine, or a business collective as on Bespin. The Republic does not seem to interfere in internal matters on these worlds, only conflicts between systems. As a result the Republic has not required a standing army.

A real world parallel might be found in the United Nations, which does not interfere in internal affairs of nations— any nation is allowed to join regardless of type of government, so long as the nation agrees to abide by the U.N. charter. Peacekeepers may be sent to "trouble spots," but the U.N. does not, per se, have its own army with which to enforce its pronouncements, rulings, and policies. Rather, it serves as an international body to which grievances may be brought and collective action may be taken on such problems that ignore national boundaries like disease, famine, or natural disasters. The U.N. may condemn aggressive action by a member nation, but cannot do much about it unless such action is universally condemned and the major parties on the Security Council are willing to use their own resources to stop the aggression, as happened in the Persian Gulf War (1991).

In opposition to the Jedi are an order called the Sith. The Sith are Jedi who have gone over to the dark side and who use the power of the Force for personal gain. Sith Lords, as they are known, developed out of the Jedi. There are only two Sith at any one time, a master and an apprentice. The Sith, Ki Adi Mundi notes in *Phantom*, have been extinct for over a millennium when that film begins. Yet the order has clearly been reestablished, and is out to destroy the Jedi and take over the galaxy.

Arguably, the entire prequel trilogy concerns the fight between the Sith and the Jedi. In *Phantom*, Darth Maul tells Darth Sidious, "At last we will reveal ourselves to the Jedi. At last we will have our revenge." When he is declared emperor in *Sith*, Palpatine cries out, "Once again the Sith will rule the galaxy." Over the progression of the trilogy, we see the master, Darth Sidious, go through three apprentices: Darth Maul, Darth Tyranus, and Darth Vader. The whole reason why there can be only two is that the Sith apparently do not share power well. In fact, the most famous Sith, Darth Plagueis, was killed by his apprentice. So is Darth Sidious, eventually. Darth Sidious also sacrifices his first two apprentices in order to consolidate his power and bring to him Anakin Skywalker as the final apprentice. He orders Anakin to kill Count Dooku (Darth Tyranus) when Dooku kneels at his feet, literally disarmed and helpless. Though Anakin admits, "It is not the Jedi way," he still beheads the apprentice, thus making way for himself to become a Sith Lord.

The very titles of the final two films also read as a battle between Sith and Jedi. A thousand years ago, presumably when the Republic was founded, the Sith were defeated by the Jedi. The Empire is their titular "revenge," taking power over the galaxy and theoretically wiping out the Jedi, though Yoda, Obi-Wan, and the Skywalker twins obviously survive to "return" by the last film of the original trilogy. One might even read the battle for the center in the prequel trilogy as being fought in the margins, much as the Cold War of the twentieth century was not fought openly between the Soviet Union and the United States, but by proxy in Africa, Asia, and Latin America.

The senior senator from Naboo, Palpatine, is actually the Sith Lord Darth Sidious. He orchestrates a crisis so as to create a demand for a strong and powerful leader of the Republic, which will ultimately allow him to seize power and become sole, incontrovertible ruler. He has taken as his apprentice a Sith named Darth Maul. When Maul is killed by Obi-Wan Kenobi, Sidious recruits Yoda's former Padawan, Count Dooku, to become Darth Tyranus, his new Sith apprentice. After the fall of the Republic, a third apprentice, Anakin Skywalker, becomes a Sith Lord, Darth Vader.

As *Phantom* begins, the opening crawl informs the audience that, "The taxation of trade routes to outlying star systems is in dispute." The specific nature of those disputes and why the Trade Federation, a member of the Republic and a collective of business worlds and systems, primarily Neimoidians, is blockading Naboo is not explained. One might assume that the Naboo object to the Trade Federation attempting to tax the Naboo's trade, perhaps in the interest of maintaining a monopoly, but none of the details are given.

Instead, we learn that the Trade Federation is blockading the planet Naboo, preventing any ships from entering or leaving the planet. The Supreme Chancellor has asked the Jedi to resolve the dispute, and the Jedi council sends the unconventional Jedi Qui-Gon Jinn and his Padawan learner Obi-Wan Kenobi. The Trade Federation attempts to assassinate the Jedi, who then escape to the planet surface onboard a landing ship that is the vanguard of an invasion. The Trade Federation plans on colonizing the Naboo and will occupy Theed, the capital city, and force the Queen to sign a trade agreement. This plan sounds remarkably like nineteenth century European colonization, in which invading Western nations forced local rulers to sign unfair trade agreements and then used the agreements as a pretext to strengthen their control when that control was threatened with resistance.

The two Jedi, confronted with the invasion, join Amidala and members of her entourage as they go to Coruscant to plead directly to the Senate against the blockade and invasion. After a stop on Tatooine to repair the ship, where they find Anakin Skywalker, a slave boy, pilot, and product of a virgin birth, free him from his master, and bring him to the Jedi Council, which initially decides not to train him as a Jedi.

Amidala pleads to the Senate to intervene in the conflict on Naboo, but the Trade Federation delegation protests and the Supreme Chancellor orders a fact-finding investigation instead of interference. The Jedi and the Queen then return to Naboo, finding it occupied and under martial law. Joining forces with the other indigenous intelligent species, the Gungun, the Naboo are able to wage a counterattack against the occupiers and succeed in capturing the Viceroy, forcing him to sign a treaty on their terms. The Sith apprentice kills Qui-Gon and is himself killed by Obi-Wan. No reason is given, but the Jedi Council then relents and allows Anakin to be trained.

In other words, *Phantom* is ultimately a film about the effort of one group to colonize another and the successful resistance to that colonization. Beneath the colonization attempt, however, was another, more sinister purpose: to create a crisis situation in which a powerful leader could seize control of the Republic, which is precisely what happens. Valorum receives a vote of no confidence from the members of the Senate and in sympathetic response to the invasion of Naboo, Palpatine, who orchestrated the crisis in the first place, is named Supreme Chancellor.

Clones is as much an overtly political film as well—from the opening terrorist attack on Amidala's ship to the senatorial debate on whether or not the Republic should have a standing army to the overriding issue of whether or not systems are able to secede from the Republic and set up their own organization. *Clones* begins almost a decade after *Phantom* ends. Amidala and Jar Jar are now senators from Naboo (the audience is never introduced to the third), which has elected a new queen. Palpatine remains Supreme Chancellor and Anakin is now Obi-Wan's Padawan, although he has received attention and support from Palpatine as well.

The Fanonian elements of the series come to the forefront in a deleted scene, available on DVD, in which the Senate debates what to do about the Separatist movement. Some are in favor of using the Jedi or other military force to keep the separatists in the Republic. Amidala, whose ship and decoy double are destroyed in the opening sequence by a bomb placed by separatist terrorists, argues, "If you offer the Separatists violence, they can only show violence in return."

Mace Windu accuses "disgruntled spice miners on the moons of Naboo" of planting the bomb that almost kills Amidala. Amidala believes it is the work of Count Dooku, which Ki Adi Mundi dismisses out of hand: "He is a political idealist, not a murderer." Windu concurs, as Dooku is a former Jedi: "He couldn't assassinate anyone. It's not in his character." Yet, though the source of the bomb is never confirmed, the fact that Dooku now uses violence to achieve his ends is a given, as Dooku is now a Sith. Windu's comment, however, indicates the prejudicial view of Jedi in the galaxy — Jedi cannot and will not use violence for personal ends, which seems like wishful thinking when one realizes Jedi are trained since childhood to use violence as a solution when necessary.

The separatists, who now call themselves the Confederacy of Independent Systems, seek to leave the Republic. While their reasons for desiring separation and secession are never made clear, it might be safely assumed that they desire freedom from the Republic's laws regarding trade and interaction between systems. The separatists are mostly, if not entirely, commercially oriented systems and species: The Corporate Alliance, the Trade Federation, the Techno Union, the Intergalactic Banking Clan, and the Commerce Guild.[41] The insect race on Geonosis work at and guard the droid factory owned by the Techno Union. These groups desire to practice predatory capitalism, which seems to be prevented by the rules of the Republic.

Yet more of Palpatine's plans are revealed in the second episode as well. He has arranged for a standing army of the Republic to be created in the name of the Jedi by the cloners on Kamino. Given that the Separatists have a droid army, which is growing, the clone army being made on Kamino is the only force large enough to fight against them. Using the name Sifo-Dyas, a deceased member of the Jedi Council, Palpatine arranges for the creation of a large clone army, based on the genetic model of a bounty hunter, Jango Fett. When Obi-Wan investigates the assassination of a bounty hunter trying to kill Amidala, he is lead to Kamino and the existence of a clone army.

Also implied is that Palpatine/Sidious, working through his agent Darth Tyranus/Count Dooku, is encouraging the separatists to be more aggressive in their confrontation with the Republic. Playing both sides against each other, Palpatine also stokes fears of the Separatists and manipulates the Senate into both granting him unlimited power and to sponsors the "Military Creation Act," which calls for the development of a "Grand Army of the Republic." His plan to become Emperor is now almost complete — he has the military, the authority to use it, and the Senate has voluntarily agreed to cede their power to him in this time of crisis.

At Geonosis, the Jedi stage a pre-emptive strike in the name of the Republic against the Separatists. The Jedi, who were in danger of being wiped out in the arena, emerge victorious. But as Yoda states in the coda to the film, "Begun the Clone Wars have." In other words, through his machinations, Palpatine/Sidious has engineered a civil war in the Galaxy.

In the third and final episode, Sidious's plans are made complete. Three years or so have passed since the beginning of the Clone Wars. Obi-Wan Kenobi has been made a general. He and other Jedi Masters now lead clone troops into battle against the droid armies of the Separatists. The opening crawl to Episode III makes the theme apparent: "WAR!" is the first word of the crawl. The battles that raged throughout the outer rim have finally made it to the center. The opening fight of the film takes place over Coruscant. Count Dooku leads the Separatists. The droid armies are commanded by General Grievous, an alien soldier whose body, severely damaged after an accident, has been made into a cyborg and kept alive with the help of a respirator. Together, they have attacked the Republic capital and "kidnapped" Chancellor Palpatine, who has actually arranged the entire affair to bring the artificial civil war to a head.

Rescued by Anakin and Obi-Wan, Palpatine has Anakin kill Dooku, while Grievous escapes. Palpatine takes Anakin into his confidence, revealing his identity as a Sith Lord and offering Anakin, who is afraid his own wife will die, the power over life and death. The Jedi Council dispatches Obi-Wan to Utapau where Grievous hides with the main body of the droid army, while other worlds, including Kashyyyk, are attacked by other droid units. Mace Windu, accompanied by three other members of the Jedi Council, attempts to arrest Palpatine who has stayed in office long after his term was over and whom Windu accuses of treason and being a Sith Lord. Palpatine reveals himself as Sidious, the Sith Lord, and a phenomenal lightsaber duelist, dispatching the other three Jedi Masters easily. Windu defeats him, but when he tries to kill Palpatine, fearing that since the Sith Lord controls both the Senate and the courts there will be no legal recourse to dethroning the Chancellor, Anakin stops him, allowing Palpatine to kill Windu. Anakin then swears allegiance to Palpatine and is named Darth Vader, the new Sith apprentice.

Palpatine announces that because they tried to arrest him, all Jedi are the enemy of the Republic and must be eliminated. In a two-pronged attack on his enemies, Palpatine sends Anakin to the Jedi temple to kill all the Jedi there, including the "younglings"—children training to be Jedi, and conveys to the clone troops to execute Order 66, a secret order he has given the clones to kill the Jedi leading them. All Jedi but Yoda and Obi-Wan are killed.

With the elimination of the Jedi, all resistance to Palpatine ends and he is proclaimed Emperor after he declares the Republic an Empire. Anakin is dispatched to Mustafar where the Separatist leaders, including the Trade Federation leader Nute Gunray, are waiting for the end of the war. On Palpatine's order, Anakin kills all of the separatists as Palpatine orders the droid armies permanently deactivated. Thus, the only army left in the galaxy are the clone troopers, who now become the stormtroopers and the personal army of the Emperor. Though Obi-Wan defeats Anakin in a duel on Mustafar, leaving him limbless and mortally wounded, the Emperor rescues Anakin and has him surgically transformed into the Darth Vader of the original trilogy, "more machine than man."

Amidala dies in childbirth bringing the twins Luke and Leia into the galaxy. The beginnings of the Rebel Alliance are seen as Bail Organa, who is the ruler of and senator from Alderaan, joins with Obi-Wan and Yoda to hide the children from Anakin and the Emperor and begin to plot the downfall of Palpatine, who begins construction of the Death Star.

Nineteen years pass while the Empire consolidates its power. The Senate, which Obi-Wan states in *Sith* is needed by the Emperor in order to rule the galaxy, is first called the "Imperial Senate," but then is eventually disbanded. The Emperor rules directly by passing his orders to the regional governors. The governors are able to exert authority over the systems and planets of the Empire through the power of the clone army, now called stormtroopers, and through military technology, most emblematic in the Death Star.

In response to the militarization and imperialization of the galaxy and the consolidation of all authority in the hands of the Emperor, a new group emerges: the Rebel Alliance. Beginning as "The Alliance to Restore the Republic," the organization, faced with persecution from the Empire, went underground and became a full scale rebellion. Utilizing a series of hidden bases and a constantly moving fleet, the Rebellion against the Empire grew. It also incorporated spies in high places, which brought information valuable for the destruction of key Empire technology.

The capture of former senator Princess Leia by Vader could have brought the Rebellion to an end. In order to demonstrate the Empire's power, her planet of Alderaan was destroyed. Leia, however, had had a duel mission: bring Obi-Wan Kenobi back into the service of the Republic and deliver stolen plans of the Death Star to the Rebellion high command. A pair of droids with whom the plans were entrusted make their way to Obi-Wan on Tatooine, where, with the son of Skywalker, who remains ignorant of his heritage, he hires a smuggler to get him to Alderaan.

Also captured, the small band manages to rescue Leia. They are allowed to escape unmolested as the Death Star plans to follow them back to the rebel base. Utilizing the stolen plans, the Rebellion discovers a weakness in the structure of the Death Star and destroys it. The Empire then locates another rebel base on Hoth and is able to destroy it.

The revelation that the son of Skywalker lives and is training to be a Jedi causes Vader and the Emperor to consider it a top priority that Skywalker be converted to a Sith. On Bespin, another marginal system which had managed to avoid imperial attention, Han and Leia are captured by Vader and used as bait to lure Luke. After singular combat, in which Vader both reveals that he is Luke's father and cuts off Luke's hand, Luke and the others escape.

First rescuing Han from the criminal who hired the bounty hunters to get him, Luke and the others then join up with the rest of the Rebellion for an all-out assault on the new Death Star. Located above the moon of Endor, the new Death Star, still under construction, is protected by a shield generated from the moon's surface. A two-pronged attack is designed. A small commando squad attacks the moon in order to destroy the shield. The fleet will then attack the unprotected Death Star. This battle becomes all the more important when the Rebels learn that the Emperor will be on board the station. Thus, its destruction is not merely a battle goal but actually an assassination attempt — kill the Emperor and the Empire falls.

The Emperor, however, is aware of the plans to assassinate him. The Death Star is fully functioning and can not only defend itself, but can also be used offensively to attack the Rebel fleet. Of far greater concern to him is the conversion of "Young Skywalker." The Death Star is ultimately destroyed by a combination of luck on the part of the Rebels and the assistance of the indigenous people of the moon of Endor, the Ewoks, who aid the Rebel commandos in the destruction of the shield generator. The death of the Emperor and the destruction of the second Death Star seem to indicate the end of the Empire and the restoration of the Republic, but this is by no means guaranteed.

The political situation in the original trilogy is overly simplistic — a conflict between an evil empire and a good rebellion. The Rebels love freedom, the Empire loves power. The Rebels are an autonomous collective, the Empire is a dictatorship. Yet there remains both nuance and implied complexities in the politics of that trilogy. It should also be noted that the Empire is the active creation of a single individual — Palpatine — who works to enhance and develop his own personal power. The Rebellion is a collective fighting for their own freedom, but also for the re-establishment of their own power. Many of the Rebels are not the poor and disenfranchised of the galaxy; they are the ones who were formerly in power.

The Rebellion against the Galactic Empire is not a rag-tag, fugitive, small group. It is a well-organized, well-funded, well-armed body, organized into military ranks with several hidden bases. These bases are well-constructed, well-hidden, and contain large amounts of military hardware (ships, weapons, shield generators, etc.). Those leading the Rebellion come from the elite of society — Princess Leia is from the royal house of Alderaan and a member of the Imperial Senate. Other characters clearly also come from establishment backgrounds. The Rebellion, growing out of the Alliance to Restore the Republic, is actually a group out to reassert its own power and dominance.

The very name, the Rebel Alliance, indicates that it is actually a group of smaller organizations that have been united into a single body against the Empire. The Alliance is multiethnic, multiracial, multicultural, and, at least in theory, egalitarian. It is mobile, moving from base to base in order to avoid direct conflict with the military might of the Empire, and has spies placed very highly within the ranks of the Empire. These spies feed technological information (such as the designs for the Death Star, or permission codes for Imperial shuttles) to the Rebels in order to enable them to better plan strikes against the Empire. There is no mention of what will happen after the Rebellion is over. The main, indeed the sole, purpose, is to bring down the Empire and destroy its military might. The Rebellion, in short, is a guerrilla war fought in space, usually on planets in the margins for the purpose of reestablishing the old order.

The audience is never shown the Rebels attacking on Coruscant — indeed, is never even shown or hears about Coruscant until the Special Edition of *Jedi*, when it is briefly shown as part of the victory celebrations. It is an interpolation, as in Greek mythology, where gods added to the pantheon are written into earlier stories — Dionysus, a god from the Levant, is made to be Zeus's son so that he is now a part of the divine family, justifying worship even though it did not exist previously — or in the writing of scripture, in which later authors add to the writings of earlier ones to justify a new belief. The Rebels fight on Hoth, Yavin, Endor, and Sullust — out of the way places. They seek to reestablish what had been — perceived as freedom yet also encoded into a hierarchy of power. The Rebellion parallels African, Asian, and Latin American independence movements, yet it also parallels the attempt by White Russians to reverse the effects of the Russian Revolution and restore the Czar to power. The new order is rejected by the old, which wishes to maintain its own privilege and power. Leia, after all, is both "Princess" and "Senator." The Senate, held up in both trilogies as the model of democracy, is hardly that. Naboo elects its queens, but the queen appoints the senators. The Gunguns had never been represented in the Senate until Padme selected Jar Jar to serve. Apparently senators serve for life, as Bail Organa, the "father" of the princess was a senator for decades, and many of the same senators serving in *Phantom* are seen still in the senate in the second and third films. Princesses, queens, and royalty serve in the senate while slaves fix ships on Tatooine.

The six films, taken together, compose a master narrative of the fall of a Republic, the rise of the Empire, and the successful revolution against that Empire by the former leaders of the Republic. A real civil war, the Rebellion, follows an artificially manufactured one, created for the purpose of allowing one individual to seize power and impose his will on the galaxy. The *Star Wars* series is part war story, part history lesson, part model for revolution, and part discourse on the nature of power and rebellion. Unasked by the films is the question of what happens after the Empire falls. Are the Rebels' motives "pure," or do they have plans for the galaxy after they conquer its rulers? In some ways, as will be argued below, the films are not so much "mythic," as some have argued, as an "ideological mirror" — so many things are left blank that the audience is left to make assumptions and see in the films the reflection of their own ideology. Leftists see the Empire as being rightist; rightists see the Empire as being leftist. The viewer is the good guy; therefore, whatever the viewer identifies as negative must be the bad guy.

Yet underneath this fluidity of meaning is the appropriation of the language of colonialism and empire. The films clearly deal with issues of colonization, imperialism, power and dominance. It is through the terminology of the films that we see them in a Fanonian sense as being both anti-colonial and yet pro–Western.

The Language of Empire

Peter Farb reports that

> In 1492 Queen Isabella of Spain was formally presented with a copy of Antonio de Nebrija's *Gramatica*, the first grammar written about any

modern European language. When the queen bluntly asked, "What is the book for?" the Bishop of Avila replied, "Your Majesty, language is the perfect instrument of empire."[42]

We use language to not only describe reality, but to create reality. To name something is to have power over it. In the *Star Wars* films, the language of archetypal colonialism is employed. *The* Empire dominates the galaxy, resisted and fought against by *The* Rebellion. *The* Emperor controls and dominates *The* Empire. And while no locality, planet, or people are termed colonies, *per se*, imperial domination, colonization, and the use of violence to impose order are apparent in all of the films.

I follow here Deborah Wyrick's definition of colonialism as "the forceful occupation of another people's land in order to extract material benefit," to which we might also add, in order to establish and maintain power.[43] Power and profit are the two engines that drive colonialism. The Empire is driven by power and profit. "Stormtroopers" are used to control and maintain order — they are given authority to use violence to fulfill that mandate. The Empire does not have "colonies," *per se*, but it has colonized the entire former Republic. It can be argued, that we see the colonization of Bespin by the Empire in *Empire*. Darth Vader goes to Bespin to capture Luke Skywalker's friends to use as bait to lure him to a confrontation that will turn him to the dark side. Lando Calrissian, the administrator of Bespin, makes a deal when confronted by the threat of violence from the Empire that Vader will be allowed to play out his trap on Bespin. Vader then "alters the agreement" by leaving a garrison, and threatens to do worse if Lando objects. Lando then suggests to his people that they flee as the Empire is now in control of Cloud City, as he himself flees and joins the Rebellion against the Empire.

We also see a kind of pre–Empire colonization of Naboo by the Trade Federation. The leader of the Trade Federation, Nute Gunray, has the title of Viceroy, itself a colonial term. The title Viceroy is particularly apt for two reasons, the first being its echo of real world colonial history, the second being the implication that the title holder is merely a deputy. The Viceroy of a colony does not rule for himself, but rather in the name of the monarch or government of the colonizer. Nute Gunray is a colonial administrator who seems to be in command of the invasion of Naboo, but actually serves as deputy of Darth Sidious. The Trade Federation Viceroy serves a master higher than himself.

One might also ask what kind of imperialism is represented in the films? There are many real world echoes to be found in the construction of empire in the series. It could be considered to be modeled on Persian, Athenian, Roman, modern European or even American models. In a sense, it is a combination of echoes, reflecting aspects of many different real world imperialisms. Yet the specific language and situations cause some critics to view specific antecedents as having a shaping influence on the idea and language of empire in *Star Wars*.

Martin M. Winkler, for example, writes that "Lucas's evil empire parallels the Roman Empire and conforms to the negative view of imperial Rome generally present in popular culture."[44] Winkler is right in that the historical process of the imperialization of Rome is echoed in the *Star Wars* saga: a republic ruled by a senate builds up its military might and a ruler is proclaimed emperor who then rules the republic as an empire. He also uses the military might of the empire to expand what is a multi-racial, multiethnic empire through conquest. Winkler sees numerous Roman echoes throughout the films, both linguistically and situationally: Grand Moff Tarkin's name suggests the Tarquins, "the last dynasty of Roman kings," the stolen shuttle in *Jedi* is named Tydirium, the senator who becomes emperor is named "Palpatine," from the Latin words for "imperial" or "chamberlain."[45]

Thus, both modern and classical models of imperialism are present in the films. Yet the specific language of the films suggest the construction of a modern colonial discourse. Senator Palpatine has dissolved the Senate at the beginning of *Star Wars*. Grand Moff Tarkin informs the men in the Death Star briefing room of this, and explains that "The regional governors now have direct control over their territories. Fear will keep the local systems in line." Governor Tarkin uses the Death Star as the colonial powers in Africa and Asia used their military might to keep the locals "in line." *Star Wars* places the theories of post-colonial political analyst Frantz Fanon in outer space: colonialism is "violence in its natural state," and "it will only yield when confronted with greater violence," i.e., armed rebellion, and, in the case of *Star Wars*, *The* Rebellion against *The* Empire.[46] Fanon claims that liberation from imperial oppression can only "be achieved through force."[47] This claim holds true in the *Star Wars* universe as well. We may add the Jedi struggle against the Empire to Fanon's Algerian insurrection, to the Mau Mau war of Kenya, to the Boxer Rebellion of China, and to dozens of other armed uprisings against politically, militarily, and economically dominant empires. In fact, Lucas's use of direct articles and capital letters (The Rebellion, The Empire) in the *Star Wars* trilogy seemingly suggests an archetypal colonial structure and struggle; *The Wretched of the Earth* becomes "The Wretched of the Galaxy."

Lucas's films thus bifurcate the universe into two camps: rebels and supporters of the Empire. The films furthermore make moral judgments on these camps: rebels are good, they are freedom-fighters, they use the

Force; the Empire and its supporters are the bad guys, they are evil, they have power and abuse it and therefore must be resisted. A parallel to real world politics is avoided being directly ascribed in the films, but the message remains that rebellion against an evil, economically oppressive Empire is "good."

In *The Star Wars Encyclopedia*, Stephen J. Sansweet defines the Empire by noting:

> [The Emperor] was bolstered by a vast war machine and the scheming of millions who also saw personal benefit in subjugating the inhabitants of the galaxy — and in killing off billions of inhabitants if necessary.[48]

In another entry, Sansweet observes that the Empire "was based on tyranny, hatred of non-humans, brutal and lethal force, and, above all, constant fear."[49] In short, the Empire is defined by its use of violence and force, its inherent racism, and its predatory capitalism.

The Empire also seems to be racially homogenous. Only humans are seen in Imperial settings. The Rebellion is multicultural and multi-ethnic, but the Empire is all-human, all-white, and primarily British. When aliens are present, they are not a part of the imperial hierarchy; they are bounty hunters, for example, hired by the Empire to find the rebels more effectively. Or they are tools in another sense, being used to build battle droids to provide an enemy for the eventual clone army, for example, or serving as informants and spies, such as in Mos Eisley in *A New Hope*. The Empire, by and large, is primarily a humans-only, or at least human-centric, human-privileged organization.

Another imperial concept present in the films is the idea of slavery. In *Jedi*, Leia, once captured, becomes a "slave girl," chained to Jabba the Hutt in a very revealing outfit, denoting her status as his sexual slave. In *Phantom* the audience learns of an entire class of slaves on Tatooine: Anakin Skywalker and his mother Shmi are slaves. Although Padme insists that the Republic has anti-slavery laws, the truth is that slavery is not only present in the galaxy, it grows under the Empire. Anakin tells Qui-Gon he wants to become a Jedi Knight so that he might free slaves. Along the way, he becomes corrupted and loses his interest in freeing slaves. Rather, he becomes committed to the Empire and serves to enslave people to the Empire. A potential slave-freer, who has known slavery himself, is corrupted into a slave-maker. Likewise, the attack of the droid army on Kashyyyk in *Sith* occurs because members of the Separatists seek to enslave the Wookiees. Between *Sith* and *A New Hope* Chewbacca served as a slave.

Although Wookiee slavery seems to carry the echo of the trans–Atlantic slave trade, the slavery of the *Star Wars* universe is not the chattel slavery of the United States for the first three centuries of its existence. Instead, it is much closer to the classical concept of slavery. Anakin and Shmi are slaves that can wager or buy their freedom. They have their own home, away from Watto's. They can own their own property. Anakin has his own room filled with electronics and is building a droid, C3PO. Watto, *Star Wars Episode I: The Visual Dictionary* reports, is "a firm but fair master" who "treats his slaves more decently than most."[50]

Even given that Watto is a sterling master, the films represent the buying and selling of human beings, but specifically white human beings. The horror of slavery in the series is that Leia, Anakin, and Shmi are subjected to slavery. There is no reminder that modern historic slavery was rooted in commercial practices instituted by European colonizers who needed cheap labor for their colonies and created a system of chattel slavery based on race — people of color (both African and Indigenous American) could be enslaved and could neither buy their freedom nor own property. Wookiee slavery, though discussed in the peripheral material of the canon, is never seen on screen or even mentioned directly.[51]

The double effect of the representation of slavery in the films is to find horror in white people suffering what millions of people of color suffered and simultaneously to assert that slavery, for all its horror, was not all that bad. This contradictory yet completely comprehensible approach to the representation of slavery absolves the viewer of any guilt for the enslavement of blacks by whites while simultaneously filling them with horror at the prospect of being a slave one's self.

Not only slavery but the idea of servitude is engaged by the series. Consider the number of times the word "master" is used, by whom, and in order to address whom. "Master" is used in the sense of a teacher (i.e., a martial arts master), thus "Master Yoda" and "Master Windu." These are titles of respect to someone who has mastered an art. There is in the film, however, the employment of "Master" to convey a sense of "owner" (i.e. slavery). "Master Luke" is how C3PO acknowledges Luke, and Anakin calls Watto "master" in *Phantom* and Obi-Wan "master" in *Clones* and *Sith*. In the latter, Anakin is no longer a Padawan learner, he is a Jedi in his own right, but still must call Obi-Wan, Yoda, Mace Windu and the others on the council "master." Vader calls the Emperor "my master," indicating both exalted teacher and owner.

The films use the archetypal language of empire to establish an imperial discourse and also use language of dominance and subjugation to convey the horror of being dominated without necessarily echoing historic injustice so that the audience can identify with the Rebellion without identifying the Rebellion with any historical uprisings against western domination. It is a tricky game of inversion to use the language of empire to absolve historic empires of their imperialism while still condemning imperialism.

A Contest of Phantoms: Language, Culture and Economics and the Erasure of Difference

In empires, culture develops as a mixture of assimilation and maintaining indigenous identity. Yet identity can also be used as a weapon in a struggle for independence from empire. Fanon and other postcolonial critics see the assertion of indigenous culture over imposed Western culture as a means of decolonizing the psyche of the colonized people and aid them in avoiding a neocolonial mindset in which the nation is technically free, but values the culture, ideas, and ideals of the former colonizer over their own.

The *Star Wars* films deal with none of these issues, or, at the very least, gloss over them by erasing cultural difference within the Empire. *Star Wars* does not deal with the issue of language in the colonial sense. All characters understand all languages unless they don't. For example, Uncle Owen clearly understands the Jawas. Han clearly understands Chewbacca and Chewbacca clearly understands Galactic basic. Han and Greedo talk to each other in their own languages, yet clearly understand each other. Anakin and Sebulba address each other in their respective native tongues and each understands the other perfectly. It is the audience that needs subtitles to understand the Dug. Yet no one other than C3PO understands the language of Ewoks. C3PO is a translator droid, among other functions. Only he understands R2-D2. He translates for Jabba, who is understood by Bib Fortuna, his major domo, but not by the other characters. Similarly, Leia disguised as Boushh speaks another language which C3PO must translate. One wonders if she learned an entire new language as part of the rescue plot and, if she already spoke it, one must wonder why. There are translator droids to translate any and all languages and most characters can understand several languages without speaking a word of them. Han Solo is never shown speaking Wookiee, a language he clearly understands when he hears it. The issue of language is never addressed.

The issue of culture is never addressed either. We hear some music — the cantina band in *A New Hope* became rather famous when that film was first released and in the special edition of *Jedi* an extended performance of the song by the band in Jabba's palace was interpolated into the film, and we see some games—the alien chess match in *A New Hope* and the podraces in *Phantom*, but other than these slim examples, no culture is actively present in the films. The characters do not go to performances or watch visual media, the décor and decorations in each shot tend to be bland and unobtrusive. There is no attempt to demonstrate the differences between different cultures. The bands of the first and third films in the first trilogy could be switched without problem as neither one is emblematic of any particular culture (granted, they are both on Tatooine). There are no aesthetic markers of specific cultures in the films. Therefore there is no need to assert one's culture as a means of determining a postcolonial, anti-imperial identity. All difference is erased.

The films display a reductivist approach to the presentation of other planets, species, and cultures. Kenneth M. Cameron argues that the same serials that Lucas seeks to recapture are reductivist. A "bastardized" kiSwahili (which was used in *A New Hope* as the language of the Jawas!) becomes "African," a language that everyone on the continent speaks. All Africans, regardless of geographic location become "Zulus," as that is the best known ethnic group in the West. Cameron: "one language and one landscape and a few physical types replacing the hundreds of languages and cultures and physical environments of that enormous continent."[52]

Thus, everyone speaks, or at least understands, Galactic basic, the language of *Star Wars*. All the beings from a single planet, regardless of geographic, religious, political, economic, philosophical and cultural differences between the beings of that planet, are presented as emblematic of all peoples of that world. Not all humans are French, white, isiZulu-speaking, Muslim, wealthy, tall, or from Greenland. But in the *Star Wars* films, planets produce only homogenous groups. Any and all difference between different members of the same species (unless they are human) is erased. And any and almost all difference between alien species from different worlds is also reduced down to the barest minimum: you are from the outer rim, I am from Coruscant, but we all love the music of the cantina band. Instead, social difference rather than cultural difference becomes the focus. Who dominates whom is the determining factor and all other cultural aspects follow from that.

In *Phantom*, Naboo serves as a model for the interaction of the world. The planet Naboo is also the name of the human-like dominant species, Naboo. They are mostly white. They have advanced technology, European-style architecture, and the veneer of "civilization." The other species, the Gungun, do not share a name with the planet. They are not represented in the Galactic Senate. Only the Naboo have that honor, until Jar Jar Binks is nominated to serve in *Clones*. The Gungun live near and in water, use spears and other non-technological weapons, use animals for transportation as opposed to space ships, though clearly they can and do have advanced technology (the ship they loan to Qui-Gon and the shield generator and energy weapons in the battle with the droids).

In addition to a lack of anti-imperial culture, the films take into account a vague sense of economics, but not the full series of economic concerns that center around imperialism. The economics of the saga are also visible in some of the occupations of the characters. Jango and Boba Fett are bounty hunters. Han Solo is a smuggler. Jawas are scavengers who resell what they find. There is a huge black market economy in the original trilogy, echoed in the second one. Yet who pays for not one but two Death Stars? At issue in *Phantom* is the concern over the taxation of trade routes, but no details are given. Are the Naboo attempting to tax Trade Federation ships that pass through their space or is the Trade Federation attempting to tax imports and exports from Naboo? Both are possibilities, neither implied for certain in the film. The difference in meaning between these two possibilities is staggering, which may be why the exact nature of the economic relationship between the Naboo and the Trade Federation is left blank. It is easier to construct the Naboo as good and the Trade Federation as bad if no complexities get in the way.

Similarly, in *Empire*, Bespin is a free planet that has its economy rooted in "gas mining." We learn nothing more about the economy of Bespin and, given that it has been able to "avoid Imperial entanglements," we know nothing of its trading partners. To whom does Bespin sell the gas it mines? It is irrelevant to the story that is being told. There are no echoes of real world economics. Instead, the audience is given a much simpler image to understand. Bespin is the home of a simple and peace-loving people. After the arrival of the Empire and the freezing of Solo, Vader announces he will leave a garrison of stormtroopers, thus bringing Bespin into the Empire. Lando, the planet's supreme administrator, tells his people to flee over a public intercom:

> Attention! This is Lando Calrissian. The Empire has taken control of the city. The Empire has taken control of the city. I advise everyone to leave before more Imperial troops arrive.

The leader of the city tells the citizens to flee their homes, give up their possessions, taking only what they can carry, but gives no indication as to where they should flee. They become refugees and, perhaps, rebels. He does not encourage them to fight, to resist, or to attempt to hold control of their own land. No fighting — only fleeing with what they can carry. The economics of empire are presented as natural disaster. Economic causes are invoked, but only as a pretext to draw one's lightsaber. By the end of *Phantom*, the issue of taxation is not mentioned at all. It was only there in the first place to give a reason to invade, which, in turn, gives a reason to rebel.

In a larger sense, then, we must note that the struggle for liberation in the original trilogy is neither a nationalistic nor ethnic struggle — it is a galactic one. The Ewoks do not fight to free Endor and thus need not assert Ewok culture. The Wookiees do not fight to free Wookiees from oppression, the Gungun do not fight for the Gungun. In fact, in the original trilogy, the evidence is fairly strong that the Empire leaves these groups alone. Instead, the Rebellion is actually a struggle to "free" (and return to power) the benevolent hegemony of the Republic. Missing from *Star Wars* is the concept of "national liberation" as Fanon would call it. Instead, the joining of the Ewoks and Wookiees to struggles that are not theirs are similar to the use of African and Asian troops by the European colonial powers during the Second World War — the "natives" fight to liberate and restore power to those being attacked by totalitarian neighbors, but retain their own second-class citizen status and oppressed situation.

Star Wars as Ideological Mirror

A New Hope was a very different film from the other science fiction and fantasy films of the same era. It was optimistic in a pessimistic era. It was conservative in a liberal era — Jimmy Carter was president and after the failings of conservatives in Vietnam and Watergate, the left seemed ascendant again. It was retro in an era driven by the novel and the new as witnessed by such films as *Alien* or *Jaws*. Yet, people see their own beliefs reflected in the films and see numerous (and often contradictory) real world equivalents of events, characters and elements.

After the completion of the trilogy, a 1986 poll asked people how the viewed "The Empire": 50 percent saw it as "the embodiment of evil," 24 percent saw it as representing right-wing dictators, and 12 percent saw it representing communism, the last group no doubt helped by then President Reagan's assertion that the Soviet Union was an "evil empire."[53] Whom one identifies as the Rebels and whom one sees as the Empire is dependent upon the ideology of the viewer or critic. As Michael Pye and Lynda Myles note, "French leftists critics thought the film [*A New Hope*] was fascist-oriented; Italian rightists thought it was clearly communist-oriented."[54] Hitler would have loved *Star Wars*, argues Tom Carson. But he would have seen the rebels as Aryan freedom fighters and the Empire as Jewish capitalists.[55] Certainly the closing victory scene in *A New Hope* is pure Leni Riefenstahl, with certain shots lifted directly out of *Triumph of the Will*.[56] And yet the Empire's troops are called stormtroopers and the Imperial Command uniforms are very suggestive of Nazi officer uniforms, which would clearly mark the Empire as Nazis and the Rebels as those who stood up against the Third Reich. Thus, *A New Hope* is both fascist and anti-fascist, Nazis are the good guys and Nazis are the bad guys, depending upon perspective. Critics tend to see the saga as reflecting their own ideology, and the Empire is clearly those who oppose that ideology.

Hale Colebatch, a writer at the Perth-based conservative think tank The Australian Institute for Public Policy, sees the *Star Wars* movies as inherently conservative and promoting "traditional, conservative, Western values."[57] In order to take this viewpoint, however, Colebatch must address the issue that the heroes are rebels against the galactic government. His argument is that "The 'rebels' in ... *Star Wars* are actually rebels against a greater rebel who has overturned the natural order."[58] In other words, it is the Emperor who is the true rebel, as rebels, in Colebatch's world view, are anti-western, anti-traditional, and dangerous. Thus, for the rebels to be the heroes that he wants them to be (traditional, conservative, free-market loving embracers of pre-sixties western culture), they must embrace law and order, and thus their enemies must be the true rebels.

Mark Thornton, of the right-wing, libertarian think tank The Ludwig von Mises Institute, has written several articles on how the *Star Wars* trilogies reflect a libertarian economic perspective. In "*Star Wars* and Our Wars" Thornton sees *Phantom Menace* as being about "British colonialism and the problem of mercantilism," as witnessed by the actions of the "increasingly evil Republic" such as "to tax trade routes, blockade, and invade in order to assert power."[59] While this book argues a very similar point, Thornton reaches a far different conclusion: that republics willingly become empires unless they embrace rightist, libertarian principles.

In the same article, Thornton compares *Clones* with the "real life analogy" of the American Civil War, which Thornton claims was fought because the Confederate South "wanted to maintain original Republican ideals (not slavery!)." He compares Lucas's separatists with Southern secessionists, holding both up as a model for sensible economic and political behavior. Lucas's Republic is an "evil democracy ... based on the Lincoln administration that sent an army of immigrants to crush the attempted separation." Thornton notes that both Lincoln and Palpatine dub their militaries "Grand Army of the Republic."

Thornton's metaphor, offensiveness aside, is neither apt nor accurate. The Separatist movement is not looking to maintain the original ideals of the Republic — they seek freedom from the laws of the galaxy to practice predatory capitalism.[60] The Viceroy of *Phantom Menace* (whom Thornton acknowledges as evil) is a member of the separatists in *Clones* (whom Thornton sees as heroically resisting oppression from the Republic). Over and above that, the entire separatist movement is the result of a plot by the future Emperor to consolidate his hold on power. It seems safe to argue that Lincoln did not secretly organize and fund the South, hoping that the threat of secession would allow him to declare himself supreme ruler of the United States. Nor are the clones "an army of immigrants." Although one could argue they come from a system outside of the Republic, they're not immigrants in Thornton's sense. One must also wonder about the analysis of democracy as "evil."

Thornton posits that the fall of the Republic and the rise of the Empire can and will be read as the dominance of the United States in the world today. "Consolidated government," he argues, "is the greatest mistake in American history and the greatest threat to the world today. As in Lucas's film, the American Republic "simply gave in to evil despite its tradition and system of government."

In an earlier essay concerning *Phantom Menace*, Thornton sees the "real phantom menace" as "public-private partnership," as embodied in "the tax franchise over interplanetary trade."[61] Thornton wonders if Lucas has not been reading Ludwig von Mises, the rightist Austrian economist, as *Phantom Menace* demonstrates the value of "sound money [and] free trade" and the evil of "consolidated government." In both of these essays, Thornton sees the *Star Wars* films as embodying a libertarian, right-wing ideology that the institute for which he works also promotes. *Star Wars*, states Thornton, reflects his beliefs. However, like Frank Allnut, whose work sees *A New Hope* as a metaphor for Christian prophesy and is discussed in the next chapter, Thornton sees his own beliefs and ideology reflected in the *Star Wars* films and yet he ignores the evidence that contradicts his interpretation. Other proponents of other ideologies see the films as reflecting their points of view.

With the release of *Sith* in 2005, yet another interpretation of the films' ideological stance has emerged, this time reflecting the current reality of the American occupation of Iraq, an interpretation that Lucas has said is intended. When the film premiered in May at the Cannes Film Festival, audiences read into it the contemporary situation of democracy being deconstructed, and an elected ruler who preaches war as the best and only way to preserve peace. "Lucas says he patterned his story after historical transformations from freedom to feudalism," the *Los Angeles Times* reported, "never figuring when he started his prequel trilogy in the late 1990s that current events might parallel his space fantasy."[62] The examples he cited influencing his story were all historical: Rome, where Caesar was killed and his nephew then made emperor, France, where the king and queen were guillotined, only to see Napoleon rise to power, and Germany, where the Weimar democracy saw the rise of fascism.

While at Cannes, Lucas gave one of the most overtly political readings of his own films, and claimed it was intentional:

> When I wrote it, Iraq didn't exist.... We were just funding Saddam Hussein and giving him weapons of mass destruction. We didn't think of him as an enemy at that time, we were going after Iran and using him as our surrogate, just as we were in Vietnam.... The parallel between what we did in Vietnam and what we're doing in Iraq is unbelievable.[63]

Lucas's original film, as noted above, was at least in part inspired by the situation in Vietnam. And there are echoes of Vietnam even in *Sith*, where the clone troopers have been adding to their armor to individualize it, based on their unit and where they have been fighting, "similar to the way American troops did in Vietnam," states *The Making of Star Wars Revenge of the Sith*."[64]

Reviews of *Sith* interpreted the film in terms of its contemporary political context. *Entertainment Weekly* observed that the Jedi "are portrayed — in a pointed parallel with our own wartime climate — as under siege liberals fighting ostracism" and Palpatine is a "corporate seducer."[65] Virtually every review in the nation cited two key moments in the film: Anakin's assertion, "If you're not with me you're my enemy," echoing President Bush's line after September 11th, "If you're not with us, you're with the terrorists"; and when Palpatine declares himself Emperor and the Senate begins clapping, Padme observes, "This is how liberty dies, with thunderous applause." *Sith* was read as a morality play on the danger of giving too much power to a leader who has manipulated a republic into war that has generated additional political power for himself.

In a case of art imitating life imitating art, politicians began referencing *Sith* during the week of its opening in order to contextualize the then-current debate about President Bush's judicial nominees and then plan by Senate Republicans to limit the filibuster in the case of said nominees. From the floor of the Senate chamber, Senator Frank Lautenberg of New Jersey noted, "In this film, the leader of the Senate breaks the rules to give him and his supporters more power. As millions of Americans go to see this film this week and in the weeks ahead I sincerely hope it doesn't mirror actions taken in the Senate of the United States."[66] Similarly, Moveon.org, a progressive political organization, created a commercial using images from the trailers of the film to show Senate Majority Leader Senator Bill Frist as the Emperor, proclaiming, "One senator wants to send an army of conservative clones to end the Republic as we know it." The commercial ended with the tag line "Stop Senator Frist — Preserve the Republic." *Star Wars* references were again being specifically used to frame a discourse within the nation and to construct a model of political reality. Lucas's remarks to the press seem to indicate that the specific context of the film was the much larger concern of leaders manipulating the public to create a war that ensures they stay in power.

This interpretation is further matched in *Sith* itself. Palpatine tells Anakin that "All who gain power are afraid to lose it," and that Darth Plagueis was so powerful he did not even fear death — he only feared losing his power. The film is thus a treatise on power and its dangers, as well as the things individuals are willing to do to gain and keep power. While many in America saw this nation as aligned with the rebels in the first trilogy, the fear was that the rising Empire was the mirror for America in the prequel trilogy.

Yet Joe Queenan argues as effectively in his article "Anakin Get Your Gun" that "It is the Empire, not the Rebel Alliance that is best equipped to bring peace and prosperity to this troubled galaxy," particularly since the Empire has technology.[67] When one strips the Rebels of their privileged position at the center of the saga, it is clear that the Empire stands for order and the Rebels for chaos and regression. The major problem with the Empire is the corruption of its leadership — the Emperor, Darth Vader, Grand Moff Tarkin — which leads it to pursue wicked ends. Yet the Empire also has a strong military, a strong economy, and can ensure the protection of trade, its people, and its technology. The Empire can also ensure the continual development of technology. The rebels are clearly using second hand equipment and thrown-together supplies. The Empire, however, has built a battle station the size of a small moon. Despite the flaws of its leadership, the Empire is a force for stability and order. Its tactics may be heavy handed, but they are effective. The Empire, Queenan concludes, "bears a strong resemblance to the United States of America," a frequent contention of many critics.[68] Richard Keller Simon, for example, argues that Darth Vader stands for "the evils of American imperial militarism."[69]

Yet the Rebels are also often associated with the United States. Many critics see in the Rebellion an echo of the American Revolution. Queenan also sees the rebels as emblematic of the Carter administration, in power when *A New Hope* was first released: "a bunch of well-meaning, badly-dressed rubes with terrible hair who could not do anything right," while the Empire seems to represent the rise of the Reagan administration, with its visions of military might and "ruthless efficiency."[70] The hero of the Rebellion is "All-American Boy" Luke Skywalker, who is blonde-haired and blue-eyed. Contradictory readings of the real world corollaries are not only possible, they define and shape the experience of viewing the films in some ways. Identity is unstable and often echoes the perspective of the viewer as much as the perspective of the artist.

In a review of *A New Hope* in *Jump Cut* in 1978, Marxist critic Dan Rubey sees that film as inherently conservative, which for him is a negative. It "reromanticizes war" in a generation for whom Vietnam deromanticized combat in cinema.[71] For Rubey, the fantasy of a galaxy a long time ago and far away serves "to disguise Lucas's conservative ideological bias, his assumption that humanity's greatest challenge still lies in expansion and the conquest of new territorial frontiers."[72]

Rubey sees in *A New Hope* the triumph of Western individualism over valuing the collective or the community.[73] The entire planet of Alderaan cannot stop the Death Star, but one blond-haired, blue-eyed young white man in a small ship can. Though many rebel spies died getting the Death Star plans, an entire Blockade Runner crew was captured, Leia was tortured, and dozens of ships attacked the Death Star, Luke and Han get the medals at the end. Rubey compares this to the Arthurian legends or the works of J.R.R. Tolkien in which huge armies may clash over many years, but it is the actions of individual heroes that really matter.

Rubey also locates Vader firmly in the American literary tradition, seeing him as "an American Faustian figure," the driven, intelligent, powerful individual, driven by negative emotions (often vengeful ones) to negate communal morality in favor of destructiveness. Such figures as Cooper's Magua, Hawthorne's Chillingworth, and Melville's Ahab are the forerunners echoed by Vader, who has bought his knowledge and power at the cost of his soul.[74]

Irvin Kershner argues for a different reading of the imperial characters, however:

> In our own time there have been people who tried to conquer the world. They sacrificed humans by the millions. We see this kind of ruthlessness going on in our film. We see the soldiers of the Emperor, faceless men who are not interested in concepts of freedom. Yet freedom is an urgency in today's world. In their way, the *Star Wars* pictures are all about that urgency.[75]

Kershner invokes the Holocaust, the Second World War, the Cold War, the genocides and purges of Stalin, Mao, Pol Pot, Rwanda, Bosnia, etc. Kershner, rather than positing the struggle against imperialism as good versus evil, argues that it should be viewed as the forces in favor of freedom versus the forces in favor of oppression. This "urgency to freedom" is manifest in the writings of Fanon and other postcolonial critics who desire to bring about the decolonization of the nation politically, culturally, and psychologically as soon as possible. There is an urgency to Rebellion, not just in a galaxy far, far away but also in real world imperialist situations.

Five years after Rubey's initial analysis, in a review of *Jedi* for *Jump Cut*, Jon Lewis also sees the saga as "conservative and reactionary," to the point where this ideological position is the reason for its appeal: "*Star Wars'* reactionary nature as a political parable, as an epic adventure in right wing American politics, offers yet another suggestion for its unprecedented box office appeal."[76] The "all-engulfing, all-encompassing spectacle" renders the "ceaselessly violent and machine-worshipping negativity" and the desire to watch destruction and war as positive things. Violence used by the bad guys is bad, but violence used by the good guys is good, the film seems to witness.

Lewis also sees real world parallels for the events of *Jedi*. The rescue of Han Solo from Tatooine offers a much more satisfying hostage rescue than that of the U.S. citizens being held in Tehran. Lewis also sees the interchangeability of human and droid as paralleling the mechanization of manufacturing, agriculture and all areas of production, which also makes workers expendable. No one cares when a droid is destroyed. Lewis also sees parallels with the American Revolution, the Vietnam War, and U.S. intervention in Central America.

Peter Biskind, in his history of seventies cinema *Easy Riders, Raging Bulls*, sees the original trilogy as an allegory of "the triumph of the counterculture," in which the Emperor is Nixon, the Empire is America, and the Rebels are the young who rose up against Vietnam.[77] Yet Biskind also acknowledges the plurality of possible, and often contradictory, readings. He also sees the films as a metaphor for the rise of the "movie brats," the generation of filmmakers who rose after the collapse of the studio system. In this configuration, the Emperor becomes the studio heads, the Empire is Hollywood, and the Rebellion consists of filmmakers making movies on their own terms: Lucas, DePalma, Spielberg, Coppola, and Scorsese, among others.[78] Biskind offers a third possible reading of the original trilogy as "the vanguard of the counterattack by small town and suburban values that were to reclaim Hollywood."[79] Thus, *Star Wars* is celebration of radical politics, celebration of a transformation of the process of filmmaking, and an embracing and rallying cry of conservative values.

Even the costumes carry ideological implications and echo contradictory real world analogues. How one sees the uniforms of the Empire is determined by one's own ideological bent. Some see them as Nazi uniforms, others as Soviet uniforms, still others as American uniforms. John Mollo, the costume designer, claims he based them on early twentieth century Japanese Imperial Army uniforms, but the others are not necessarily wrong. The uniforms are generic enough that one looking at them sees them as echoing the uniform of the group the viewer most associates as "evil."

J. Hoberman, reviewing *Phantom Menace* for *The Village Voice*, observes that Lucas's "creatures dwell in a perpetual present, devoid of sexual activity ... historical consciousness, or even the most debased form of cultural expression (like advertising)," which may be true to a certain extent in *Phantom Menace*, but not so much so in the other films. [80] Advertising is present in *Clones*, music (a "form of cultural expression") is present in the cantina in *A New Hope* and in *Jedi* in Jabba's palace, and Chewbacca and R2-D2 play a game somewhat similar to chess in *New Hope*. The Jedi have an entire library, Han and Lando clearly play games of chance, and there is a sense of history, if not historical consciousness, in many of the characters, and while they "dwell in the perpetual present" in *Phantom*, there is a strong sense of history haunting the original trilogy in terms of the nostalgia for the old Republic and the desire to turn Darth Vader back into Anakin Skywalker in *Jedi*.

Likewise, the films and the creatures in them do have knowledge of economics, politics, and religion. Even such things as inflation and devaluation of material goods are present: Luke complains in *A New Hope* that the sale of his speeder does not get them much money: "Ever since the XP-38 came out, they just aren't in demand." Boba Fett objects to Vader's testing the freezing chamber on Solo in *Empire* because "He's worth a lot to me." Money, trade, and economics are very much present in the *Star Wars*. This entire chapter is dedicated to the presence of a variety of politics in the series as well, of which the characters are very much aware, at least on certain levels. The Jedi are referred to several times as practitioners of a religion (Admiral Motti and Han both call it an "old religion").

The new series adds to the sense of religiosity in that we learn that Jedi are not allowed to marry — in other words, they take a vow of celibacy. The greatest sin of Anakin in *Clones*, other than his arrogance and anger, is that he secretly marries Padme, which is forbidden: a Jedi shall not love. Based on the relationship of Padawan learners and their masters and between Jedi and the Jedi Council, it would seem that they take vows of obedience as well. It would seem that the Jedi have much in common with both Catholic priests and Buddhist monks, as will be discussed in the next chapter.

In a larger sense, the Jedi are colonial administrators—they keep the peace, resolve local disputes, and take punitive action, if necessary. Obi-Wan refers to the Jedi as "the guardians of peace and justice in the Old Republic" in *A New Hope*. The purpose of the Jedi, however, is to preserve the status quo within the Republic. Power is maintained and wealth continues to flow. In *Phantom*, despite the film's clear position that the Trade Federation is evil, the Jedi are sent to negotiate a solution to the blockade of Naboo. Nute Gunray asserts the legality of the blockade and then orders the assassination of Qui-Gon and Obi-Wan, first through poison gas, then by battle droid, as the case may be. Yet the Jedi have been sent to negotiate between an aggressor culture that is preventing all traffic and trade with another, subordinate culture. The film makes the "right position" clear from the beginning, yet never do Qui-Gon or Obi-Wan order the blockade to end or instruct the Trade Federation to cease its predatory capitalism. Nor do they view the attempts to kill them as inherently aggressive acts. Given the power and status of the Jedi, it should not be too difficult for them to end the blockade. Instead they choose to treat all parties, regardless of aggression, equally and fairly, even in the face of assassination attempts.

In the new trilogy the role of Jedi as administrators and diplomats is made all the more clear. In the opening of *Clones*, Kenobi and Skywalker have just returned from settling a border dispute. The Jedi Council orders Obi-Wan to serve as liaison with the cloners of Kamino. It is only with Jango Fett that such liaising results in violence. The Jedi may not be bureaucrats, but their sole purpose seems to be the maintenance of the status quo—to keep the powerful (including themselves) in power and prevent any significant resistance to the domination of the Republic.

The role of the maintaining of power and asserting dominance in the name of freedom has a real world connection in the form of the popular name given to SDI. President Ronald Reagan's March 1983 speech concerning the Strategic Defense Initiative (SDI) generated comparisons with *Star Wars*, eventually coming to be called "Star Wars" by not only the press but by the administration as well. Both Reagan and General James A. Abrahamson quoted the film, claiming not to be from "the dark side."[81] Reagan later referred to the Soviet Union as the "Evil Empire," using terminology familiar to the nation from the *Star Wars* films. The movies were used by Reagan to make his policy palatable to Americans. Lucas, however, saw it as both infringement of his trademark and intellectual property rights as well as a corruption of his vision. He sued to have people stop referring to the SDI program as "Star Wars," but lost the case.

Beyond protecting his own rights, Lucas also recognized the power of association. Reagan sought to link SDI to *Star Wars* because of its positive associations and the connotation that American science was as advanced as what was on the screen — we may not have lightsabers, but we can protect you from the Death Star of the Soviet Union. *Star Wars* also then is linked with a Cold War weapons system and the Reagan agenda. *Star Wars* is transformed into an advertisement for Reagan by association. As noted, anyone can look at the ideological mirror of the films and see their own beliefs reinforced and reflected. The SDI association would fix the ideology of the films in the conservative camp. The values of the Rebellion, according to Michael Ryan and Douglas Kellner, are "individualism, elite leadership, and freedom from state control," which they compare to the values of Neoconservatives under Reagan.[82] Through the very image of an elite, powerful establishment figure, Reagan could use the association with *Star Wars* to posit himself as a rebel, as one of the good guys. Ryan and Kellner call the original trilogy "the paradigmatic conservative movie series of the period because it also makes conservatism revolutionary."[83]

Further problematizing the issue of real weapons associated with the weapons of the film is the lack of consequence of the use of violence. There is a willingness by the characters in all of the films, even the good guys, to use violence unquestioningly to achieve ends, but without the attendant negative results of violence. For example, Hoberman further observes that the battle of *Phantom* is "virtually cost free" — battle droids feel no pain and Gunguns aren't human, nor are Neimoidians: "Ani learns the magic of strategic bombing (or is it a video game?), blasting away at largely unseen as well as nonhuman targets."[84] Obi-Wan is not above cutting off an arm in the cantina to stop violence, and the Jedi are more than happy to use the clone army to fight droids in *Clones*. Luke kills Jabba's guards without a second thought. Han remarks in *A New Hope* that "Hokey religions and ancient weapons are no match for a good blaster at your side, kid." Anakin and Obi-Wan talk and even joke about "aggressive negotiations," in other words, using lightsabers. The only actual dead bodies showing the results of violence are in *A New Hope*: the bodies of Uncle Owen and Aunt Beru. All other dead bodies (rebels stormtroopers, Ewoks, etc.) killed in battle or otherwise never show the marks of violence upon them. They look as if they died in their sleep. Except for *A New Hope*, violence has no consequence for the bodies of those it is enacted upon.

In the next section, the idea of violence and its uses, a major theme of Fanon's, as expressed in *Star Wars* is explored, especially considering the idea that the major metaphysical/divine principle is called "The Force." Force can also mean violence or power, and all three meanings intermix in the films.

The Force and Force

The first chapter of Fanon's *The Wretched of the Earth* is entitled "Concerning Violence," and discusses the role of violence in colonization and its effect on colonized people. Fanon, as noted above, defines colonialism as "violence in its natural state."[85] Violence "rule[s] over the ordering of the colonial world."[86] Violence, argues Fanon, is the only logical response to colonialism. Violence, as a tool of the oppressor, is the only means to combat the oppressor. Thus, violence is used by both Empire and Rebellion, both in Lucas's world and Fanon's.

Lucas uses the word "Force" to describe the "energy field created by all living things. It surrounds us and penetrates us. It binds the galaxy together," as Obi-Wan Kenobi tells Luke in *A New Hope*. "Force," however, can also refer to military force, strength, and, in particular, power, particularly coercive violence. In this case, *A New Hope* and the subsequent films present three different types of violence: primitive violence (striking with hands, feet, pushing, or choking), technological violence (lightsabers, blasters, the ability to destroy a planet with a beam weapon, etc), and spiritual violence (using the Force to hurt or kill).

"The Force" was, in the original draft of *A New Hope*, called "the Force of others," utilizing Lucas's idea of a communal energy pool that both is derived from and binds "all living things."[87] But there is also a suggestion of communal force as well. The next chapter deals with the Force as religion. It is perhaps valuable, however, to take a moment here to analyze how Lucas also shows the Force as force, meaning power and/ violence. After all, as Vader argues in *A New Hope*, "The ability to destroy a planet is insignificant to the power of the Force."

In *A New Hope* we first see technological violence: the film begins with ships firing at each other, which rapidly segues into stormtroopers exchanging fire with rebels. Vader then employs primitive violence, holding a wounded rebel commander by the throat, choking him in order to get information. When the man is not forthcoming, the music swells and an audible snap is heard as Vader breaks the mans neck and tosses his body aside. Later, in the Death Star conference room, Vader uses the Force to choke Admiral Motti in order to make a point:

> MOTTI: Don't try to frighten us with your sorcerer's ways, Lord Vader. Your sad devotion to that ancient religion has not helped you conjure up the stolen data tapes or given you clairvoyance enough to find the rebels' hidden fort ... (Begins to choke and grasps his throat).
> VADER: (making a squeezing motion with his hand) I find your lack of faith disturbing.

This process is repeated twice in *Empire*. First, when Admiral Ozzel brings the fleet out of lightspeed too close to the rebel base on Hoth, Vader, from the distance of another ship, chokes Ozzel to death with the words, "You have failed me for the last time." Subsequently, Captain Needa, who has lost the Millennium Falcon in the asteroid field, goes to report his failure and take responsibility in person. His lifeless corpse drops to the floor at the beginning of the following scene as Vader replies, "Apology accepted." This choking is echoed in *Sith* when Anakin chokes Padme on Mustafar, believing she is aligned with Obi-Wan against him.

The Force is employed most violently by the Emperor, who discharges purple lightning bolts from his hands in the attempt to destroy Luke at the end of *Jedi*. Luke is clearly writhing in pain from the violence of the Force. After Vader throws the Emperor from the balcony, the discharge from the lightning clearly illuminates the skull inside Vader's helmet. The Emperor is twisted and disfigured because of his use of this lightning to attack Mace Windu in *Sith*. Windu deflects the lightning with his lightsaber, and it rebounds back on Palpatine, melting his face. The Force is quite clearly a force — something that can be employed for violent ends, to cause pain, or even to kill.

Nor is the violence of the Force limited to the Dark Side. The Force is also used by the Jedi in battle. It is by using the Force that Luke is able to destroy the Death Star in *A New Hope*. It is by using the Force that Luke is able to defeat first Jabba the Hutt and his minions and then Vader in *Jedi*. In the prequel trilogy, the violence of even the good side of the Force is apparent in the battles of Obi-Wan Kenobi and Qui-Gon Jinn against the battle droids and the Neimoidians. A simple gesture is all it takes for Obi-Wan to destroy a group of droids, shattering them to pieces. In *Clones*, a variety of Jedi are shown using the Force on Geonosis to fight and defeat both droids and others. Lastly, in *Sith*, Dooku uses the Force to throw Obi-Wan and collapse machinery on him, and Anakin and Obi-Wan use the Force to throw each other about the room in their climactic fight, as do Yoda and the Emperor.

The Force is even employed by both Dark and Light sides for psychological violence. Ben tells Luke, "The Force can have a strong influence on the weak minded," after they escape stormtroopers looking for them by using the "Jedi Mind Trick," as it has come to be known. The Jedi Mind Trick is used several times throughout the saga: by Obi-Wan in Mos Eisley, by Luke at Jabba's palace in *Jedi*, and by Obi-Wan in a bar on Coruscant to a "death stick" dealer. Other creatures pride themselves on their ability to resist the Jedi mind trick: both Jabba and Watto claim immunity from it. The Emperor and Vader can read minds: "Your thoughts betray you," is said more than once during *Jedi*. Luke even says it to Vader once. The Jedi's mind is a weapon, one which can be used to invade, influence, and betray.

The Jedi are also not above using technological violence or primitive violence to achieve their ends. The sole purpose of a lightsaber, elegant weapon though it is, is violence. Anakin refers to "aggressive negotiations" in *Clones*, by which he means "negotiations with lightsabers." He says it jokingly, as if it were fun. In *A New Hope*, Obi-Wan slices off an arm and cuts down another opponent in the cantina. In *Empire* Luke is shown fighting the wampa, stormtroopers, and eventually Vader and in *Jedi* he kills dozens of Jabba's guards, the rancor, and more stormtroopers, and fights Vader and the Emperor. Granted, when Luke responds with violence, it is in self-defense and for the seemingly good cause of the rebellion.

In *Wretched of the Earth*, Fanon posits, "Decolonization is always a violent phenomenon."[88] The Rebellion is inherently violent, not least of which because the Empire is violent. As Fanon argues, colonialism "is violence in its natural state, and it will only yield when confronted with greater violence."[89] Great violence must be met with great violence: the Rebellion destroys the Death Star, the planet destroyer. As Fanon asserts, "The colonized man finds his freedom in and through violence."[90] Violence not only overthrows the oppressive order, by being proactive through violence the colonized subject reasserts his or her own identity and reintegrates him or herself.

The new trilogy, however, features extensive violence performed by Jedi. And it is the image of violence and how that violence and its cost are depicted that tell us something more than Fanon's assertion of the use of violence. Obi-Wan does not merely cut down Darth Maul, he cuts him in half after Maul rams his lightsaber through Qui-Gon Jinn. In *Clones*, Mace Windu does not merely fight Jango Fett, he decapitates him. Yoda, Obi-Wan, and Anakin all fight Darth Tyranus, who employs the force to throw objects at his opponents or pull down structures upon them. Yoda is shown to be able to project a beam from his hand, as can Darth Tyranus, which seems to be pure violent energy from the Force. In *Sith*, Anakin decapitates Dooku at Palpatine's bequest. The sheer number of literal disarmings—hands being cut off with lightsabers in them — in the film is tremendous: Dooku by Anakin, Mace Windu by Anakin, General Grievous by Obi-Wan and Anakin by Obi-Wan. Yoda slams Palpatine's guards against the wall with a wave of his hands. Once he converts to the Dark Side, Anakin kills all the Jedi in the temple and all of the Separatist leaders on Mustafar. The Force is a force to be reckoned with, it would seem.

The Dark Side, we are also assured, is very seductive. The major danger in *Jedi* is not even that the second Death Star is fully operational, but that the last Jedi, all–American Mark Hamill, might willingly go over to fascism and imperialism. The presentation of violence as a solution to many, if not all problems, is also seductive, especially if that violence is cost free. A million voices cried out and were silenced all at once when Alderaan was destroyed, though the audience did not hear it. Instead the audience is meant to identify with the pain of Leia watching the destruction and of Obi-Wan hearing it. We do not feel those million deaths ourselves, nor do we feel anything about it. We should not forget that a million voices most likely cried out and were silenced all at once when the Death Stars exploded as well. But since those were the agents of the evil empire, not only are their deaths not worthy of sadness or horror, they are actually a cause for celebration.

In *Sith*, the climactic duel (admittedly one of two) between Yoda and Palpatine involves a complicated series of violent actions. The two use the Force, lightsabers, force lightning, and even physical objects to attack each other. The fight, which began in Palpatine's office, escalates and climaxes in the Senate chamber itself. In the literalization of a metaphor, Palpatine destroys the chamber by throwing the seating platforms at Yoda, who stands below him, deflecting them into other parts of the chamber. Even as the Senate's power is destroyed, the two destroy the physical space of the Senate. Yoda escapes with his life, but his defeat in the Senate chamber is a literal and metaphoric defeat by the Emperor. It seems appropriate that liberty dies, not merely to thunderous applause, but by a maniac who gleefully uses the Force to throw platforms violently at a three foot tall, 900-year-old Jedi Master.

The violence of *Star Wars* is also seen in the control of information by the Empire. Even greater than the power of the Force is the power of P.R. When Vader captures the Rebel Blockade Runner and imprisons Leia at the beginning of *A New Hope*, one of the imperial commanders grows concerned:

> COMMANDER: Holding her is dangerous. If word of this gets out it could generate sympathy for the Rebellion in the Senate.
> VADER: I have traced the Rebel spies to her. Now she is my only link to finding their secret base.
> COMMANDER: She'll die before she'll tell you anything.
> VADER: Leave that to me. Send a distress signal and then inform the Senate that all aboard were killed.

While the Commander is concerned that the little remaining power in the Senate could be rallied against the Emperor because of the popularity of Leia, Vader, in order to be able to hold and torture Leia indefinitely, fakes the destruction of her ship and announces that she is dead. He does so with impunity. By informing the Senate that all died, the implication is that all on board the ship will be killed to cover up the reality. The Empire controls the media and therefore controls the reality. This control allows them to capture diplomatic ships, capture and kill the crew, torture the passengers, and the Senate, with its limited power, makes decisions on the false information fed them by Vader and the Emperor. This model directly echoes the oft seen situation in the real world when dictatorships control the media and "spin" the news in order to maintain the government's power.

For a series of films aimed at a young audience, the two trilogies are remarkably violent. The very title — Star Wars, originally The Star Wars — indicates the subject matter: war. The opening crawl of A New Hope, the film that introduced the saga begins:

> It is a period of civil war.
> Rebel spaceships, striking
> from a hidden base, have won
> their first victory against
> the evil Galactic Empire.

The audience learns that we are watching the beginning of a violent revolution against the authority figures in the galaxy. The phrase "first victory" asserts either that this moment is the beginning of the revolution, or only the first success after long losses. Very likely, given the narrative of the film, it is the latter that is true. We further learn that the Emperor has just dissolved the Senate and order will be maintained by regional governors. The Death Star, the ultimate weapon, conceived of by the separatists under Count Dooku (really Darth Tyranus), has also just become operational. A New Hope in therefore about the growing militarism within the galaxy. In a direct reference, the crawl that begins Sith starts with the word, "WAR!"

In Phantom, Anakin blows up the Trade Federation ship. Unlike the battle on Naboo, in which the only enemy killed are droids, we are shown a ship full of Neimodians, living beings, who are effectively destroyed by an eight-year-old boy. In A New Hope, Alderaan is destroyed as a demonstration — a means of openly displaying the power of the Death Star and the Empire. The stakes are very high in all films — entire worlds and huge numbers of intelligent beings are destroyed right before the audience's eyes.

Yet clearly a distinction is made in the use of violence. Violence is good when "we" use it and bad when "they" use it. This argument extends out to the ideologies behind the Empire and the Rebellion, which, after all, both use violence and the deaths of large numbers of people to assert their primacy in the galaxy: "From the outset, we encounter a clear distinction regarding relative imperialisms. The empire represents bad imperialism because it opposes freedom. Bad imperialism is connected with high-powered military warfare, a tendency to use devastating weaponry and a will toward totalitarian rule. The rebels, elite-led, expose the brighter side of imperialist action: their activity is licensed in the name of liberation."[91] The primary end is liberation, but the means, violence, remains the same, and the secondary goal is to return the rebels to power.

Irvin Kershner, the director of *Empire* sees a fundamental difference between the approach to violence of the Empire and the Rebellion:

> Princess Leia's Rebel forces will not do anything in order to win. They will not sacrifice lives. They do not descend to the level of the enemy. That's the difference between Rebels and the Empire.[92]

This assertion, however, is simply not true — many Rebel spies died to get the Death Star plans to Leia. Many Rebels die attacking the Death Star. Many Rebels are sacrificed on Hoth in order to allow the others, including the Princess, to escape. More spies die getting shuttle codes allowing the elite commando squad to infiltrate the shield generator on the moon of Endor. More die attacking the second Death Star. The Rebels are constantly sacrificing lives. The key difference, arguably, is that for the Rebels the sacrifice is voluntary. But the reward is the same — with victory comes authority and power.

In fairness, there are also key differences in the representations of individual violence and suffering between Rebel and Imperial — the Rebels do not appear to torture anyone. Vader clearly tortures Leia and Han in the first two films, respectively. He also appears quite sadistic when dealing with his own son in the second and third films. On the other hand, all being fair in war, the Rebels are not above killing, deceit, spying, stealing and using the peoples they encounter to aid in the fight against the Empire. Clearly the imperial base on the moon of Endor has existed for quite some time. No indication is given that the Empire and the Ewoks have had any conflict. They coexist on the planet without a problem. The Rebels arrive and the Ewoks begin to fight a proxy battle for them, resulting in the deaths of at least a few Ewoks. One wonders if the Ewoks even know why they are celebrating at the end of *Jedi*. The Rebels follow the example of the Empire — they use violence to achieve power, they use violence to achieve their ends, and they are not above involving uninvolved others in that violence if it will help them win.

Gender and Colonization

I have already discussed at length how *Star Wars* is centered on the white male. Chapter 4 discusses at length the presence and absence of people of color in the films. Attention should also be paid to how gender and gender roles are constructed in the series. In the first trilogy, there is only a single significant female presence, and she is a princess. In the second trilogy, the only significant female presence is a queen, but a queen younger than the princess of the first trilogy. Both are also Senators. The construction of the female characters, despite their positions of power, follows the model of fairy tales—wealthy, beautiful young women who are often in need of rescuing. Leia must be rescued from the Death Star in *A New Hope* and from Jabba in *Jedi*. She might be considered a strong female character, but the image of her in the slave girl costume on Jabba's barge, being grabbed by Luke who has just fought off the guards with his lightsaber, and carried by him as he swings himself and her over to the rescue ship summarizes her position in the trilogy: she is an object to be rescued.

Amidala must be rescued by the men in her life from the Neimoidians in *Phantom* and later, despite her prowess with a blaster in the arena in *Clones*, she must be protected by the Jedi. While flying to confront Count Dooku, she falls out of the ship and is rescued by clone troopers, which ends her participation in the battle, while the men — Obi-Wan, Anakin and even Yoda, go on to battle Dooku with lightsabers. In *Sith* she is even less active, seeming to exist only to be pregnant and die. She does nothing in the Senate, is ineffective is mitigating Anakin's seduction by the Dark Side, is not shown in any position of power or combat. She was at her most powerful in *Phantom*; by *Sith* she is a housewife and mother to be who dies as soon as she is done naming Luke and Leia.

In *Empire* Leia does not need to be rescued directly, but neither is she an active presence. Han must remove her from Hoth once the way to her shuttle is blocked. She does nothing but wait while the Millennium Falcon is repaired in the asteroid field, offers no resistance in Bespin, and needs Chewbacca and Lando to escape from Cloud City. The main women in *Star Wars* are young, beautiful, headstrong, and titled; but they are not active presences in the manner that the men are.

Other female presences are minimal or ineffective. The most powerful one that the audience is shown is Mon Mothma, the architect of the Rebellion and a rebel general that never fights—Admiral Ackbar is the leader of the attack that Mon Mothma planned. Shmi Skywalker, present in *Phantom* and *Clones*, is Anakin's virginal mother who exists only in relation to him. She is present to tell Qui-Gon that Anakin is the product of a virgin birth and then to remain behind as a slave when Anakin is freed and goes to Coruscant to become a Jedi. In *Clones*, she serves to tie the two trilogies together by being sold to the father of Owen Lars, "Uncle Owen" and Luke's foster father, who frees her and makes her his wife. When they meet, Owen acknowledges that he and Anakin are now step-brothers. Shmi then serves her final purpose by being kidnapped and assaulted by Tusken Raiders, which gives Anakin a reason for giving into anger, hate, and fear and killing an entire village of Sand People, including the women and children. In other words, Shmi is not so much a character in her own right but rather exists to give purpose to Anakin. She exists to be a victim so that he might have a reason to go to the Dark Side.

The other women present in the films serve as background or to present an exotic (and perhaps once or twice, erotic) presence. Jabba's dancers, such as Oola, and the nameless others exist to provide background in Jabba's palace. Oola exists to resist Jabba's advances and thus serve as a victim for the Rancor, alerting the audience to the threat and making Luke seem all the more heroic for defeating the monster.

In the new trilogy, apart from Amidala and the new queen of the Naboo in *Clones*, female characters are again backgrounded and marginalized. Amidala's handmaidens have names, but the only way one would know them is by reading the credits or going to the website or other Lucasfilm-affiliated sources. They are indistinguishable from each other. They serve no purpose than to surround the queen. One of them serves as decoy at the beginning of *Clones*, gladly giving her life. As Amidala's security chief says of her, "She did her duty, now you do yours." This statement might summarize the role of women in *Star Wars*—to serve as a brief presence, a motivating purpose for the male characters. The same holds true for the few female Jedi whose names would not be known if not for action figures and Lucasfilm publishing: they are background at best and mere tokenism at worst. In *Sith*, for example, there are four female Jedi Masters—Luminara Unduli, Aaya Secura, Barriss Offee, and Stass Allie, none of whom are named in the film or given much to do other than sit in the council and then get killed by their clone troopers when Order 66 is executed. No lines, just quick deaths.

In addition to the lack of strong female characters in the series, there is a lack of sexuality, either overt or covert. Han Solo, Leia, and Lando are the only sexual beings in the original trilogy. In the second trilogy, Amidala and Anakin fall in love and get married, but despite the knowledge that they will give birth to Luke and Leia, theirs is also represented as a fairly sexless relationship. Held hands and brief kisses are the extent of their sexuality. The Jedi are nonsexual — they must be celibate. *Clones* repeatedly announces that a Jedi must not love. Luke competes with Han for Leia's interest in *Empire*, but by *Jedi*, with the completion of his training and the recognition that she is his sister, he renounces her and seemingly any other sexual relationships in exchange for an asexual existence as the last of the Jedi. Leia might be the object of the male gaze in *Jedi* as a result of the slave girl costume, as opposed to *A New Hope* where she is covered from neck to feet in a flowing white gown, but the sexual threat comes from Jabba, not Han and Luke. As soon as she is freed, she is completely covered again.

In writing about gender, sex, and films depicting the British Empire, Kenneth Cameron observes:

> One effect of the imperial films, then, was to suggest that imperial men do not have sexual selves— that they are eunuchs of empire. Indeed, so severe is their sexism that the absence of women can be taken as an iden-tifying mark of the imperial film....[93]

There are no women in the Empire and Rebel women (Leia, Mon Mothma, etc.) tend to be nonsexual. The only other woman in the original trilogy who demonstrates any kind of sexuality, Oola, Jabba's dancer, dies. In the second trilogy we only have Amidala, who is too young to be sexual in *Phantom*, and her relationship to Anakin, which ends in marriage at the conclusion of *Clones* remains virtually non-sexual — we only see a scattering of kisses between the two. To top it all off, Anakin is the product of a virgin birth. Women are valued for their reproductive ability, but not for the actual reproductive act, which is either nonexistent or not mentioned or discussed in any way.

That women exist to be threatened with rape and give the asexual white males the reason for rescue is a mark of colonialist cinema. Ella Shohat notes,

> The orientalist films tend to begin in the city — where European civi-lization has already tamed the East — but the real dramatic conflicts take place in the desert where women are defenseless, and a white woman could easily become the captive of a romantic sheik or evil Arab. The positioning of a rapable white women by a lustful male in an isolated desert locale gives voice to a masculinist fantasy of complete control over the Western women.[94]

Leia disguises herself as a (male?) bounty hunter, much as Dale (Brooke Shields) disguises herself as a male race car driver in *Sahara* (1983, the same year as *Jedi*) in order to enter a race. Dale is captured by desert tribesmen and must be rescued. Leia must be rescued from Jabba in *Jedi*, where Jabba is presented as a sultan-type character threatening to rape the white woman. Chapter 5 will explore this echo of orientalist cinema in the Tatooine scenes of *Jedi*, but it is worthwhile to note here that the cumulative effect of first completely covering Leia, then objectifying her as a slave girl, threatening her with rape from Jabba and then rescuing her is to demonstrate the complete control that males (even alien males) have over women.

This is not the first time that Lucas has been critiqued for subjugating the women in his narratives for the men. Kenneth von Gunden reports many critiques of *American Graffiti* for treating its female characters as second class citizens. The film, he reports, suffers from a "lack of well-defined female characters," to the point where at the end of the film the audience is told of the fates of the male characters but not the female ones.[95]

End of the Empire/End of the Rebellion

Jedi ends with the death of the Emperor, the destruction of the new Death Star, and the celebration of the end of the Empire. The end of the Empire, however, would also indicate the end of the Rebellion, as well. There is no need for a revolution to continue when the order it seeks to overthrow is overthrown. As many a revolutionary throughout history has learned, however, leading a nation is very different than leading a revolt. There is no indication that the rebels have a plan for "winning the peace," or for dealing with the issues that resulted in the rise of the Emperor.

Lucas changed the ending for the Special Edition of *Jedi*. The original ending featured a celebration on Endor only. Now, the galaxy rejoices in the form of celebrations on Bespin and Coruscant as well. The statue of the Emperor falls before the Imperial Palace on Coruscant, reminiscent of the fall of communism in Eastern Europe and presaging the toppling of the statue of Saddam Hussein at the end of the Iraq War.

The original ending is more realistic, however, citing the localization of the victory. The destruction of the Death Star and the death of the Emperor does not immediately remove the apparatus of empire — the vast majority of the fleet and its office corps, as well as those who have a vested interest in the continuing of the Imperial system, will attempt to keep it alive and well. Not every stormtrooper in the galaxy was on the Death Star when it blew up. It seems illogical to suppose that the moment the news of the Emperor's demise occurred that all the clones stripped off their armor and began a celebration of their new non-military existence.

Even if such a thing occurred, the victory of the Rebellion indicates a shift in power. Supreme authority now reverts to the Senate and the old system of government, although it, too, will take time to organize. The Rebels also have a great deal of military hardware now, which did not exist in the Old Republic, not only their own but the Empire's as well. Robin Wood asks, "What will the rebels against the Empire create if not another empire?"[96]

The popularity of the films and the presence of its archetypal language of Empire present in the popular lexicon indicate not only the power of the films, but also the appeal of imperialism on some levels. Martin Green, in his study of imperial narratives, argues that "imperialism has penetrated the fabric of our culture, and infected our imagination more deeply than we usually realize."[97] *Star Wars* certainly demonstrates how unrealized imperial dreams have infected our popular culture. At the very least, the first trilogy represents a military fantasy about the triumph of violence. Might makes right. Just as ideology shapes our understanding of *Star Wars*, the films shape our understanding of ideology:

> Colonialist fiction is generally predominated by the ideological machinery of the Manichean allegory. Yet the relation between imperial ideology and fiction is not unidirectional: the ideology does not simply determine the fiction. Rather, through a process of symbiosis, the fiction forms the ideology by articulating and justifying the aims of the colonialist.[98]

The Manichean allegory of good versus evil oversimplifies complex situations and allows for the Othering of one's enemies. One does not have to think of one's enemies as human if they are evil. In fact, if one's enemies are evil, one has a moral obligation to destroy them. If an action is good we do it and if we do it, it must be good. The logic is circular but results in an ideology that justifies militarism, imperialism, and conquest.

The connection of SDI to *Star Wars* greatly benefited the Reagan administration because it allowed citizens to think of SDI in a positive manner. Likewise, the need espoused by Geoffrey Nunberg that the insurgents in Iraq not be called "Rebels" for fear of also linking them to a positive association demonstrates the fiction justifying the ideology in addition to the ideology justifying the fiction.

Film offers the audience a way to encounter, view, and think about the unfamiliar as well as new ways to encounter and think about the familiar. Words mean things and nomenclature is important for this reason. In a recent column in the *Los Angeles Times*, Nunberg ruminated on what to call the "bad guys" in Iraq, or as he put it, "Just which movie are we screening here?"[99] "Resistance," he argues, is associated with the French fighting against the Nazis in the Second World War and Americans do not want to cast themselves as the Nazis. Other terms such as "assassins" or "thugs" have emerged out of Orientalist enterprises and fictions in the Middle East and India, respectively. The problem with "Rebellion," Nunberg posits, is that the term has "awkward heroic resonance," as it reminds listeners and readers of *Star Wars*. If the people of Iraq who are resisting the American presence are the Rebels, then the United States becomes the Empire, again, an uncomfortable association, if not entirely inappropriate as discussed above.

As with Reagan and SDI, the Iraq conflict not only demonstrates how the real world instructs audiences how to understand film, but also demonstrates how film instructs the audience how to understand the real world. *Star Wars*, while presenting rebellion in a positive light, as Fanon does, actually maintains the powerful white male as the center of the universe and even posits him as the true rebel, fighting against evil aliens. The series inverts Fanonian notions of colonialism, asserting the importance of freedom from oppression while ignoring issues of language, culture, and representation, and, in fact, representing non-westerners and non-whites as dangerous, cute, or buffoonish aliens. It does this in part by appropriating elements of Asian cultures and relying upon stereotypical constructions of race, gender, and foreign cultures. The series despises the Empire, but posits the value of colonialism and the colonial mindset, which, as the examples of SDI and Iraq above imply, can be translated by the audience into real world equivalencies: violence is a good solution to problems, white males are the heroes of the world and the center of the culture, and there is no inherent difference between cultures. This mindset is far more dangerous than the Dark Side, but just as destructive.

CHAPTER 2

The Power of Mythmaking / May the Tao Be with You: Myth, Religion and *Star Wars*

RANDAL: *If the head of the Empire is a priest of some sort, then it stands to reason that the government is therefore one based on religion.*
DANTE: *It would stand to reason, yes.*
RANDAL: *Hence the Empire was a fascist theocracy, and the rebel forces were therefore battling religious persecution.*
DANTE: *More or less.*
RANDAL: *The only problem is that at no point in the series did I ever hear Leia or any of the rebels declare a particular religious belief.*
DANTE: *I think they were Catholics.*
— Kevin Smith, *Clerks*[1]

A glorious place, a glorious age, I tell you! A very Neon Renaissance — And the myths that actually touched you at that time — not Hercules, Orpheus, Ulysses and Aeneas — but Superman, Captain Marvel, Batman.
— Tom Wolfe, *The Electric Kool-Aid Acid Test*

I find your lack of faith disturbing.
— Darth Vader to Admiral Motti, *A New Hope*

As part of an attempt to have it declared an official religion in Australia, 70,509 people declared their faith as "Jedi Knight" in a recent census. One in 270 respondents, or 0.37 percent of the entire population of Australia, responded to the census question by writing in the name of Lucas's creation under "Religion." Fans in New Zealand began the drive in 2001, but it was in Australia that fans worked to have "Jedi" declared an official religion in Australia by sending an email noting that if 10,000 people wrote in "Jedi" the government would have to recognize it. This assertion, however, proved to be untrue as those who wrote "Jedi" on the census form were subsequently categorized by the government as "not defined."[2]

Fans have compared the potential of a religion based on the teachings of the Jedi to Scientology, the religion founded by science fiction writer L. Ron Hubbard. In fact, there are "Jedi Temples" in London and Romania. Americans are also organizing "Jediism" a religion based on the teachings in the *Star Wars* films.[3] What was an interesting fusion of Eastern religion and mythic structure by Lucas may become something of a genuine philosophy or life path, if not a real religion.

In humor there is often truth, and the first epigram from the screenplay of *Clerks* above is no exception. The *Star Wars* series contains religious and mythic elements, and the world of the films contains a developed religious faith that is defined as such. In fact, many commentators have observed the conflict between technology and spirituality beginning in *A New Hope* and continuing through the series. The commanders at the Rebel base on the moon of Yavin grow concerned when Luke turns off his targeting computer. The audience has already seen one run by the Rebels at the weak point of the Death Star using targeting computers which deflected off the surface. Luke hears Obi-Wan tell him to "use the Force," and by his faith he is able to successfully destroy the battle station.

There is also a union of technology and spirituality, especially in the prequel trilogy. In *A New Hope*, Obi-Wan uses a "remote," a floating robot designed to teach and test combat, to train Luke in the use of a lightsaber. In *Clones* the audience is shown an entire class of Jedi children training with the same style of remote. The Jedi use starships and speeders, employ technology to determine one's abilities with the Force (for example, Mace Windu tests Anakin Skywalker in *Phantom* using a hand-held viewing screen). The lightsaber itself represents the ultimate combination of technology and spirituality — each Jedi Padawan learner must make his or her own lightsaber before he or she is considered a Jedi. Lightsabers take years to master and therefore require lengthy training and dedication. Lastly, lightsabers themselves are weapons that are created by technology and could not function without it, requiring the projection of an energy field from their bases to work. It is this combination of technology and disciplined spirituality that embody the Jedi.

In *Skywalking*, Dale Pollock argues that "The message of *Star Wars* is religious: God isn't dead, He's there if you want him to be."[4] In a sense, he is correct, although whether that is the dominant message, or even one of the most recognizable messages is arguable. What is incontrovertible is that in the *Star Wars* films the Force is a divine presence whose effect is both concrete and visible. The lightsaber flies into Luke's hand on Hoth. Yoda can raise the X-Wing Fighter out of the swamp on Dagobah. Vader clearly can use the Force to kill, even at great distances. The acknowledgement of a greater metaphysical reality that has efficacy in the real world is comparatively rare in American cinema. To not acknowledge the divine presence is not only wrong, it is dangerous. As Vader tells Motti in the epigram above, "I find your lack of faith disturbing." *Star Wars* values and promotes a surfeit of faith.

Star Wars and Religion

In *The Movies as History*, Peter Krämer sees *Star Wars* as a film that celebrates the primacy of the Force over technology — Luke does not use his targeting computer to fire his torpedoes into the Death Star, he "trusts his feelings" and "uses the force." This action, Krämer argues, represents the primacy of metaphysics over physics and religion over science.[5] Others have seen this hierarchical dichotomy, the power of religion, metaphysics, and irrationality over science, technology, and rationality, as central to Lucas's series as well.

The notes in the published annotated screenplays discuss the Force when it is first introduced in *A New Hope*. In the rough draft of what would become *A New Hope*, the greeting is given as "May the force of others be with you," which Laurent Bourzereau observes is an "obvious variation" on the Christian phrase "May the Lord be with you and your spirit."[6]

Some critics have argued there is not only a strong spiritual and religious presence in the films, there are specific echoes of specific religions within the films. While Lucas does not see *Star Wars* as "profoundly religious" he does note that "almost every single religion" found the film to contain elements of and be suggestive of their faith: "They were able to relate it to stories in the Bible, in the Koran, and in the Torah."[7] Indeed, within a few months of the release of the original film in 1977 Frank Allnut wrote *The Force of Star Wars* which viewed Lucas's film as a "prophetic parable" about the coming of the Antichrist in which the Force is God, the Emperor is Satan and the Rebellion represents the Church.[8] Allnut offers a fundamentalist Christian analysis on the film that attempts to make the *Star Wars* narrative fit the Book of Revelation, but fails. In Allnut's reading, admittedly done after *A New Hope* and before any other film in the series, the Force is God, Obi-Wan is Jesus, Luke represents Hebrew Christians, Han represents Gentile Christians, Leia is Israel, the Emperor is Satan and Darth Vader is the Anti-Christ. Allnut sees *A New Hope* as "a prophetic parable" and an endtime narrative along the lines of Hal Lindsey's *Late Great Planet Earth*, one of many popular books in the seventies proclaiming the end of the world and the beginning of Armageddon.[9] In the absence of a true Christ figure (Allnut suggests Obi-Wan, who does not share the relationship to the Force that the Christ shares with God the father in traditional Christian theology), and subsequent revelations in the series (given Allnut's schema, the Anti-Christ is the father of Hebrew Christians who will eventually turn on Satan), the reading does not work. *Star Wars* cannot be read as Christian metaphor.

Robert Jewett analyzes *Star Wars* in terms of Pauline theology in *Saint Paul at the Movies: The Apostle's Dialogue with American Culture*, a book in which he compares the cinematic text of popular American films with the text of the letters of Paul in the New Testament in order to determine the reflection, or lack thereof, of Pauline theology in popular culture. Chapter two, entitled "*Star Wars* and 'the Force' of Paul's Gospel," considers Lucas's film in light of Paul's Letter to the Romans. Although *Star Wars* "seemed to embody the ultimate Christian value of right triumphing over wrong," and multiple, repeated viewings of *Star Wars* serves as "a ritualistic reenactment of a story of salvation," ultimately Jewett rejects the film as not being compatible with Pauline theology.[10] In Paul's letter to the Romans, Jewett argues, it is clear that salvation is open to all, but in *Star Wars*, knowledge of the Force, which Jewett also reads as the Judeo-Christian God, is open only to a select few: "selected warriors and saints," i.e., the Jedi.[11] An "unintended implication," Jewett concludes, is that *Star Wars* promotes a "fascist ideology," which is incompatible with Christianity.[12]

There is also the implication that Anakin was a virgin birth. In *Phantom*, Shmi tells Qui-Gon that there was no father, that she simply conceived and gave birth. Qui-Gon seems to believe the child was conceived by the Force, but in *Sith* Palpatine implies that he has learned how to create life through the Force, making one wonder if Anakin is not a custom-made apprentice, whose master is also his "Force father." This virgin birth was not inspired by the Gospels, however, but from Joseph Cambell's studies of the virgin birth motif in myth.[13]

The world of *Star Wars* is seemingly morally dualistic — good versus evil. Yet inherent in the names of these concepts is recognition of a more Eastern world view — "light side" and "dark side." The use of the word "side" indicates that there are both sides of the same coin, so to speak.

Good and evil in the Western moral sense are not aspects of the same thing, whereas light and dark aspects of the same "force" is very common in Eastern philosophy and religion. Christianity rejected the Manichean heresy of evil being equal in strength and presence to good. Spiritual evil in the West is ultimately subservient to the divine principle, and the divine principle itself contains no inherent evil or dark side. It would seem, then, that if the Force consists of both light and dark sides, and that neither is ultimately ascendant over the other, then real world religions that embrace duality are more echoed by the concept than Western monotheism. Anakin is the "chosen one" who will bring balance to the Force, which also has no equivalency in Western religion. Jesus did not come to bring balance to good and evil, according to Christianity. Balance, however, remains a key element in Taoism and Buddhism. Thus, Asian religions are more strongly echoed in the films, as are the alternative spiritualities and alternative consciousness that rose to prominence in the sixties and seventies.

In his biography and film analysis of George Lucas, Chris Salewicz argues that the term "the Force" came out of Carlos Castaneda's *Tales of Power* (1974), in which the Yaqui shaman Don Juan Matus, who had been teaching Castaneda "the Yaqui way of knowledge," talks to him about a "life force" that unites and binds all things.[14] Castaneda began writing about an indigenous Mexican spirituality in *The Teachings of Don Juan* (1968). *Tales*, the fourth book in the series by Castaneda, was released in 1974. One might even see Don Juan Matus as an Obi-Wan type figure, teaching Castaneda about an ancient religion.

The sixties and seventies, when Lucas was in graduate school and then making films, also saw the rise of awareness of Eastern spiritualities in the United States, particularly in California. Many critics and scholars see a good deal of Asian religions present in the doctrines of the Jedi. Either a general Eastern spirituality or Zen Buddhism specifically are cited as the most similar real-world equivalent of the Force. This book will also argue that Taoism is very strongly echoed in the text of the films.

Critics, scholars, participants in the films, and Lucas himself have acknowledged the variety of Asian religious echoes in the film. Chris Salewicz states of the philosophy of the Force and the way of the Jedi, "Many of the essential precepts are those of Buddhism."[15] Richard Keller Simon sees the Force as "a generalized inner spirituality that echoes Eastern mysticism."[16] Bill Moyers, in his interview with Lucas, suggests that the Force is an "Eastern view of God — particularly Buddhist — as a vast reservoir of energy that is the ground of all our being."[17] Lucas agrees that "it's more specific in Buddhism," but also argues that "it is a notion that's been around before that," without specifying what he means or to which religious philosophies he refers. Lucas's own view notwithstanding, the language the various characters use to describe the Force suggests Taoism. Moyer's "reservoir of energy" implies the Tao. Obi-Wan tells Luke, "The Force is what gives a Jedi his power. It's an energy field created by all living things. It surrounds us and penetrates us and binds the galaxy together." The theology of Buddhism maintains that this world is an illusion that generates misery and must be transcended.

It is in Taoism that the idea of energy is a principle tenet. Lao Tzu writes in the *Tao Te Ching* that the Tao (the Way) "gives them [people] life and rears them. It gives them life yet claims no possession.... It is the steward, yet exercises no authority" (I:x). Unlike the Western notion of God, an authoritative, anthropomorphic patriarch, the Tao is both life giving and binding, yet does not actively control human beings or demand worship or authority. The Tao is a non-present presence: "The way is empty, yet use will not drain it" (I:iv), which further suggests Moyer's "reservoir of energy," albeit one which will never be emptied. The theology and cosmology of *Star Wars* constructs an ultimate reality much closer to Taoism than any Western religious philosophy.

Western religious philosophy does not have the idea of "flow" on which both Taoism and the Force are centered. The famous metaphor in the *Tao Te Ching* compares the Tao to water:

> In the world there is nothing more submissive and weak than water. Yet for attacking that which is hard and strong nothing can surpass it. This is because there is nothing that can take its place (II: lxxviii).

The ideal follower of the Tao flows with the Tao as water flows. While seemingly weak and submissive, one will overcome any difficulty by flowing. Likewise, both *A New Hope* and *The Empire Strikes Back* contain repeated lessons for Luke by Obi-Wan and Yoda to learn how to flow:

> OBI-WAN: Remember, a Jedi can feel the Force flowing through him.
> LUKE: You mean it controls your actions?
> OBI-WAN: Partially, but it also obeys your commands.

Yoda repeatedly tells Luke, "Feel the Force flow." This idea of the divine being an energy which flows and is both controlling and can be controlled is Taoist, not Western.

A further example of the Taoist nature of the Force is its resistance to intellectual understanding. Ingrid Fischer-Schreiber, writing in *The Shambala Dictionary of Taoism*, observes, "All Taoists strive to become one with the Tao. This cannot be achieved by trying to understand the Tao intellectually; the adept becomes one with the Tao by realizing within himself its unity, simplicity, and emptiness."[18] During the training session on the Millennium Falcon, Obi-Wan tells Luke he is thinking too much: "This time let go your conscious self and act on instinct.... Stretch out with your feelings." The Force cannot be understood or used intellectually, only be experiencing within one's self, by *feeling* can one become one with the Force and use it. At the climactic battle of the Death Star, Luke turns off his tactical computer and "uses the Force" to hit the Death Star with his torpedo. It is only by "trusting his feelings," "letting go," and "letting the Force flow" can the huge, mechanical Death Star be beaten and destroyed. Like water, a single man in a small ship seems weak and defenseless against the huge mechanical (read: Western) terror of the Death Star, and yet, through the use of the Force, the living being overcomes the mechanical monster. By learning the Taoist-like teachings of the Jedi, Luke is able to defeat the Dark Side and save the Rebellion repeatedly.

Yoda is the Taoist master of the *Star Wars* universe. Once Vader and Palpatine have destroyed the Jedi, Yoda, like Lao Tzu, turns his back on civilization and goes off to the wilderness, in Yoda's case, the planet Dagobah. In *Empire*, similar to Zen masters and Taoist teachers who initially play the fool to test potential students, Yoda pretends to be an insignificant native in order to evaluate Luke while teaching him valuable lessons in Taoist thought. When Luke claims that Yoda is a great warrior, Yoda responds, "Wars do not make one great," and Luke then learns that this small creature is powerful in the Force but does not resemble what Luke believes to be a warrior. This sentiment echoes the *Tao Te Ching*: "One who excels as a warrior does not appear formidable; One who excels in fighting is never roused in anger..." (II:lxviii). The Jedi, likewise, is not roused in anger when he fights, for this leads to the Dark Side.

It is in the dualistic nature of the Force what Lucas comes closest to Western religious philosophy. While Taoism recognizes that good and evil, light and dark, are merely opposites in which balance must be sought, Western philosophy judges light to be good and dark to be bad. The yin-yang symbol is the embodiment of Taoism — both light and dark aspects are present and balanced. Western religious philosophy acknowledges a dualistic nature but one from which the darkness must be purged. Evil is seen as separate from good and must be not only resisted and rejected but overcome. The Dark Side is the result of Taoism being subjected to the Western concept of evil.

Susan Mackey-Kallis identifies the Force as another name for Chi, specifically citing Yoda's levitation of Luke's X-Wing in *Empire* as an example of his similarity to "a Zen master able to harness and move 'Chi.'"[19] I have argued above that the Force can be seen as a manifestation of the Tao, which can be seen as the equivalent of "chi," or "life energy" in Buddhism. The levitation of the X-Wing is proof that the Force and the ideas behind it are Asian, not Western, in origin. In Western religions, God allows one to do something and works through one, and God is free to decline to do what one wishes as well. One cannot command God in the West, one can only pray and hope that one's prayers are answered positively. In Asian religions, however, one harnesses power — one's own power, the power of the universe, the power of the Tao, the power of the chi, etc. and allows it to flow through one, directing it to its purpose. Obi-Wan tells Luke that the Force "obeys your commands." God in the Western sense does no such thing.

Zen Buddhism had a profound shaping influence especially beginning with *Empire*, not least of which because director Irvin Kershner was deeply interested in Zen Buddhism himself. In his own writings and comments on the film, Kershner continually and repeatedly conceptualizes the events of *Empire* in terms of Zen Buddhism:

> Having Ben come back is almost like Zen, a Buddhist notion that you don't die, that you come back and have to suffer again until you do enough good and decide you don't want to come back.[20]

Kershner later states of Kenobi that "he is a Zen master, he is almost Godlike."[21] It is Kershner's conceptualization of Yoda and Obi-Wan as Zen Masters that both drive the echo of Zen in the film and subsequently frame the film as an example of the shaping influence of Zen.

Buddhist teaching is also made manifest in *Sith*, when Anakin, having dreams of Padme's death, consults with Yoda. He fears the loss of Padme. Yoda tells him:

> The fear of loss is a path to the Dark Side. Rejoice for those around you who transform into the Force. Mourn them do not. Miss them do not. Attachment leads to jealousy. Let go of everything you fear to lose.

This philosophy is remarkably close to Buddhism, where attachment to this world and the things in it is seen as a source for suffering. If one lets go of attachments, one grows closer to enlightenment. There is even a saying, "When you meet the Buddha, kill the Buddha," as one should not be attached to anything, even the Buddha. One might even argue that it is his attachment to his mother and his wife that are responsible for Anakin's embracing of the Dark Side.

Despite being warriors, the Jedi are also religious figures. Jedi may not marry, nor even love. Though *Star Wars* is virtually devoid of sexual content, it is clear in *Clones* that becoming a Jedi involves some kind of vow of celibacy. One of Anakin's great sins, after his anger, pride and arrogance, is that he secretly marries Padme against the Jedi code and his own vows. The Jedi Council demands that the Jedi follow the Jedi code. Obi-Wan reminds Qui-Gon that he would be on the Jedi Council if not for his disobedience. The Jedi Council forbids Qui-Gon to train Anakin, and despite his beliefs to the contrary, he agrees. The Council orders Obi-Wan, Qui-Gon and Anakin to a variety of tasks in the second trilogy, and, though those orders are occasionally circumvented, such circumvention never occurs without multiple characters commenting that such disobedience to the Council is both unwise and morally wrong. It would seem that in addition to a de facto vow of celibacy, a de facto vow of obedience also occurs.

The combination of these vows echoes the vows taken by both Catholic priests and Buddhist monks. The Jedi are part of a larger religious community that undergoes martial training as well. Though such warrior priests or warrior monks existed in the West, the cinematic history of warrior priests is much more Eastern in origins. In that sense, the Jedi are Shaolin monks, who train in kung fu and a variety of weapons in addition to their religious training. They also take vows of obedience and vows of celibacy. The training sequences we see of both Luke and the Jedi of the second trilogy would not be out of place in martial arts films concerning the training of Shaolin monks, such as Gordon Liu in *Shaolin Master Killer*. Such films will be discussed in depth in the next chapter, but let it suffice to say at this point that the Jedi are warrior priests in the Shaolin tradition, taking vows of celibacy and obedience and dedicating themselves not only to spiritual mastery, but mastery of combat as well.

Dale Pollock, as noted above, sees the existence of a divinity that shapes our ends as one of the key messages of the films. He also sees the representation of that divinity as being a fusion between Eastern and Western religions: "The Force embraces positive Oriental philosophies and the Judeo-Christian ethic of responsibility and self-sacrifice."[22] Perhaps so, but it would seem that the major religious echoes in the film come from Asian, not Western, sources. The larger frame of comparative mythology demonstrates how Lucas and his critics have rooted the *Star Wars* films in the idea that they are not only a modern mythology, but that they echo recognizable, predominantly Western myths.

To return to where this section began, those who practice Jediism see it as a form of Asian religion. In interviewing fans waiting for *Sith*'s premiere, the *Los Angeles Times* interviewed a group of Jediists. Their leader, Aaron Mosny, states emphatically, "*Star Wars* is simply a vehicle to bring these Eastern beliefs to Western people."[23] That the films are seen as embodying Eastern religion and philosophy and as "vehicle" for their dissemination in the West not only stands as proof of the Eurocentrism of the films and the fans, but the identification of Jedi teaching with Buddhism and Taoism.

Star Wars as Myth

Lucas has worked rather hard to reinforce the idea that his films form a modern mythology. *Star Wars* has admittedly been shaped by myth, packaged as myth, called "modern myth" or "American myth" by numerous critics, and is now used in comparative mythology. Stuart Voytilla calls it "truly our modern myth," raising the larger questions of who is the "we" behind the "our" and how, specifically, do the films function as a myth for a modern, pluralistic, multicultural society?[24]

Alan Arnold reports in his journal of the making of *Empire* that Lucas's studies in mythology in college anthropology courses served as the originating point for the desire to use the cinema to create a myth or mythology. He quotes Lucas as saying, "Through anthropology I had gotten interested in folklore and mythology and in their role as an anchor for societies. I came to realize that America has no modern fairy tales. You could say that the Western movie is the last of our myths."[25] Again, the larger question is raised of what is the role of myth in modern society, and can cinema serve the same function within a pluralistic society?

Irvin Kershner states, "In *Empire* we're dealing with legend, myth and magic—forces that are ineffable and indefinable."[26] This statement is simply not true, all three of which are actually not only effable but quite easily definable. Joseph Campbell, perhaps the best known scholar of mythology in the world and who shared a mutual admiration with George Lucas, states that "The dictionary definition of a myth would be stories about gods."[27] Campbell then further distinguishes between myths that relate the individual to the natural world and myths that relate the individual to society. Myths serve to define and unite the community. In a more modern sense, the word myth has come to mean something that is legendary, but most likely untrue. To say that something is "just a myth" means that it is false. Campbell, however, argues that historic myth has a greater truth behind it than the reality of the narrative. Myth, in this sense, is a meaning maker, as are legends.

Magic, the third thing invoked by Kershner as "indefinable" is both definable and multifaceted. Magic comes from the Greek *magikē*, meaning "sorcery," or the Greek *magikos*, meaning "of the Magi," the Magi being the priestly caste of ancient Media and Persia. Magic is the attempt to have efficacy in the real world through individual acts such as rituals, incantations, and mimicry. The use of the Force often mimics magic, but does not fall under the anthropological definition of magic. The Jedi do not use spells, incantations, or rituals in order to achieve power and control over the real world. Their "magic" is, in a sense, profane, meaning "everyday," as it is a skill they master which has a direct effect. Magic, in a sense, is always indirect. The Rain Dance is not actual rain, it is a dance designed to bring rain when needed. The levitation created by the Force is actual, direct levitation. Magic, in the anthropological sense, is an attempt to control the world, as opposed to myth, which is an attempt to explain the world.

In this sense, Lucas is correct, but not just about Westerns. All film is meaning-making. Specifically, film does not mean, but it generates meaning by connecting the life experience of the viewer with composed visual images, aural experiences, intellectual content and narrative. Ernest Ferlita and John R. May argue in *Film Odyssey: The Art of Film as Search for Meaning* that film is a "quest for meaning," that film is a medium entirely designed to generate meaning.[28] In writing on *Star Wars*, John Seabrook observes that "The purpose of a myth, after all, is to give people a structure for making sense of the world."[29] Both myth and film are meaning-makers.

To posit *Star Wars* as "modern myth" then, is to argue that it is an overall narrative that explains the world to the viewer and also explains his or her place in it. Numerous commentators and critics have offered various mythic interpretations of *Star Wars*, sometimes contradictory, and often with ultimately a leveling effect by making all myths serve the same function and achieve the same ends within any society regardless of context. Joseph Campbell, for example, among others such as Henderson and John (analyzed below), place *Star Wars* images alongside images from classical Western mythology (Greece and Rome), pagan mythology (Norse, Frankish, etc.), folk stories, legends, and, occasionally, Eastern mythology, although, problematically, Eastern religion is often presented as "mythology." In *The Power of Myth*, Campbell sees echoes in the first trilogy of the Faust myth, the world navel, the story of Jonah, and *The Odyssey*.[30] He also sees in the films the embodiment of the "monomyth" that he posits in *The Hero with a Thousand Faces*, which places Luke Skywalker in the same category as Beowulf, Gilgamesh, Osiris, Dionysus, Jesus, Arthur, Jason, Heracles, Theseus, the Buddha, and Mohammed.

Campbell, however, has also come under criticism for the reductive nature of his comparative mythologies. As Mary Lefkowitz observes, Campbell begins with the "rather questionable assumption that all myths, from all cultures, conveyed the same basic messages and followed virtually the same narrative patterns."[31] Campbell creates a metapattern to overlay on all myths, ignoring the elements that do not fit the pattern. Campbell also changes context, reading myths anachronistically, charges Lefkowitz. He gives myths modern, psychological readings that may not have been the emphasis or focus in the original context. Campbell, like Lucas, adds modern spirituality to his readings of ancient myths. All religions do not function in the same way, nor do they serve the same purpose. By modernizing and psychologizing myths, Campbell deprives them of their origin and their original context. This criticism is one that can be leveled at many of those who seek to compare *Star Wars* with the myths of a myriad of cultures.

One solution to the problem of reductivism is to ignore the original context in favor of psychoanalyzing the myths. Looking for Jungian archetypes, or looking for the psychological meanings beneath the surface context is one way of comparing movie to myth. Steven A. Galipeau, for example, in his *The Journey of Luke Skywalker* uses his "personal Jungian approach" to analyze the original trilogy and *The Phantom Menace*.[32] He goes so far as to state:

> Indeed, the entire *Star Wars* saga can be approached as a *cultural dream*, one that has meaning for numerous people and symbolically depicts in important aspects the psychological and spiritual shifts taking place in our age.[33]

To a certain extent, one can argue that the series is highly symbolic and one that makes meaning for numerous people. On the other hand, however, unlike myths, which are created by a community over the course of generations—a "cultural dream"—the *Star Wars* films are the artistic product of an individual, Lucas, and the other artists whom he hires to shape that narrative. *Star Wars* is not a cultural dream — it is an artistic (and commercial) product. While the product of the ear and the culture that produced it, the series is also undeniably the result of an individual's vision, not for religious purposes, as Jesus, Buddha, or Mohammed's visions were, but for the purpose of making a commercial film. Campbell calls this "creative mythology," but it is significantly different from the myths created by a culture to explain the relationship between the individual, the natural world, and society.

Galipeau, like Campbell, John, and Henderson before him, links events and characters in the film to other myths. Tatooine, for example, becomes the Egypt of Moses, and Luke the promised leader who will free his people.[34] The films are subjected to a Jungian analysis in which each event or character corresponds to an element in Jung's theories. Leia's message in R2-D2 in *A New Hope* is a manifestation of "the anima archetype," the Force is the "collective unconscious," the destruction of Alderaan is symbolic of "the soul's struggle to live," and Lando is Han's "shadow side."[35]

Likewise, James F. Iaccino sees the original trilogy as a fable of Jungian archetypes, specifically the struggle of the Self with the Father archetype and the Shadow archetype. *A New Hope* concerns the need of Luke to find father figures to replace the abandoning father. Uncle Owen clearly is not a good replacement, but Ben Kenobi is. *Empire* shows the Father trying to reclaim a lost offspring, yet Luke's battle on Dagobah with Vader, whose mask shatters to reveal Luke's own face, also demonstrates that the fight is with the archetype of the Shadow, one's own negative side. Lastly, despite the death of another mentor, Yoda, *Return of the Jedi* concerns a reuniting with the Father.[36]

In addition to underlying psychology, one can consider the *Star Wars* films as myth from a structuralist perspective. Stuart Voytilla performs a structural analysis in his *Myth and the Movies*, analyzing the morphology and mythic structure in fifty films, including the original *Star Wars* trilogy individually and collectively. "Following Campbell," Voytilla states, "but making adjustments to reflect the unique conditions of movie storytelling, [he] described the Hero's Journey as a twelve-stage adventure for the hero."[37] Each film in the trilogy follows the twelve steps of the hero's journey, and the cycle as a whole can also fit into the same structure, argues Voytilla. In each episode, the hero is separated from the ordinary world after being called to adventure and meeting a mentor. The hero is then tested and meets allies and enemies, finally going through a central ordeal, after which he is rewarded, journeys back out of the special world, and is resurrected, sharing the elixir of life which he shares with the community.

As with all predetermined structures, Voytilla's is a procrustean bed in which all things cannot be made to fit without violence. Some aspects of each film he considers must be ignored, and other aspects, perhaps not as important, are played up or focused upon. In order to fit on the bed of Procrustes, one must either be stretched or have limbs cut off. In order to fit in Voytilla's structure, things must be stretched or cut. Furthermore, to argue that a group of major films all follow a particular structure is to ignore the differences that separate the films. Not all myths function in the same way. Not all myths follow the same structure. Not all myths serve the same purpose. The same holds true for films with supposed mythic structures.

Others locate the mythic content of the films in the similarity to other quest narratives, yet retain the psychological function of the myth. Susan Mackey-Kallis, for example, sees the original trilogy as a hero quest, but not for a boon or Holy Grail. Instead, she interprets many American films, including *Star Wars*, as heroic quests to establish Self and to find a home.[38] *Star Wars* is a uniquely American myth as it involves self realization and self actualization. The narrative concerns not only becoming whole but also establishing one's own identity.

Lucas, as quoted above, also claims that his films are designed to fill a gap because "America has no modern fairy tales." Fairy tales and myths are different things. Fairy tales, unlike myths which serve the entire community, are aimed at the education and indoctrination of children. "Little Red Riding Hood" warns of the danger of talking to strangers. "Cinderella" is a rumination on the benefits of humility, hard work, and dedication to family, extolling these qualities by showing them rewarded. Fairy tales also address the anxieties of children, demonstrating how to successfully negotiate the issues of concern and assume one's rightful place in the world. Adults neither believe nor use fairy tales in the manner that children are meant to. By his statement it would seem Lucas looks to create a filmed fairy tale that teaches moral lessons to an audience of children.

In *Manufacturing Desire: Media, Popular Culture and Everyday Life*, Arthur Asa Berger sees *Star Wars* as a fairy tale. Focusing on the Oedipal aspects of the films, Berger performs a Proppian analysis of the film, listing the events as a morphology.[39]

Star Wars gives the audience a cautionary tale emphasizing the anxiety over the destructive and consuming father who must ultimately be killed by his progeny so that they may assume their place in the world.

Similarly, in an article for *Harpers* Bruno Bettelheim, whose *The Uses of Enchantment* remains one of the primary texts for analyzing the role and purpose of fairy tales, argued that movies do form a kind of modern mythology, or at least serve the purpose that myths served in pretechnological societies. He makes several observations about the nature of *Star Wars* as psychologizing myth:

> Science-fiction movies can serve as myths about the future and thus give us some assurance about it. Whether the film is *2001* or *Star Wars*, such movies tell about progress that will expand man's powers and his experiences beyond anything now believed possible, while they assure us that all these advances will not obliterate man or life as we now know about it. Thus one great anxiety about the future — that it will have no place for us as we now are — is allayed by such myths.[40]

In other words, the *Star Wars* series gives audiences hope for the future which they do not get from the news or from their own assessments of the real world. Even adults are anxious about the future, especially when living under the threat of nuclear attack during the Cold War when the first trilogy was made. Bettelheim argues that *Star Wars* is valued because it assures us not only will we still be here tomorrow, we will be here for a long time to come. The problem being that the series is not about future, it is about "a long time ago in a galaxy far, far away." From its opening visual, the film establishes itself not as the promise of a future, but a cautionary tale about history.

Bettelheim continues:

> They also promise that even in the most distant future, and despite the progress that will have occurred in the material world, man's basic concerns will be the same, and the struggle of good against evil — the central moral problem of our time — will not have lost its importance.[41]

Bettelheim sees "the central moral problem of our time" as being "good versus evil," but this supposition is both reductivist and simplistic, particularly when given the complexity of the many conflicts, moral and otherwise, around the world in the seventies and eighties. Bettelheim sees *Star Wars* as ultimately a moral film, or, more accurately, a morality film — it shows that "evil" does not triumph so long as "good" continues to fight it. But "good" and "evil" are not only relative terms, they are interchangeable ones. The good and evil sides of the Second World War are apparent, but what was "good" and what was "evil" in Vietnam? In Biafra? Good and evil are ultimately formulations for children, who as they grow must learn more complex moral formulations. Even Vader, arguably the embodiment of evil in the films, is capable of being redeemed. Even Luke, by moving to save Han Solo from Jabba the Hutt or prevent the Death Star from destroying the Rebel base is forced to take many lives, including those who are not necessarily "evil."

Bettelheim sees the original trilogy as conflating all of history, as myths and fairy tales often do, in order to speak to the present moment:

> Past and future are the lasting dimensions of our lives; the present is but a fleeting moment. So these visions about the future also contain our past; in *Star Wars*, battles are fought around issues that also motivated man in the past.[42]

As noted already, the films are not "visions of the future," although the cinema has taught us to read space travel and laser weapons as indicative of the future, not the past. In this sense, Bettelheim is correct: we are encouraged to see the past as the future by combining the visual tropes of futuristic cinema with the narrative tropes of history.

Bettelheim concludes with a return to the idea of optimism for the future inherently contained in science fiction. Science fiction is not only a promise of the future, it also represents a regression to infancy, in Bettelheim's viewpoint.

> There is good reason that Yoda appears in George Lucas's film: he is but a reincarnation of the teddy bear of infancy, to which we ever turn for solace; and the Yedi Knight [sic] is the wise old man, or the helpful animal, of the fairy tale, the promise from our distant past that we shall be able to rise to meet the most difficult tasks life can present us with. Thus, any vision about the future is really based on visions of the past, because that is all we know for certain.[43]

Yoda as a Teddy bear? His is an initially amusing and disarming presence, but he is both a powerful warrior and a threatening presence. When Luke states that he is not afraid, a close-up on Yoda's face reveals his almost delight in stating, "You will be … you will be." This statement is not the comfort of a teddy bear. In fairness, Bettelheim wrote right after *Empire* had been released, the lightsaber-wielding Yoda of *Clones* was still two decades in the future — the teddy bear did not yet have claws. Yet the two trilogies are not about an infantile regression. They contain too many other elements. Fairy tales teach and comfort because of their simplicity. The anxieties of childhood are readily apparent in "Little Red Riding Hood" and "Hansel and Gretel."

It is also easy to do a psychoanalytical reading of the "myth" in the original trilogy. In *A New Hope*, Ben, an alternative father-figure, gives Luke his father's lightsaber, a phallic relic, and sets up a need for him to confront and defeat his father. Luke's mother is gone, but he retains an incestuous interest in his (admittedly unknown to him) sister. In *Empire*, Luke undergoes a symbolic castration by his father by losing his hand which holds his father's lightsaber. In *Jedi*, Luke has made his own lightsaber and has grown confident in his own powers and ability to use it, as witnessed during the rescue of Han Solo from Jabba the Hutt. Luke gains his father's respect and subsequently performs the same symbolic castration on his father, defeating him, which therefore allows a reconciliation between the two. Luke achieves wholeness as an individual but also does not have to bear the guilt of estrangement from his parents. Yet, as this book has argued in previous chapters and will argue in upcoming chapters, a much more complex pattern of real world relations plays out on the screen, rather than a simple Oedipal cautionary tale.

In addition to the myth criticism of the series, which Lucas has not only encouraged but actively participated in, interviewing with Joseph Campbell and sharing his mythic intentions with all biographers who interview him, all of the elements of filmmaking have been utilized to establish the mythic credentials of the saga. James Buhler even argues that the music is used to reinforce the mythic aspects of the film. He observes that the words "Star Wars" on the screen at the exact moment the first note of the theme is played after teaser of "A long time ago, in a galaxy far, far away...," arguing that "the mythic aura of *Star Wars* is born of this synchronization of music and image."[44] Buhler quotes composer John Williams as wanting to conjure "mythic archtypes" with the music: "some memory of Buck Rogers or King Arthur...."[45]

It is these memories of other myths, of other meaning-makers, of other emblems of popular culture that recall myth and legend, that ultimately show the purpose of defining *Star Wars* as modern myth. Hal Colebatch, a "well known writer" from the Australian Institute for Public Policy, a conservative think tank in Perth, sees *Star Wars* as "reveal[ing] strong underlying elements of traditional Western values."[46] Colebatch sees postwar Western culture as focusing on anti-heroes and embracing moral relativism and nihilism, and he turns to *Star Wars* and *Lord of the Rings* as modern epics that embrace conservative Western values, capitalism, and free enterprise. The mythic aura of *Star Wars* is embraced by audiences, he argues, because it reinforces their own beliefs and because it offers an alternative to believing in nothing. In other words, if *Star Wars* is a myth, then we can embrace and believe in the world it shows us. If myth defines the relationship between the individual and the natural world and the social world, the definition in Lucas's films is a very positive one.

The films not only make meaning, they reinforce belief and, conversely, allow one to ignore more negative potential meanings. The reality is that calling the films "myth" elevates them from the realm of popular culture and makes them into something both greater and deeper. It also further depoliticizes the films, allowing them to avoid or ignore any real world comparisons. Yet dangers lurk in doing so.

Myth is a distancing device — it allows us to view the Other as distant, monstrous, or even "evil." We not only can kill evil beings, we have a moral obligation to do so. Myth allows us to justify oppressing or attacking other cultures. We do not need to engage other cultures on their own terms under myths; the gods have already explained who those people are and what their place in the world is, and if they exist to be slaughtered, it is the will of the gods.

Myth is also used to exoticize and distance the Other. Lucas, quoted in Pye and Myles, stated that since he wanted to create a mythic world, "[t]here had to be strange savages and bizarre things in an exotic land."[47] By calling *Star Wars* myth, it is placed into the same category as other myths which posit that other peoples are not human. The anthropomorphic creatures of Greek mythology were not only psychological symbols, they were also representations of the people who lived in foreign lands. Africa is radically different than Greece, the myth states, as there are people there whose heads are below their shoulders, men with only one leg, and men who are covered in fur. Therefore, they are not human. They are different. "They" are not like us. They are Other.

Myth criticism erases difference between cultures. The cultural and social forces that created the Arthurian legends of England are not the same as the ones that created Greek mythology, which are not the same as the ones that produced *Star Wars*. By placing all myths side by side, regardless of original context, we ignore at our peril underlying differences which may shape the meaning and reception of those myths far greater than an underlying structure, psychology, or morphology. Every myth has historicity — the conditions that created the myth in the first place, which often includes a religious function — and a transhistoricity — how that myth is read by later and different peoples. Greek myths made different meanings for the fifth century Athenians than they do for twenty-first century Americans.

Myth criticism also ignores the impact and influence of the material conditions under which the myth was created. Even more, much myth criticism ignores the complicity of myth in establishing and maintaining social dominance and power structures. Many myths are created in order to explain why those in power are in power and why those who are oppressed or dominated are (and should be) oppressed and dominated. The "divine right" of kings to rule in medieval Europe, for example, is a myth that allowed no questioning of the authority of those in power. The myth of British racial and cultural superiority means the colonial enterprise goes unquestioned, and the "White Man's Burden" is to civilize the colored nations of the Earth.

Ian Barbour, after Malinowski, argues that "Myth sanctions the existing social order and justifies its status system and power structure, providing a rationale for social and political institutions."[48] While such myths can unify a society, ordering experience and defining identity, it can also Other those outside that society and create a duality where none exists. As Tina Chen writes of the Fu Manchu novels (discussed in detail in chapter five), the danger to the real world from the fictive one is that the novels of Sax Rohmer feature "a political conflict cast in mythic terms of opposition."[49]

The "good" British agents must fight the evil Dr. Fu Manchu in order to do no less than save the world. The anxiety in England over events in the East generated the Fu Manchu novels, which have served as source material for films that continue the mythic fight of East versus West. To employ myth in this circumstance is to use mythic archetype for political aims. In short, the use of myth creates a distorted way of ordering experience and casts outside groups as an Other that one is morally obligated to destroy.

Furthering that idea, Manichaeisms permeate the *Star Wars* saga: the universe is split into two opposing camps. One is either good or evil. One either embraces the light side of the Force or the dark side of the Force. Such Manichaeisms are useful in myth, but make for a remarkably uncomplex view of the world. When using real world material, including mythic structure, real languages, recognizable environments, and characters rooted in actual ethnicities, to construct an imaginative geography and history and then posit a simple duality as the method for defining what everything is—either good or bad, light or dark, helpful or adversarial—the narrative can then be used to define the real world equivalents. The "myth" of *Star Wars* allows us to see Asians as evil, as outlined in Chapter 5, or that black people are of no consequence, as outlined in Chapter 4. Uncomplex myth can serve to justify uncomplex views of reality.

Roland Barthes takes this critique even further in his book *Mythologies*, arguing that myth is "a system of communication," "depoliticized speech," and "has the task of giving an historical attention a natural justification."[50] Barthes also argues that myth can be used to exoticize others when they cannot be reduced and difference erased.[51] If we cannot understand other people on our own terms, myth allows us to remove their humanity and make them something other than people.

Another especially troubling aspect of the use of myth in the *Star Wars* series is that in the associate publications and materials put out by Lucasfilm and those who study the mythic structure of *Star Wars*, the focus is on linking *Star Wars* to Western myths, despite the extraordinary amount of material appropriated from Asian cultures and stories. If, as argued above, the Force is mostly Asian in derivation, and the Jedi more like samurai or shaolin than Western knights, and if, as argued in the next chapter, that much of the culture and visual look of the films has been appropriated from non–Western sources, then much of the myth to which the film should be compared should be Asian and other non–Western.

Yet in such books as *Star Wars: The Power of Myth* and Steven A. Galipeau's *The Journey of Luke Skywalker* the focus is on linking the two trilogies to Western myth almost exclusively, with the Eastern elements added as an afterthought. Released to coincide with the opening of *Phantom*, *Star Wars: The Power of Myth* compares Luke to "mythic heroes" such as Wilhelm Tell (Switzerland), Siegfried (Germany), Thor (Norse), Fionn (Ireland), King Arthur (Britain), Aeneas (Troy), Jaime (Spain), Viriato (Lusitania), Tijil (Belgian), and Roland (France).[52] Obi-Wan, whose name, as will be argued in the next chapter, denotes that he is Japanese, is compared to Merlin as "The Wise Guide."[53] The book compares Chewbacca, the "Hero Partner," with Jason and the Argonauts or the Knights of the Round Table.[54] The sources of these heroes are legend, myth, epic, and in a few cases, remote history. Some of the comparative heroes in these books were real, others fictitious. It is the culture of origin and the source of the comparative material, however, where these books posit a Eurocentric, Eurosuperior view of the world.

In other words, in the first three-fifths of the book, which is, admittedly, aimed at younger readers, the characters and events of the *Star Wars* saga are solely compared with Euromyths and Western stories. The echoes that are proposed in this official publication associated with the films are solely Western ones. It is not until page thirty-two (out of forty-eight) that the first non–Western reference is given, and that is not even a mythic reference, but rather a religious one. "Jedi Training" is compared to "Zen Buddhism:"

> Jedi philosophy shares similarities with Zen Buddhism, which holds that truth and enlightenment can be found through personal insight and self-mastery.... As with Jedi training, Buddhist knowledge is handed down as an inspiration to students who are "awakened" by a teacher who has experienced the truth of the teachings.[55]

The next page then shares that "in Japan, the training of Zen Buddhist monks often combines meditation with fencing, archery, and jujitsu."[56] Neither of these statements are particularly accurate in terms of summarizing what Zen Buddhism is or how it is experienced in Japan. At the very least these statements greatly oversimplify what is essentially a complex socioreligious practice in Japan. This reductivist approach to comparing the Jedi with Zen Buddhists only makes sense if you understand what the book is actually doing — not explaining the cultural influences on *Star Wars* saga to young fans, in which case Zen Buddhism should not only be included but given a much more detailed and accurate description, but explaining other cultures and other mythologies in terms of *Star Wars*.

Star Wars: The Power of Myth does not say that the Jedi are similar to Buddhist monks; it states that Buddhist monks are similar to Jedi. It privileges "Jedi" over "Buddhist," marginalizing the latter and Othering it. By claiming mythic status for his work, Lucas elevates above the realities of other cultures. We can now explain a major religion to young fans via its similarities to a popular film that appropriated elements of that religion in the first place. Even worse, however, in terms of representation, is that "Zen Buddhism" is placed side by side with pre–Christian European mythologies. While there are few people who worship Thor anymore, while few believe that King Arthur or Merlin are going to return to restore Britain to her pre–Roman glory, Buddhism is a major world religion with hundreds of millions of adherents, reduced by this book to a "myth." By calling *Star Wars* "myth," and then including Buddhism in with the list of mythologies to which the films are compared, then the young reader is left to conclude that Buddhism must be an equally discredited myth, as that of Thor and Jason and the Argonauts.

The personal combat of the *Star Wars* saga is also compared with "Samurai Swordfights," acknowledging the similarity between lightsaber duels and kendo (which will be further discussed in the next chapter, but not acknowledging that kendo not only came first but served as an inspiration for the former).[57] Again, *Star Wars: The Power of Myth* inverts the appropriation by placing Lucas's invention at the center and the Asian source from which it is appropriated as a comparative.

The much larger question begged by this book, however, is what is so "mythic" about samurai and kendo, both of which are historical realities in Japan in ways that Merlin, Thor, and Siegfried were not in their culture. In *Star Wars: The Power of Myth*, European myths are myths and Japanese history is also myth. Zen Buddhism, a religion still practiced not only in Japan but around the world, is the equivalent in this book of the worship of Thor. Such questionable leveling and erasure of difference does a disservice to Zen Buddhism and to the reader of the book.

Similarly, in both the 1997 exhibit at the National Air and Space Museum of the Smithsonian Institution called *Star Wars: The Magic of Myth* and the companion book, edited by exhibit curator Mary Henderson, Henderson calls *Star Wars* "one of the great myths of our time."[58] Like *Star Wars: The Power of Myth*, *Star Wars: The Magic of Myth* places Western myth and Asian history side by side and calls both myth. Luke is compared with Jason, Oedipus, Icarus, Heracles, Theseus, Robin Hood, King Arthur, Siegfried, Odysseus, and David. The rescue of Princess Leia in *A New Hope* is compared to the waking of Sleeping Beauty.[59] Likewise, the fight against the monster in the trash compactor is compared to Theseus in the labyrinth fighting the Minotaur.[60] Luke's fight with the Rancor is comparable to Beowulf's fight with Grendel.[61] Other works of art, both visual and performing, that employ myth are referenced: Wagner's *Ring* cycle is referenced, as is Goya's painting *Saturn Devouring His Children* (compared to Vader's dismembering of Luke in *Empire*), and Mallory's *La Morte d'Arthur*.[62] Although the occasional Western historic reference is made, such as Joan of Arc or Old West gunfighters (both of which might be argued have taken on mythic qualities of their own), the overwhelming majority of references is to myth, folklore, and legend. A few short pages are dedicated to similarities with the Nazis and the Cold War, but these come late in the book and are rather brief (two to three pages each, after entire chapters on myth).

When the culture of Asia is used comparatively with the saga, it is not the myth but the history which serves as the majority of referenced. The Force and the Jedi are compared with Zen Buddhism. Henderson compares Yoda with Gama Sennin, an 18th century Taoist sage. Once again, Kurosawa's cinema is held up as a model for the series.[63] Samurai culture, which is not mythic but historic, is referenced as a comparative to the Jedi, Boba Fett, and the stormtroopers.[64]

Both Henderson and John rely on Western culture for the vast majority of referents to which the mythic elements of *Star Wars* might be compared. The vast majority of those referents in both books are myth, legend and folklore. The few times that Eastern culture is used comparatively it is history or religious culture that is used as the referent. Western myth and Eastern history are equated — both are equally distant and strange and similar to the fantasy that is *Star Wars*.

Luke is a hero like Heracles, Robin Hood or Beowulf, but not like the heroic legends of Asia, which go unmentioned. Even historic figure who are larger than life, such as Minomoto no Yoshitsune and his companion Benkei, are ignored. Zhong Kui, the legendary demon fighter of China could be referenced, but it is not. Numerous folk heroes such as Wong Fei Hung, considered by many to the greatest folk hero of China and the subject of numerous films from Hong Kong and China, are never referenced.[65] No single hero of Chinese, Japanese, or other Asian derivation, from legend, folklore, or even history is referenced by Henderson, Campbell, or John. Instead, according to these books, the Jedi are like the Asians— mysterious, powerful, and dedicated to their art. These books use the distance of Asia and Asian culture from the West to distance and Other the Jedi in order to make them seem more mysterious and powerful.

In this study, I attempt to locate the visual and cultural elements of Asia which shape the *Star Wars* series, and certainly they are present in all six films, as will be detailed in the next chapter, as are Western elements as well, obviously. The argument here is simply that in the *Star Wars* industry, which posits the mythic stature of the films in the first place, Western influences are privileged and Eastern influences downplayed. Western influences that are claimed as "mythic" by the industry are just that: myths, legends, folklore — fantastic stories involving monsters, long journeys, and larger than life heroes. Eastern influences that are claimed as "mythic" by the industry are actually history, religion, culture. Christianity is not held up as "mythic," though Zen Buddhism and Taoism are. The religions of the West are posited as religion in the books that analyze the myth of *Star Wars*. The religions of the East are posited as myth. Western culture, religion, and history are privileged in the analysis of mythic *Star Wars*.

While I agree with Janice Rushing when she observes in her own analysis of the *Alien* films, "The new myth for humankind needs to be a *quest*, not a *conquest*; its purpose to search, rather than to search and destroy" (emphasis in original), that does not necessarily mean that the mythic aspect of *Star Wars* is without its functions within the individual viewer, within the fan community, and within the larger community.[66] The larger, and arguably final, critique is that for all of the assertions of the mythic aspect of *Star Wars*, it is not quite the new American mythology, as it serves many, but not all, of the functions of myth.

Joseph Campbell, who, as noted above greatly admired *Star Wars* and used it in his writings, just as George Lucas greatly admired and incorporated Campbell's theories into his work, offered as the fourth volume in *The Masks of God* series *Creative Mythology*, which considers how old myths are made new and new myths are generated by artists engaging the cultural material. "Creative mythology ... springs not, like theology, from the dicta of authority, but from the insights, sentiments, thought and vision of an adequate individual, loyal to his own experience."[67] Individuals like Shakespeare, the Greek tragedians, Mozart and others create works that function as myth. Yet later in the volume, in a section entitled "Towards New Mythologies," Campbell posits four functions necessary for "a complete mythology." First is "the metaphysical-mystical prospect": "to waken and maintain in the individual an experience of awe, humility, and respect, in recognition of that ultimate mystery, transcending names and forms...."[68] Second is "the cosmological prospect," which is "to render ... an image of the universe."[69] Third, myth must serve "the social prospect," which is "the validation and maintenance of an established order."[70] Lastly, "the psychological sphere" must be addressed by myth: "the centering and harmonizing the individual."[71]

Taking these functions in reverse, it could easily be argued that the *Star Wars* saga is almost but not quite a new mythology, despite its reliance on mythic structure and the enormous number of people insisting that it is new myth. For many individuals, the saga does meet the needs of the psychological sphere, the social prospect, and the cosmological prospect. Repeated viewings of the films can and do center and harmonize the individual, validate and maintain an established order, and offer an image of the universe. While the films, it could be argued, "waken and maintain in the individual an experience of awe, humility, and respect," especially in the face of cutting edge special effects in each film, what is missing from making the mythology complete is the recognition of an "ultimate mystery, transcending names and forms." Frank Allnut and the Australian Jedi notwithstanding, there is a lack of connection with a sense of the divine. Only someone with no connection to reality believes the Force is an actual principle that influences and shapes our lives. We might compare the Force to the divine, the numen, the holy, or specific deity-figures, but it is not real nor does it have a social or cultural effect as other religious belief structures do. The *Star Wars* films can give an individual's life meaning, create a social order within its fan culture, inspire their viewers individually and collectively, offer a life-changing experience, and even give the viewer a transcendent experience. But for all that it still does not offer a complete "metaphysical-mystical prospect." In the end, the politics of the film outweigh its metaphysics, the technology outweighs the theology, and the Empire triumphs.

Lastly, myth is communally owned. All myth-having cultures' members are free to understand and experience their myths, even reinterpret them and rewrite them. Reinterpretation and rewriting of myth is the basis of Greek tragedy, as well as much of Renaissance art. Never before has myth been the sole legal and intellectual property of one individual, who may add to or change that "myth" at will. Lucas owns all of the rights to the characters, concepts, worlds, narratives, images, and elements. Only he may give the *Nihil obstat* of Lucasfilm to any additions or changes in the stories. Never before has myth had a team of attorneys charged with maintaining those intellectual property rights. Myth has always had marketing, and even, it might be argued, action figures. But the "modern myth" of *Star Wars* allows no reinterpretation, no rewriting, no variation of myth. In being so, it is therefore ultimately a wonderfully creative, mythically-inspired artistic product with billions of dollars of merchandising, but is not truly myth.

CHAPTER 3

"Help Me, Kurosawa Akira, You're My Only Hope": Asian Culture and *Star Wars*

If I think of John Ford as my father, I guess that makes you my children.
— Kurosawa to George Lucas and Francis Ford Coppola, 1979[1]

Hidden Rebel *Fortress*

George Lucas has acknowledged the myriad of debts which the *Star Wars* trilogies owe to Asian cultures, especially Chinese and Japanese cultures. Cinematically, the films have been impacted by the film work of world renowned auteur Kurosawa Akira. James Goodwin observes that "Lucas has acknowledged the debt *Star Wars* owes in story and style to Kurosawa's comic adventure epic *The Hidden Fortress* (*Kakushi Toride no San-Akunin*, 1958)," whose Japanese title is better translated as "Three Bad Men in a Hidden Fortress."[2] So open is this debt that the Criterion Collection DVD of *Hidden Fortress* contains a brief interview with George Lucas, recorded in 2001, in which Lucas discusses his admiration for Kurosawa and acknowledges learning from Kurosawa's use of long lenses and camera movement.[3] The published screenplays of the original trilogy contain an extended annotation about the shaping influence of *Hidden Fortress*, particularly in structure and point of view.[4]

Lucas lists as his four favorite Kurosawa films *Seven Samurai*, *Yojimbo*,

Ikiru, and *The Hidden Fortress*. John Baxter reports that John Milius urged Lucas to see Japanese films at the Toho cinema in Hollywood on La Brea when both were film students at USC, which is where Lucas first encountered them.[5] These films also introduced him to the world of Japan. Baxter discloses that Lucas wanted to shoot the commercial version of *THX-1138* in Japan in order "to capture that sense of alienness and focused will," as well as "clinical emptiness," qualities that he felt were endemic to the Japanese landscape and culture.[6] This attitude of Japan-as-alien may have begun with Lucas's encounters with Kurosawa, but as will be argued in Chapter 5, aliens then adapt stereotypical cinematic Asian qualities in the *Star Wars* films. In the attempt to mimic Kurosawa, the Japanese are rendered as aliens on Earth.

Lucas notes that what impresses him most about Kurosawa's films is how the director tells his stories, especially visually — the graphics, the framing, the movement of the camera are all tools for advancing a narrative. Lucas acknowledges *Hidden Fortress* as a minor inspiration for *Star Wars*. He notes that Kurosawa told the story "from the point of view of the two lowest characters," which Lucas then decided to do with his film, using the droids C3PO and R2-D2 as the characters to whom the audience are first introduced and whose adventures the audience follows. Lucas then calls the other parallels between his film and Kurosawa's "coincidental," but comparative viewings of both films demonstrate that this is not so.

Kurosawa's film is set during Japan's civil war era and relates the story of a bold princess named Yukihime (Uehara Misa), rescued by an old general, Rokurota Makabe (Mifune Toshiro), who must travel through enemy territory to reach the hidden fortress, much like in *A New Hope*, in which General Kenobi must bring the bold Princess Leia to a hidden fortress, the Rebel base on the fourth moon of Yavin.

The film begins with a pair of bickering farmers (Chiaki Minoru and Fujiwara Kamatari) on the edge of a large battle. Mounted samurai ride past them and kill a fleeing samurai but disregard the farmers as insignificant, allowing them to escape. They are subsequently and inadvertently drawn into the conflict, much as *A New Hope* begins with a pair of bickering droids in a large battle, who are ignored and allowed to escape (the pod in which they escape to Tatooine is ignored and unharmed by the Imperial troops who detect no life signs). It is around these two seemingly insignificant figures that this story also develops. Similar to the plans stored in R2-D2 which must be brought to the hidden rebel base, Kurosawa's characters secretly transport gold which will allow them to turn the tide of war when they reach their home territory.[7]

In the earlier drafts of *A New Hope*, Luke was not a young man, but rather a Rokurota figure: "a large man, 'apparently in his early sixties but actually much older.'"[8] In fact, in the first draft, Anakin Skywalker's father's name is "Akira Valor," named specifically after Kurosawa Akira.[9] Later, when Lucas chose to focus on Luke Skywalker, the father figure became the mentor figure of Obi-Wan Kenobi, who, it might be noted, is greeted by the hologram of Princess Leia as "General Kenobi," who "served my father in the Clone Wars." Mifune Toshiro was strongly considered to play Obi-Wan Kenobi.[10] Such a casting would certainly echo *Hidden Fortress*, with Mifune again playing a general rescuing a princess and delivering her safely through enemy territory.

As the project developed, it began to resemble more and more its inspiration. Baxter comments that

> With each change, the script came closer to *The Hidden Fortress*, to the point where Lucas and Kurtz briefly considered buying the remake rights. They decided instead to play down the parallels, though Japanese-isms still abound, from the style of the swordplay to words like "Jedi," suggested by "Jidai-geki," the term for period TV samurai stories.[11]

Baxter is incorrect in his etymology for *jidai-geki*, which is much more than a "period TV samurai story." *Jidai-geki*, also called *jidai-mono*, was originally used to describe a particular type of Kabuki or Bunraku play which is rooted in history (and quite often based on original Noh plays), as opposed to *sewamono*, the domestic plays about the lives of merchants, courtesans, and other middle class people of Tokugawa Japan. *Jidai-mono* plays feature rulers, gods, samurai, and nobility. The events in the plays are rooted in history, but have often accumulated a level of myth or popular legend.[12] The term *jidai-geki* specifically means "history piece," and is used to refer to a film set in the distant past, traditionally the Tokugawa period. Lucas would have encountered the term as a description of Kurosawa's samurai films. *Jidai*, the word from which "Jedi" is derived, literally means "age," "era," "period," or "antiquity," rather an appropriate term for a film set "a long time ago" and glorifying a long-gone warrior caste.

Charles Champlin reports that Alan Ladd, Jr., Lucas's supporter at Twentieth Century Fox, disclosed that at one point Lucas "thought of it with an all Japanese cast."[13] At another point, he considered having Luke and Leia played by Asian actors. Lucas said:

> At one point Luke and Leia were going to be Oriental. I played with various ethnic groups, but when there are four main characters, it seemed better to have them all be the same race.[14]

Lucas never explains why it "seemed better" to have an ethnically homogenous group rather than an ethnically diverse one, particularly since so many films have not followed the former formula. The point, however, is that Lucas at one point envisioned a very Asian, if not a very Japanese film. Kurosawa, Donald Richie reports, had a similar cinematic preference as Lucas, observing that he "is also fond of the never-never land of the *chambara*."[15] *Chambara* are a particular type of *jidai-geki*, a sword film, a genre aimed primarily at children, just like Lucas's films. Lucas seeks to remake the Saturday serial. Both the *Star Wars* films and chambara pictures are nostalgia-driven — they celebrate and romanticize a lost past. Whereas Kurosawa questions both the myth and the history, however, Lucas is content to accept the nostalgia at surface level, never questioning its veracity or its ideology. *Yojimbo*, *Seven Samurai*, and *Hidden Fortress* all interrogate the feudal society that posit the samurai at the top of the social pyramid and demonstrate the ugly reality behind the romanticized past. Lucas still romanticizes war and battle. Whereas the young man of *Yojimbo* runs home to his mother at the first sight of blood, all the characters of Lucas's saga continue on in the face of injury, death, and even the entire destruction of a planet.

Other moments from the series also reflect moments from Kurosawa's films. The cantina scene in *A New Hope* echoes *Yojimbo*, Lucas's acknowledged second favorite Kurosawa film. As Luke sits at the bar with a drink, he is approached by two aliens. The first belligerently barks at Luke in an unrecognizable language and the second then translates:

> ALIEN: He doesn't like you.
> LUKE: I'm sorry.
> ALIEN: I don't like you either. You just watch yourself. We're wanted men. I've got the death sentence in twelve systems.
> LUKE: I'll be careful.
> ALIEN: You'll be dead!
> BEN: This little one's not worth the effort. Come, let me get you something.

When the alien draws his pistol and the other alien throws Luke across the bar, Ben draws his lightsaber, killing one and cutting off the arm of another. The camera cuts to the arm on the floor and then back to Obi-Wan standing still with his weapon.

Compare this exchange with the initial fight for Sanjuro (Mifune Toshiro) in Kurosawa's *Yojimbo*:

> GANGSTER 1: See this prison tattoo! I wasn't in there for nothing!
> GANGSTER 2: The law is after me! I'll hang if I'm ever caught!

GANGSTER 3: Me, too. They'll cut off my head some day! I've done
everything bad.
SANJURO: You're all tough then?
GANGSTER 3: What? Kill me if you can!
SANJURO: It will hurt...

When the gangsters draw their swords, Sanjuro cuts down two immediately and then cuts off the arm of a third. The camera cuts to the arm
on the floor and then back to Sanjuro standing still with his weapon. Both
the exchange between the hero and the belligerent adversaries from the bar
and the visual narrative which follows of *Yojimbo* are clearly echoed in *A
New Hope*.

We might also note a similarity between *Hidden Fortress* and *The Phantom Menace*, with the numbers slightly shifted. Two warriors, Obi-Wan
Kenobi and Qui-Gon Jinn, known for their prowess with swords, must
escort a disguised queen through enemy territory. Rather than two comic
figures, the farmers are replaced by the sole comic figure of Jar Jar Binks.
Amidala and Leia, warrior women and royalty, are the daughters of Yukihime, metaphorically speaking.

In an interview with Mary Henderson, Lucas ultimately admitted
how Kurosawa-as-foreign-film shaped his vision of science fiction:

> I was very intrigued by a lot of his movies because they were samurai
> movies, feudal Japan. The look of them was very exotic ... and I found it
> very interesting that nothing was explained. You are thrown into this
> world and obviously if you know about feudal Japan then it makes sense
> to you; but if you don't, it's like you're watching this very exotic, strange
> thing with strange customs and a strange look. And I think that influenced
> me a great deal in working in science fiction because I was able to get
> around the idea that you have to explain everything or understand what
> everything is.... You just put yourself into this environment. It's like the
> world of the anthropologist. You walk into this strange society; you sit
> there and observe it.[16]

Many admissions and assumptions are revealed in this statement.
Lucas freely admits Kurosawa's shaping influence, as well as the influence
of Japanese culture on his work. He sees Japanese culture as "exotic," alien
and unfathomable, in other words, the traditional, comfortable Eurocen-
trist view of Asia. He was able to "get around the idea that you have to
explain everything," but does not seem to realize that one need not explain
things easily understood by all members of a culture. Nothing needs to be
explained to the Japanese about Japanese culture and history. Lucas fails
to realize that when watching the films of Kurosawa, it is he who is the Other,

the outsider, the one who does not necessarily recognize what would be apparent to someone from the source culture.

In other words, even when encountering Kurosawa's films, Lucas remains a Self and continues to view the original, intended audience as Other. This conception of experiencing the films is equally interesting, as Lucas insists on controlling meaning in the *Star Wars* films himself, rejecting alternative viewings, but he watches Kurosawa from own perspective. The repeated use of the word "exotic" demonstrates that Lucas has exoticized Japanese history — the samurai are "exotic" in a way that Western knights clearly are not. He equates feudal Japan with the words of science fiction and science fantasy. Japan is "strange" in the same manner that the cantina scene in *Star Wars* is strange.

Not only does seeing Japanese as Other firmly set Lucas's perspective on Asia within the Eurocentric camp, it more or less proves the contention of Chapter 5 of this book, namely that Asians are presented in the *Star Wars* films as aliens. Asian actors are absent, but Asians and "Asianness" is present in the form of Jedi, Neimoidians, Darth Maul, and other "strange" or "exotic" beings.

By this quotation, Lucas sees himself as anthropologist when he views the films of Kurosawa. He is studying a foreign society when he views Kurosawa's films, but he fails, as any good anthropologist would not, to site himself as the one whose gaze shapes his understanding of the world he is experiencing. One might ask, does this make the *Star Wars* films a kind of anthropology? If so, what kind? Lucas substitutes literal aliens for the alienness of Japanese culture.

Those who inscribe and describe Lucas in a myriad of biographies, film analyses, and hagiographies continue to perpetuate the Asian-as-alien anthropological approach to the understanding of how Kurosawa has shaped the saga. John Baxter relates that

> Eighteenth century Japan, when Kurosawa set most of his films, was so alien it could well have been Mars: the ankle-length robes and rural settings, the castles and sword play, the culture of imperial power and privilege, opposed by daring and belief — all recalled Edgar Rice Burroughs.[17]

Baxter literally equates feudal Japan with the planet Mars. Like Lucas, Baxter is the Self for whom Kurosawa's films are utterly alien. Not so to the original Japanese audiences, who would have seen and perceived them as historical, not alien. Not so to Westerners with knowledge of Japanese history, cinema, or culture, who would have seen the embodiment of these in the movies, not utter alienness. Again, the fifth chapter of the current volume will explore in much greater depth the idea of Asian as alien, but it is in the analysis of Kurosawa through the retrospective lens of his influence on Lucas that begins with the idea that things Japanese are really things alien.

We should also note that, by Baxter's analysis, it is both concept and visual content that makes Kurosawa "alien." What "we" see on the screen is alien — it looks different, weird, foreign. But what "we" also experience in terms of the themes, philosophies, and intellectual content of the films of Kurosawa ("the culture of imperial power") is also presented as utterly alien. Rather than see Lucas as proceeding from Kurosawa, Baxter (and other critics) see Kurosawa, if not proceeding from Lucas, at least serving as a forerunner to him. It is Lucas in the center, not Kurosawa. Kurosawa's films are experienced in terms of Lucas's, instead of Lucas's in terms of Kurosawa's.

Star Wars shares something else in common with the *jidai-geki* and *chambara* films of Kurosawa Akira: both sets of films are about traditional societies in transition to new orders. *Yojimbo, Hidden Fortress* and *Seven Samurai* all feature the advent of guns into Tokogawa Japan. Most *chambara* feature swordplay — in fact, it is what they are known for. Kurosawa introduced guns into his films both as historical markers and to emphasize the passing of the samurai culture. It is no coincidence that all four samurai who are killed in *Seven Samurai* are killed by guns — Heihachi (Chiaki Minoru) while raiding the bandits' fort, Gorobei (Inaba Yoshio) while repelling the first attack, Kikuchyo (Mifune Toshiro) during the final battle, and even Kyuzo (Miyaguchi Seiji), the master swordsman who has trained to perfect his technique and is an unbeatable warrior, are killed by guns. Each death is preceded on the soundtrack by the sound of a rifle firing — an audible reminder that even as the samurai kill bandits with their swords and their superior organization and fighting techniques, the guns will eventually defeat the sword. The gun is not only the "great equalizer," its use in battle marks the transition from the samurai to the modern army. Technological advances mean that a warrior culture of personal combat (be it Jedi or samurai) will be replaced by standing armies of common people (or clones) who will fight huge impersonal battles.

Obi-Wan calls the lightsaber "a more elegant weapon for a more civilized time," and Mace Windu notes that the Jedi are "keepers of the peace," not an army in the traditional sense, and should the separatists opt out of the Republic, the Jedi cannot fight them. For a thousand years the Jedi kept the peace in the galaxy, but the advent of both the droid army and the clone army make them easy prey for Darth Sidious and Darth Vader. Many Jedi die in the battle in the arena on Geonosis — none are killed by lightsaber. All who die are killed by the blasters of droids and the separatists. In fact, in the five movies released to date, only one Jedi has been killed by lightsaber — Qui-Gon Jinn in *Phantom*. One might argue that Obi-Wan Kenobi is also struck down by a lightsaber, but the film makes rather clear he does not "die" in the traditional sense. Han Solo tells Luke in *A New Hope*, "Hokey religions and ancient weapons are no match for a good blaster at your side, kid." While the films want us to believe Solo is wrong, in the world of *Star Wars* he is proven right. Jedi who die are killed by blasters. Samurai who die are killed by guns.

The first *Star Wars* trilogy deals with two transitions. The first is that of Republic to Empire. When *A New Hope* begins, the Senate still exists and the Imperial Commander of the Star Destroyer that captured Leia is worried that her imprisonment "will generate sympathy for the Rebellion in the Senate." Clearly the Emperor's control is not yet complete if the Senate is still of some concern. It is only later in the film that Grand Moff Tarkin announces to the Death Star command staff that "The Imperial Senate will no longer be of any concern to us." The Emperor has just dissolved the Senate, and "the last traces of the Old Republic have been swept away." Thus it is only during *A New Hope* that the Emperor's power becomes complete. Bespin, in *Empire*, has not yet attracted Imperial attention — one might argue that the Empire is still conquering the galaxy and shoring up the Emperor's power. Then, in *Jedi*, the death of the Emperor and destruction of the Death Star shows the end of the Imperial transition and the beginning of the New Republic.

Likewise, the films of Kurosawa are often set in the period right before the Meiji restoration in Japan. If the Old Republic of *Star Wars* stood for a thousand years, the Tokugawa Shogunate stood for two and a half centuries. The films of Kurosawa are set at the end of the Shogunate and right before the modernization of Japan. The importation of guns and their use in battle begins to spell the end of the samurai. Lucas's films deal with a transitional period in which a warrior culture of personal combat is replaced by a military culture of uniform soldiers using blasters. Kurosawa's films deal with a transitional period in which a warrior culture of personal combat is replaced by a military culture of uniform soldiers using guns.

Very few periods (and period films) feature both swords and guns in combat. Kurosawa's samurai films, set at the end of the Tokugawa period, feature guns and swords. Only in science fiction and science fantasy is such a combination possible or believable. In the writings of Edgar Rice Burroughs and the Flash Gordon films we see laser guns side by side with sword combat. *Star Wars* features blasters and lightsabers used side-by-side in combat. We even see the lightsaber used to deflect blaster shots by some Jedi. Similar to Luke's being shot in the hand on Jabba's sail barge by one of Jabba's guards armed with a blaster, and subsequently killing that guard with his lightsaber, Kukichiyo in *Seven Samurai* is shot by a bandit, whom he then kills with his sword before dying of the bullet wound. Kurosawa's use of sword and gun alongside each other is echoed by Lucas's use of lightsaber and blaster. Jedi and droid echo samurai and bandit.

Even beyond the religious aspects of Yoda as argued in the previous chapter, that he is a "Zen master," the character is also perceived (by Lawrence Kasdan at least) as an echo of the mentor figures in Kurosawa's work as well. Kasdan states that the training sequences in *Empire* are also rooted in Kurosawa's *jidai-geki* films: "All through Kurosawa's movies you have the idea that it's one thing to be physically adept and something else to be spiritually adept."[18] The training sequences of *Empire* echo the door test of *Seven Samurai*, in which Katsushiro (Kimura Isao) hides behind a door and attempts to strike samurai entering through a door to test their martial abilities. One samurai catches the stick and throws Katsushiro, displaying his fighting skills and quick reactions. He does not join the group, however. The next samurai to be tested, however, Gorobei, stops outside the door, smiles and says, "No tricks, please." He sensed the danger before it could even be a threat, very much a lesson that both Obi-Wan, who places a helmet over Luke's head and has him fight a remote in *New Hope*, and Yoda, who tells Luke not to take his lightsaber into the cave under the tree, would like their young trainee to learn.

Kurosawa uses a number of mentor figures in his films, and Lucas echoes those mentor figures with ones of his own. Though it will be argued below that the training sequences echo Chinese martial arts films more than Kurosawa films, one cannot deny the shaping influence of Kurosawa in many, if not all, aspects of the *Star Wars* saga.

Hal Colebatch argues that the *Star Wars* films are inherently "Western" in that they have "a distinct affinity to historic Western cultural values.... The fundamental outlook behind [them] is traditional and conservative."[19] While I would not disagree that *Star Wars* is inherently conservative and has an affinity for certain "Western values" (indeed, those are two of the contentions of this volume), I would argue that Star Wars in not inherently "Western," particularly given the amount of cultural appropriation from Asian cultures evident in the film. In the previous chapter I explored how Asian religions, far more than Western religions, shaped the idea of "The Force," and certain key characters as being emblematic of Asian religious figures. Given the admitted embracing of Kurosawa's influence on his work by Lucas, as described above, in this chapter I shall move beyond Kurosawa's presence in the *Star Wars* films to the role of Asian martial culture and visual influence on the films.

Kurosawa's influence on the *Star Wars* films even moves beyond the first trilogy. So open and obvious the influence on the saga is Kurosawa that to prepare for his role in *Phantom Menace*, Liam Neeson not only watched the original trilogy, he watched *Seven Samurai*.[20] His performance as Qui-Gon Jinn, providing object lessons for his young student while also defending a small planet (read: village) with a small group of mismatched outcasts against a larger, more heavily armed bandit force echoes Kambei in Kurosawa's masterpiece. Unlike his predecessor, however, Qui-Gon does not live to see the village defeat the bandits.

Lastly, we should note that Lucas paid two of the greatest possible tributes to Kurosawa as an influence. First, he secured funding for Kurosawa for his film *Kagamusha* when no Japanese producer would agree to help. Along with Francis Ford Coppola, Lucas served as executive producer on the film. Lucas in a sense paid Kurosawa back by allowing him to continue to produce films on his terms. The second tribute, and the one which more or less proves my contention in this chapter, is, as noted above, that Lucas derived the name "Jedi" for his warrior priests from the Japanese term for period film, *jidai-geki*.[21] The Jedi are literally "*jidai*"— Japanese history. By their very name they demonstrate their debt to Japanese culture and cinema.

Star Wars as *Wuxia:* Asian Martial Arts in the Films

Kurosawa's influence in the films is clear, and the Japanese presence in the visual elements of the films is detailed below. Yet there is also a Chinese presence in the *Star Wars* films in their echo of *wuxia*— the Chinese martial art film. *Wuxia* is an umbrella term meaning the use of force (there's that word again) by a righteous person. As David Chute observes, "*Wuxia* stories depict heroes who are prodigious martial artists, but the emphasis is on how the prowess is used and to what end."[22] The two *Star Wars* trilogies can be taken as a pair of *wuxia* narratives— the first depicting a martial artist (Jedi-in-training Luke) using his prowess for good to redeem his father and end the Empire and the second depicting the converse, a martial artist (Jedi-in-training Anakin) using his prowess selfishly and ultimately to his and the galaxy's ruin.

In the program of the Fifth Hong Kong International Film Festival (1981), Koo Siu-fung describes the traditional narrative of *wuxia* cinema:

> The standard plot of a martial arts film invariably centres on the slaying of a father or *sifu*. From the call of duty, the hero vows to avenge his

death. He seeks out a master (his surrogate father) to tutor him in the martial skills. After long years of hardship, during which vengeance becomes his *raison d'etre*, he confronts his enemy, and by eliminating him, upholds and restores the moral order.[23]

In the first trilogy, Luke, out to avenge Anakin, whom he believes slain by Vader, seeks out two masters, Obi-Wan and then Yoda. Obi-Wan Kenobi is the surrogate father who teaches Luke martial skills; Yoda is the master who can complete his training. Luke has long years of hardship in which rebellion against the Empire (headed by the man who both is his father and killed his father) becomes his *raison d'etre*. He confronts Vader above Endor's moon and "upholds and restores the moral order" by redeeming his father while also slaying the one who "killed" him.

Another trope of the American martial arts movie, as observed by David Desser, is "the seemingly and deceptively harmless, wizened, crafty, benevolent, a little bit mysterious Asian man who is, in reality, a martial arts master."[24] Desser locates this figure's mainstream American origin on television in *Kung Fu*'s Master Po, played by Keye Luke. Many of the martial arts films of the seventies, eighties, and nineties use this trope, perhaps most notably in American popular culture in *The Karate Kid* (1984, also cited by Desser as a significant moment in the history of this trope), in which Mr. Miyagi (Pat Morita), a deceptively harmless small Asian man teaches a young boy (Ralph Macchio) karate. Yoda is, arguably, yet another embodiment of the idea of the mysterious Asian man who is discovered to be a martial arts master, and who teaches this knowledge to the young, all–American (white) hero.

There is a more general trope of the older man who trains the hero, common to much of cinema. Yet the key in martial arts films is that the teacher is, as Desser argues, "deceptively harmless," "crafty," "benevolent," and "mysterious," as well as being Asian. One author argues of *The Karate Kid* that it is merely *Rocky* in which the director has "replaced the Burgess Meredith character ... with former stand-up comic Pat Morita."[25] Yet the Burgess Meredith character of *Rocky*, apart from his serving as a mentor figure and his knowledge of boxing training, contains none of these other characteristics: he is not deceptively harmless. He is not crafty or mysterious. One might argue that his character is not these things because he is not Asian.

Yoda, as introduced in *Empire*, however, fulfills Desser's trope admirably. Upon first meeting Luke, who draws his gun, sees a "strange, bluish creature not more than two feet tall. The wizened little thing is dressed in rags."[26] Yoda cries out, "Away put your weapon, I mean you no harm." Within the first exchange of Yoda with Luke, much of Desser's trope is already established. Yoda is presented as a mysterious creature. He is deceptive in that he is other than he appears to be. Luke tells him, "I'm looking for a great warrior." Yoda laughs and responds, "Wars not make one great." (Ironically, William O. Stephens argues that "Yoda" is Sanskrit for "warrior," a reputation confirmed in *Clones* and *Sith* by Yoda's lightsaber fights with Count Dooku and Palpatine and his leading of clone and Wookiee troops in battle.)[27] Yoda proceeds to rummage through Luke's belongings, pretending to be simple, even foolish. Yet the whole thing is a test, to see if Luke can see beyond the surface appearance of things.

Yoda offers Luke multiple opportunities to see the truth of what is before him. At his house, Yoda offers Luke food. When Luke declines, Yoda responds, "For the Jedi it is time to eat as well," and sits down to dine. When Luke mentions his father, Yoda responds, "Ah, father. Powerful Jedi was he...," angering Luke who cannot understand how this little creature on the swamp planet could know Anakin Skywalker. Yoda then announces, "I cannot teach him. The boy has no patience," revealing himself as the Jedi master Luke has come to Dagobah to find.

Yoda is small, wizened, mysterious, seemingly harmless, crafty, and benevolent. He is also a Jedi master, and, as we see in *Clones*, a great martial artist. Later, when Luke cannot raise his X-Wing out of the swamp, Yoda chastens him: "Size matters not. Look at me. Judge me by my size, do you?" Yoda then proceeds to levitate the craft out of the swamp and onto dry land. Everything Yoda does is an object lesson for his young Padawan.

We see the same type of character in the films of Kurosawa: the older, slightly mysterious man who does not meet one's expectations for a great warrior. In *Seven Samurai*, Kambei allows his head to be shaved and disguises himself as a priest to trap a thief who has kidnapped a child. He teaches Katsushiro how to determine the ability of a samurai to recognize the truth of a situation through the aforementioned door test. He teaches all of the samurai on one level or another. He is the mysterious teacher whose appearance does not match his reality.

Likewise, Mifune Toshiro's character is deceptive in order to be benevolent as well as to test those around him. He cleans up a town of gangsters by pretending to be bad, and setting them against each other. It is only by pretending to be that which he is not that he is able to achieve his ends and teach those who surround him (the innkeeper, the young man who ran away to the town to avoid being a farmer, etc.) the reality of the situation.

Yoda falls into the mentor figure trope, whether the Japanese one of Kurosawa or the American Asian one of Desser. He trains Luke, played by all–American Mark Hamill to be a Jedi. As noted above, Yoda is a "Zen master." To this we must now add "martial arts master" and American martial arts movie trope.

Until *Clones*, Yoda was never seen with a lightsaber or even fighting. He teaches Luke to fight without ever fighting himself. Although Mr. Miyagi is seen fighting early on in the film *The Karate Kid*, his method of teaching (the famous "wax on" and "wax off") involves learning how to fight without having to fight. Martial knowledge is passed on through seemingly unrelated techniques that force one to learn technique in the body, so that one responds naturally. This trope, too, is common to martial arts movies. In *Shaolin Master Killer*, a film that *Empire* strongly echoes, discussed below, the main character, having trained in a series of seemingly pointless activities, learns that they have made his reactions to being attacked a series of natural defenses. Likewise, Daniel in *The Karate Kid* has learned that by painting the fence and waxing the cars he has learned the *kata* to block punches. Luke learns to fight on Dagobah without ever actually fighting, a martial arts trope.

As noted in the previous chapter, the Jedi share much in common with the samurai, with the warrior monks of Japan, and mostly with the Shaolin monks of China, at least within the popular cinematic history of that tradition. The Shaolin temple was established in Hunan Province in Central China in 495 B.C.E. as a Buddhist monastery. In addition to religious training, however, martial arts were also developed there and until the temple ceased to be a center of religious and martial study in 1928 it was renowned as the home of the best warriors in China. Often, Shaolin monks would be "loaned" to the Emperor or others who needed assistance in defense. The Shaolin were peacekeepers—celibate warrior monks who underwent a long and rigorous training. The Shaolin are remarkably similar to the Jedi, and the Shaolin have proven to be remarkably popular in Chinese cinema.[28]

The two trilogies, concerning as they do the training of the two most significant Jedi in the history of the Republic, Luke and Anakin, respectively, echo Chinese martial arts movies, especially those that focus on the training of the Shaolin. For the purposes of this study, let us consider Chia Hui Lui's *Shaolin san shi liu fang* (*Shaolin Master Killer*). Though made the year after *A New Hope*, it exemplifies the structure and narrative of Shaolin kung fu films, stretching back not only through the history of martial arts cinema, but even into the history of *jingju* and *kungchu*, the traditional Chinese operas.

Generally regarded as one of Chia Hui Liu's (known in the United States as Gordon Liu) finest films and one of the best martial arts movies ever made, *Shaolin Master Killer* tells the story of San Te, whose family is killed by the Manchus. He tries to join the Shaolin temple, but is dismissed as unfocused and untrainable. Eventually he is allowed to begin training at the Shaolin temple and must work his way through thirty-five chambers, each one teaching him a different skill or building a particular strength. He builds endurance and strength through carrying buckets of water, ringing a bell with a weighted twelve foot bamboo pole, and hitting sacks filled with sand with his head. He learns to control his body and his movements through a series of devices using candles, mirrors, and burning sticks of incense, which burn him if he moves the wrong way or goes too far in a move, and to kick through a burning hoop. He learns forms of fighting, both unarmed and armed. He spends a long time training with a sword and a bo staff. Every time he thinks he has mastered shaolin kung fu, however, he learns how much more skilled his masters are, and that he must continue training.

Likewise, Luke goes to Dagobah, having studied somewhat under Obi-Wan during their short time together. Obi-Wan tells Luke to go to study with Yoda. Yoda quickly begins instructing Luke for endurance, strength and fighting techniques. Luke must run through the jungles and swamps of Dagobah with Yoda on his back. Luke must climb vines, flip through the air, and perform one-handed handstands with Yoda standing on his foot. He must raise rocks with his mind. He must train with his lightsaber. Luke is assured by both Ben and Yoda that the training will be long and hard and that he must not be tempted to take the easy route. In other words, his training is rigorous and complete — mind, body and soul. In order to become a Jedi, a warrior-monk, Luke must train like a Shaolin.

In addition to learning how to be a fighter, San Te also learns humility, patience, and self-control. He learns to humbly ask his masters to train him and thank them for his lessons. Luke must first learn that the small Yoda is the great warrior he seeks and then learn humility, patience, self-control, and even to be afraid without giving into the fear. The Luke Skywalker of *A New Hope* moves from innocent wonder to cockiness and bravado and impatience in *Empire*. By *Jedi*, however, he is humble, self-assured. His promises of destruction to Jabba are not idle threats but simple statements. Luke has no desire to fight Jabba — he simply wants Han freed. If Jabba will not free him, Luke will be forced to fight. But he does not come in to Jabba's palace lightsabers blazing. Nor does he attack the Emperor and Vader openly, instead biding his time and choosing not to kill — he shows he is a true Jedi.

Eventually, proving himself worthy of Shaolin after mastering all thirty five chambers in record time, San Te is offered a teaching position in the chamber of his choice. Instead, he asks to open a thirty-sixth chamber in which non–Shaolin would be allowed to train. For this radical idea, he is exiled from the Shaolin temple. During his wandering, he invents the three-sectioned staff, a new type of weapon which allows him to fight and defeat any other weapon, even someone armed with two swords. By using his training, he develops his skill in this weapon and eventually defeats the Manchu who killed his family. It is only through mastering himself and his martial art that San Te can become the master killer of the title.

Subsequent films featuring Gordon Liu have him in similar roles as a Shaolin sifu — a teacher of martial arts. Again, though these films come after *A New Hope*, the series still echoes dozens of martial arts films from the sixties and seventies. The training sequence, however, is a staple of *wuxia* cinema. Films such as *One-Armed Swordsman* (1967), *The Chinese Boxer* (1970), *Vengeance!* (1970), *Five Fingers of Death* (1971) and even Bruce Lee's *The Chinese Connection* (1972) make the training of the hero a focal point of the plot.[29] Luke's training in *Empire* so follows the martial arts model that David Chute includes it in a listing of films that have "the classic plot of the normative kung fu movie" because they include the pivotal training sequences.[30] The first trilogy also echoes *One-Armed Swordsman* (written by the same screenwriter as *Shaolin Master Killer*), as it involves Fang Gang (Jimmy Wang Yu) losing his sword hand in a fight with his teacher's daughter and having to learn to fight left-handed with a sword of his own creation. He returns after his training to fight and defeat his enemies, including the one who maimed him. The character returned in *Zatoichi and the One-Armed Swordsman* (1970) and was echoed in such films as *The One-Armed Boxer* (1971). Another common trope of the martial arts film is the hero who must overcome a physical defect, most notably the loss of a hand, in order to fight and defeat his enemy, most often the one who dismembered him in the first place.

Luke loses his sword hand to Vader and learns to fight again with his mechanical hand, using a lightsaber he made himself. Vader even comments on the weapon, noting that Luke's manufacture and mastery of it indicates the conclusion of his training: "I see you have constructed a new lightsaber. Your skills are complete." Luke is another one-armed swordsman, just in a galaxy where mechanical prosthetics are available. He is subsequently joined later in the saga by Darth Vader, who loses a hand and sword in *Jedi*, and Anakin, who loses the same hand in *Clones*.

Wuxia films often combine realistic swordplay and historical conflict with magical powers and fantasy figures. In films like *Zu: Warriors from the Magic Mountain* (1983) and even *Crouching Tiger, Hidden Dragon* (2000), warriors have seemingly supernatural abilities to fly through the air, walk on treetops, communicate with animals, and other seemingly impossible feats. There are ghosts and monsters in *wuxia*, some of whom will fight alongside the heroes, and others serve as villains and obstacles. Sam Ho notes that "Fights against monstrous creatures became a staple ingredient in Cantonese *wuxia* films of the 1950s and '60s, along with secret scrolls, magic potions, and cameo appearances by monks, nuns and wizard-like Daoists."[31] By this summary, the *Star Wars* films qualify as *wuxia*; after all, the films are full of fights against monstrous creatures, along with secret scrolls (the *wuxia* equivalent of the secret Death Star plans hidden in R2-D2), magic potions (the bacta-tank in which Luke is healed after his encounter with the Wampa and Han's freezing in carbonite, both in *Empire*, are science fantasy versions of the magic potion), and cameo appearances by Obi-Wan Kenobi, Yoda, and other Taoist (Daoist) wizards (read: Jedi).

Wuxia films are also an extension of a much greater Chinese cultural tradition — that of the *yu-hsia*, translated by James J.Y. Liu as the "knight errant," but also suggesting and embodying the idea of the wandering warrior — one who ventures around righting wrongs, fighting on the side of justice.[32] The *yu-hsai* has usually undergone rigorous training in the martial arts, is noble in nature (if not by birth), and often is forced by situation to fight evil generals, corrupt politicians, and supernatural beings. In *The Chinese Knight Errant*, James J.Y. Liu analyzes the figure and its recurrence in Chinese literature, legend, theatre, and folklore. The cinema of *wuxia* has seized upon the figure of the *yu-hsia*, of which Luke Skywalker might also be seen as an embodiment. Likewise the Jedi, as individual peacekeepers as opposed to a military order, might be seen as *yu-hsia*. Qui-Gon Jinn and Obi-Wan Kenobi seem to fit the model of wandering warriors who right wrongs and fix problems in the Chinese model, rather than the Western model of the questing knight.

This Chinese echo is matched by a Japanese one. Joseph Campbell, writing of *Star Wars* in *The Power of Myth*, observes that Ben Kenobi as presented in *A New Hope* is "a Japanese sword master" seemingly implying that the character is more similar in philosophy and action to a samurai than a Western knight.[33] Likewise, the two-handed lightsaber suggests the Japanese *katana* of a samurai more than Western swords, and the style of fighting is closer to Kendo than to fencing. The Jedi is meant to be dispassionate in battle, like a samurai.

Nick Gallard, who choreographed the fights for *The Phantom Menace*, developed the style of lightsaber fighting by combining epée, kendo, rapier, tennis, and "tree chopping" moves.[34] This summary contains mostly Western-style fighting techniques, but it must be remembered that Ray Park, the Scottish martial artist who portrayed Darth Maul, "has been training in Chinese martial arts since he was seven (including *Wu Shu* and Northern *Shaolin* Kung Fu, to name only a couple).[35] In other words, Darth Maul's style of lightsaber fighting, with his double-bladed lightsaber, is primarily derived from Chinese styles of fighting. The fights in *Phantom* and *Clones* are much closer to *wuxia* films than the fights in the original trilogy, but even then, elements of Asian swordplay outweigh elements of Western swordplay. Garry Jenkins reports that while preparing to film *Jedi*, Lucas instructed director Richard Marquand not to let Hamill use the lightsaber with just one hand: "You hold it like a samurai sword."[36] The Jedi train like Shaolin and fight like samurai.

Asian Costume Elements

When Lucas asked artist Ralph McQuarrie to design the *Star Wars* look, he cited feudal Japan as a source for images, and gave him pictures of samurai to design the Jedi.[37] Although McQuarrie and costume designer John Mollo state that their designs for the Jedi are rooted in medieval Europe, they also admit that the garments for Ben and the Emperor are raw silk kimonos, beige for Ben and black for the Emperor. In another context, Mollo admits that he "modeled the Imperial uniforms on those of the Japanese army of the 1920s."[38] In other words, the Jedi are samurai, or feudal Japanese. The Empire are Japanese Imperial Soldiers, or modern Japanese in appearance.

The visual influence of Japanese film and culture is quite evident in *Star Wars*. Obi-Wan Kenobi (whose name even sounds Japanese, as further discussed below) wears a costume that, with its long brown robe and white underrobes, suggests the kimono of a samurai.

The shape and sweep of Darth Vader's mask, his breastplate, and cloak suggests the formal armor of a *samurai* or *daimyo*. Vader's helmet is a *kabuto* helmet with a *mempo* faceplate.[39] The helmet flairs out in back, much more common in Japanese feudal armor, as opposed to Western medieval helmets, in which the back of the head is protected by the metal curving back in to meet the neck plates. The *mempo* is an iron mask, usually made more fearsome for battle by resembling a demon or monster. The robes Vader wears are reminiscent of the robes of samurai, which are designed to disguise the movement of the feet. Vader dresses as a samurai general.

Left: Eighteenth century Japanese helmets (courtesy of Dover Publications, from *Weapons and Armor*, edited by Harold Hart). *Right:* Medieval European helmet (courtesy of Dover Publications, from *Weapons and Armor*, edited by Harold Hart). Compare Darth Vader's helmet and mask with the helmets in the images above. Clearly the Japanese helmet, not the European one, are the source of the design of Vader's helmet.

He fights, as noted above, two-handed, with a lightsaber that is handled like a *katana*.

Visually, the followers of the Light and Dark sides of the force are much more Asian in appearance than the more Western clothing of Han Solo or Grand Moff Tarkin, both of whom disbelieve in the Force, though both have seen evidence of its power. If the Force is more similar to Asian philosophy than to Western, as argued in the previous chapter, then this fact is reflected in the costuming of the characters in the epics. The characters closest to the Force wear Asian costume, the characters most rooted in science or cynicism wear Western dress.

In designing *Empire*, John Mollo "wanted to give Bespin a flavor of India," resulting in Leia's silk costume colored "nutmeg brown," presumably an Indian color, and the lining of Lando's cloak contains Chinese-style dragons.[40] The costumes of all five films, in fact, contain strong Asian elements by choice of the designers. For example, Nilo Rodis-Jamero, the costume designer for *Jedi*, based Luke's first costume for that movie on samurai and Zen Buddhist monks' robes: "If you look at Luke's costume, it's all derivative of Japanese designs ... Ben also wore some kind of Japanese kimono."[41]

The Asian influence on the visual look of the original trilogy becomes even more apparent in the new trilogy. The costumes for *The Phantom Menace* were designed to reflect a "cultural/historical basis," claims "The Official Souvenir Magazine": "Many of Lucas' costume ideas were based on fashions, styles, history and color schemes of various countries in which he is interested including Japan, Mongolia, China, North Africa and Europe."[42] One should note, however, that only the first three refer to countries, the other two are geographical locations containing over a dozen countries (and many more cultures and ethnic groups) each. The dresses of Queen Amidala's handmaidens are based on kimono, and, in fact, according to Trisha Biggar, the costume designer, the entire throne room of Naboo and the costumes and furnishings are meant to suggest "a sort of Chinese Imperial feel."[43] Biggar also cites an overall "Asian influence," as well as "North African" and Renaissance European influences on her designs for the Jedi and other characters.[44] In his review of *Phantom Menace* for the *Village Voice*, J. Hoberman refers to Natalie Portman as "a walking piece of Japanaiserie."[45]

In short, much of *The Phantom Menace*'s costume (and *mise-en-scène*) is inspired by non–Western and particularly Asian culture. Iain McCaig, a "concept artist" for *Phantom Menace*, shares that Amidala's costumes are rooted in Mongolian and Tibetan clothing.[46] Design director of *Phantom Menace* Doug Chiang modeled the hair of the Jedi, specifically Qui-Gon, after the Samurai — he wanted long hair with "Samurai-style pigtails on the side," presumably referencing the topknot of the samurai.[47]

What has essentially happened in the two trilogies is that designers and conceptual artists have appropriated visual elements of Asian cultures (among others) in order to represent alien cultures. The previous chapter has argued that the philosophies, religions, and intellectual traditions of Asia were appropriated to shape the philosophy and religion of the Jedi. The Jedi, we now learn, are meant to visually remind the audience of Asian culture as well — their costumes and hair styles have been appropriated from Asian culture. In the next section, we shall consider how some characters (especially Jedi) have Asian-derived names, in contrast to the Western names of the bad guys. Yet none of the Asian-named, Asian-dressed, Asian-thinking characters are played by Asian actors.

Asian Names / European Faces

Lucas's Asian appropriations suggest an East/West binary in which the Empire is Western and the Rebellion is Eastern. The films posit a universe in which Asian-derived characters rebel against an Empire which is

European in nature and name. All of the "good guys" have names derived from Asian or Asian-sounding languages. Obi-Wan Kenobi and Yoda suggest Japanese names. Qui-Gon Jinn suggests Chinese or Japanese. The "bad guys" have Western names: Darth Vader, which is Dutch for "dark father," Senator Palpatine, who becomes Emperor, has a Roman name, and the others—Grand Moff Tarkin, Nute Gunray, Darth Maul, Darth Tyranus, Darth Sidious, etc., just to name a few—are all derived from Western names.

When Luke first stumbles upon the message from Leia hidden inside R2-D2 in *A New Hope*, she repeats, "Help me, Obi-Wan Kenobi, you're my only hope." Luke wonders aloud to his aunt and uncle if she might mean "old Ben Kenobi." "Ben" is the name Obi-Wan has taken since moving to Tatooine and going into hiding as a Jedi, since Vader and the Emperor were hunting and killing Jedi. "Ben," short for "Benjamin," is a decidedly Western name. Obi-Wan then rescues Luke from the Sand People and Luke asks if "Obi-Wan" is a relative. "That's a name I haven't heard in a long time," Kenobi confesses, then admitting that he is, in fact, Obi-Wan and not "Ben," though Luke continues to identify him as "Ben" for the rest of the film.

Perhaps the name Ben is merely taken as a disguise, but if so, why keep "Kenobi," which is just as recognizable as "Obi-Wan"? Perhaps the name change signifies something other than a desire to hide from the Empire. Obi-Wan Kenobi takes the name "Ben" when he moves to Tatooine to watch the growth of Luke Skywalker, Anakin's son. If, as argued above, the Jedi are emblematic of samurai, among other Asian religious warriors, there is a history in Japan of warriors retiring as Buddhist monks and taking a new name. Once one leaves the service of one's master to become a monk or nun, the swords are given up, the head is shaved, and the person takes a new name. Could we read Kenobi's change from "Obi-Wan" to "Ben" as the retirement name of a Jedi warrior?

Alternatively, the name change can also be seen to signify the shift in his purpose from being located in the Asian world to being located in the Western world. Perhaps the name change might even signify the Westernization of Asia at the end of the nineteenth and beginning of the twentieth century. In Japan, for example, after the Meiji Restoration (1868), the Japanese embraced things Western and sought to modernize their culture, which oftentimes entailed westernizing it as well. The use of Western names by the Japanese, particularly among those converted to Christianity, was not uncommon. Obi-Wan, with the death of the Jedi order, must become a part of the new Empire-dominated galaxy, which entails changing his identity, and therefore, changing his name.

The name Obi-wan Kenobi is actually nonsense Japanese. "Obi" means a belt. "Wan" may be translated as a bowl, a bay, or an inlet. It might also be seen as a corruption of the particle "wa," used in Japanese to indicate topic, but also as a form of the verb "is," as in the play *Higashi wa Higashi* (*East Is East*, 1933) by Iwata Toyō. "Kenobi" is a combination of the word "ken" and a repetition of the word "obi." "Ken" has a variety of possible meanings: healthy, heaven, prefecture, sword, tendon, authority, sphere (meaning "range," as in "sphere of influence") or ticket. If we read "wan" as the particle "wa," the most likely meaning of "Obi wan Kenobi" is "The belt is a sword belt." Although the implications are martial, the name is Japanese-sounding without really meaning anything in Japanese.

Similarly, Qui-Gon Jinn can either be nonsense Chinese or Sinized Japanese (Japanese transliterated into Chinese). The words mean nothing in Chinese, although they sound like other words. In Japanese, if the name is rendered phonetically, kuwai gon jin, a few possible meanings present themselves. "Kuwai" can mean arrowhead, mulberry fruit, or the color light yellow. "Gon" is a philosophical term, used in Buddhism to express earnest aspiration, seeking rebirth, or another name for the Buddha's Pure Land. "Jin" literally means "person," and can also be used as suffix to place names to indicate origin of a person. An "Amerikajin" is an American; a "Doitsujin" is a German; a "Chugokujin" is a Chinese person, and so on. Qui-Gon Jinn's name, therefore, also suggests several possibilities, including implications of spirituality or martial activity. One way to read the name (depending on which characters it is written with) may be "The arrowhead person from Heaven," or "The yellow person seeking rebirth," or even "Heaven's arrow person." However, it can also read "The earnest mulberry person." The name is suggestive of some possible meanings, but again, like "Obi-Wan Kenobi," though Asian sounding, the name does not actually mean anything in Chinese or Japanese.

Yoda, whom it was argued above and in the previous chapter is *Star Wars*'s Zen master, also has a Japanese-sounding name with potential meanings in that language. "Yoda" is an auxiliary adjective which expresses the likelihood of something. It is also indicative of something that appears to be, or seems like, or looks as if it is something. One uses the adjective to mean something like "It appears it will rain today," or "That really was Mr. Johnson." Use of the phrase "yoda" indicates that the statement "is based on firsthand, reliable information."[48] "Yoda," therefore, expresses the reality of a likelihood and is reliable. "Yoda" is used to confirm something already suspected. It is a useful Japanese expression. As noted above, William O. Stephens claims that "Yoda" is Sanskrit for "warrior." In the *Star Wars* films, "Yoda" again serves as an Asian-sounding, but ultimately meaningless name. The pattern is common among Jedi Masters—the names are meant to be alien, but many of them come across as Asian. Walter Ritoku Robinson, for example, believes that Ki Adi Mundi's name was inspired by the Japanese martial art "Aikido."[49]

The introduction of Count Dooku in *Attack of the Clones* further verifies this schema. As a Jedi, and one who began his career as Yoda's Padawan learner, his name is appropriately Japanese, although one that suggests his duplicitous nature. In Japanese, Dooku means several things. It can translate as "poison" or "alone." As a verb, "Dooku" can mean "to step aside or make way for." Dooku himself is a separatist who is actually poison to the separatist cause. He is using his associates to foment civil war within the Rebellion. He sets up the war in order to "make way for" Darth Sidious to proclaim himself Emperor. Interestingly, at the end of *Attack of the Clones* when Dooku is revealed to be Darth Sidious's new apprentice under the name "Darth Tyranus," his "evil name" is, in fact, Western. He moves from a Japanese name to a Western one as he moves from Jedi to Sith. Tyranus from the Greek root which gives us the English word "tyrant," and also sounding like "Tyrannosaurus," the "Tyrant King of Lizards" and most memorable in recent cinema history as one of the most fearsome of adversaries in *Jurassic Park*. "Dooku" the Jedi becomes "Tyranus" the Sith. Jedi are Asian, bad guys are Western.

The other characters in the series have names that also are indicative of Asian/Western dichotomies. Han Solo's name suggests a mix of characteristics: Han is Chinese, suggesting his possible allegiance to the Force, whereas Solo is Western, suggesting his "rugged individualism" and selfish desire to "look out for number one—me;" the part of the character that is ambivalent and ignorant of the Force. Over the course of the first trilogy Han moves from the latter aspect of his character to the former, punctuated by the increased use of the name "Han" instead of "Solo" by the other characters in the later films. Of the Jedi, only Anakin Skywalker and Luke Skywalker have names that are not Asian in origin. They are also the only two Jedi about whom there is genuine concern over their going to the Dark Side. Anakin becomes Vader, and the entire question behind *Jedi* is whether or not Luke will follow his father by giving in to hate, anger, and fear and become yet another tool of the Emperor.

The names of the Empire figures are all European—"Darth Vader" resembles the Dutch words for "dark father." Similarly, Rune Haako, Nute Gunray, Daultry Dofine, Boba Fett, Grand Moff Tarkin, and Palpatine to name several of the antagonists, are all Western names. Tarkin and Palpatine are Roman. The Neimoidians, like Vader, have Dutch sounding names. Bad guys in the *Star Wars* universe have European names.

The danger, however, is that the Asian-named characters, wearing Asian clothing and expressing Asian ideas, are all played by European actors. Japanese Obi-Wan Kenobi is played by British Sir Alec Guinness and Ewan McGregor. Chinese Qui-Gon Jinn is played by British Liam Neeson. Japanese Yoda is played by American Frank Oz. The characters with Asian names have European faces. The characters with European names and who are the Imperialists, the colonialists, the bad guys, are also played by white actors, or are represented as utterly alien and are equally Asian-derived. Brian Crow writes in his study of postcolonial theatre:

> A characteristic feature of the development of Western art forms during the twentieth century has been the frequent and highly fruitful exploitation by artistic practitioners of all kinds of materials drawn from non–Western cultures.[50]

What Crow says of theatre can also apply to film. Some of the elements that make *Star Wars* popular and innovative are actually borrowed from Asian cultures. Recently there has been a growing influence in Hollywood of Asian cinema, particularly Hong Kong martial arts cinema and Japanese horror. As such, there is also a greater awareness of the shaping influence of Asia on contemporary film. The rise of Jackie Chan, Chow Yun Fat, Jet Li, and other martial arts stars in Hollywood is indicative of the appreciation of and demand by American audiences for both Asian martial arts and novelty. *Crouching Tiger, Hidden Dragon* brought *wuxia* films to a whole new level of awareness and acceptance for American audiences.

As such, now Hollywood openly mines Asian culture for source material to make new films. From *The Matrix* trilogy to the American remake of *Ringu* (*The Ring*), Asian influence is pervasive and appropriation of Asian culture rather obvious. The majority of Asian appropriated films, however, have openly acknowledged their origins and sources. *Ringu* (the Japanese original) received wide release in the United States after the success of the American remake. Quentin Tarantino not only openly acknowledges how much *Kill Bill* was shaped by Asian cinema, but also cast Gordon Liu in a key role and has used his influence to bring greater attention to Chinese and Japanese cinema. The Asian appropriations are acknowledged and are used to elevate the status and attention of the cinema of Asia.

In fairness, as noted above, Lucas has put his money where his appropriations have come from by serving as executive producer on Kurosawa's *Kagemusha* (1980), which most likely gave Kurosawa enough credibility to then create *Ran* (1985), *Dreams* (*Yume*, 1990), *Rhapsody in August* (*Hachigatsu no kyôshikyoku*, 1991) and *Madadayo* (1993) before his death in 1998.

More recently, Lucas's presence on the *Hidden Fortress* DVD brings new levels of awareness to its shaping influence on the trilogies. Acknowledgement of the influence of Asian culture is also present in some of the books about Lucas and the films, but it is subsumed into the greater purpose of giving shape to the films. Asian culture is not as important in itself as it is for what the films have taken from it. One can hope that the more recent willingness to admit to the shaping influence of Asian culture and cinema on the two trilogies will also raise awareness in the target audience of that culture and cinema. In that sense, if *Attack of the Clones* or *Revenge of the Sith* lead fans and Fanboys to Kurosawa, *wuxia* films, other *jidai-geki,* or even the performing arts and history of Asia on their own terms instead of as source material for American movies, then they will have performed admirable service.

CHAPTER 4

"Making the Galaxy Safe for White People": People of Color in the *Star Wars* Universe

This chapter takes its admittedly offensive title from Kevin Smith's film *Chasing Amy*. Smith is obviously a knowledgeable fan of the *Star Wars* films as he continually references them in his own movies, including extended dialogue sequences discussing Lucas's work.[1] In *Chasing Amy*, Holden (Ben Affleck) and Banky (Jason Lee), the main characters, attend a comic book convention panel on "Minority Voices in Comics." Hooper X, an angry African-American comic book writer speaks on racism within the comic book industry and the balance that his own book, *White-Hating Coon*, provides. He asserts that "The Black man's no longer gonna play the minstrel in the medium of comics and Sci-Fi/Fantasy." Holden responds from the audience that Lando Calrissian is "a positive black role model in the realm of science fiction/fantasy." Hooper's response is indicative of the relative position of Lando in both the Star Wars films and people of color in science fiction:

> HOOPER: Fuck Lando Calrissian! Uncle Tom Nigger! Always some white boy gotta invoke "the holy trilogy"! Bust this—those movies are about how the white man keeps the brother man down—even in a galaxy far, far, away. Check this shit: You got Cracker farmboy Luke Skywalker; Nazi poster boy—blonde hair, blue eyes. And then you've got Darth Vader: the blackest brother in the galaxy. Nubian God.... Now Vader, he's a spiritual

126

brother, with the Force and all that shit. Then this cracker Skywalker gets his hands on a light-saber, and the boy decides he's gonna run the fucking universe — gets a whole Klan of whites together, and they're gonna bust up Vader's 'hood — the Death Star. Now what the fuck do you call that?

BANKY: Intergalactic civil war?

HOOPER: Gentrification! They're gonna drive out the black element to make the galaxy quote, unquote safe for white people.... And *Jedi* is the most insulting installment, because Vader's beautiful black visage is sullied when he pulls off his mask to reveal a feeble, crusty old white man! They're trying to tell us that deep inside, we all want to be white!

BANKY: Well, isn't that true?

HOOPER: BLACK RAGE! BLACK RAGE![2]

Hooper then pulls out a nine millimeter gun and "shoots" Banky, causing a panic in the mostly white audience. The confrontation and gunplay, however, are immediately revealed to be a prank which Hooper and Banky often carry out in public. Hooper is revealed to be not an angry black man, but a flamboyant and effeminate homosexual who plays the stereotypical angry black man because his publisher insists that the image improves his sales.

Smith clearly intends for the audience to initially side with Banky, who sees the struggle in *Star Wars* as "intergalactic civil war" and having nothing to do with race. The reality of Hooper's character, when finally revealed, undercuts his analysis and instead shows an Afrocentric reading of *Star Wars* to be a mere pose for the sake of promotion and personal gain. "Black Rage" is, in the end, the means to a prank's end.

The analysis that Hooper gives is, admittedly, highly flawed — though we must recall that Smith wrote it as a parody of angry Afrocentrists within the popular culture community. The point that Hooper (and Smith) unintentionally raises, however, is the lack of a strong African-American presence in *Star Wars*, in the comic book world, and in the realm of fantasy and science fiction. One might ask why Smith chooses to parody a minority within a minority.

Yet, as Michael Pye and Lynda Myles note in 1979, "The iconography [of *A New Hope*] is bizarre. Darth Vader, the dastardly villain is black. That is common in science fiction," then observing that in *Planet of the Apes*, the warlike gorillas are also black.[3] We might further note that the voice of Darth Vader is provided by James Earl Jones — a "black voice" for the only "black presence" in *A New Hope*. The most evil thing on the screen in *Star* Wars is a character entirely dressed in black from head to foot, including face and hands, given voice by a black actor. In *A New Hope*, evil is black and good is white — Luke, Leia, Han, and Obi-Wan. Pye and Myles conclude, "The closer to the color of a California WASP, the better the character; it is a fair rule of thumb."[4]

Yet the other "bad guys" are the stormtroopers, dressed entirely in white, with a name from the Nazis, and the members of the Imperial Command, wear grey-green uniforms based on the Nazis. Grand Moff Tarkin (Peter Cushing) has a British accent, as does most of the Imperial Command. In short, black and white are intermixed on the evil side. The problem is that no such commingling of black and white occurs on the heroic side. Not all bad guys are black, but no good guys are.

In this chapter, I shall take seriously what Hooper and Smith do not: the role and representation of the person of color in the *Star Wars* films.

Vader and the Presence of an Absence

During the casting of *A New Hope*, several different actors were considered for the main characters, including performers of color. Lucas had originally considered using African-American actor Glynn Turman as Han Solo, and an Asian-American actress for Leia. Lucas, however, decided that "an interracial romance could cause problems."[5] He does not state what those problems would be, although in 1977 it could be argued that an interracial romance in a family-oriented movie would not play as well in certain parts of the nation. One could also argue, however, that as a family-oriented film, *A New Hope* had very little romance, interracial or otherwise — Leia kisses Luke briefly "for luck" and there is some flirtatious banter between Leia and Han, but there is absolutely no genuine sexuality in the film.

Furthermore, science fiction had already cleared the way for "interracial romance." Almost a decade had passed since the first interracial kiss on television, in *Star Trek's* episode "Plato's Stepchildren," and many films of the sixties and seventies had featured interracial romances. Lucas states, "I didn't want to make *Guess Who's Coming to Dinner* at that point, so I sort of backed off," to explain why he ended up casting the actors he did.[6] As a result of his desire not to make a socially relevant, if not socially active film, Lucas ended up making a film without a single actor of color in a speaking role.

In postproduction, James Earl Jones, known for his deep, booming voice and his phenomenal stage work, especially in productions of Shakespeare, was hired to give voice to Darth Vader. David Prowse, who played Vader, had no idea his voice would not be used. Instead, an uncredited Jones was paid ten thousand dollars to perform Vader's lines, which were then dubbed over Prowse's performance. Thus, Vader, who is Luke's father, is the only "black" presence in *Star Wars*. Lucas may not have wanted to make *Guess Who's Coming to Dinner?* or feature an interracial romance, but the black father of a white son did not appear to bother him.

Vader, after all, is black, in a sense — vocally (James Earl Jones's voice is very recognizable) he is voiced by a person of color and in terms of actual color — Vader is dressed, head to toe in black. He is the major black presence in *A New Hope*, no other actors of color are heard in the film; no other actors of color have any significant presence in the film. Chris Salewicz observes that "The fact that Jones was black was possibly not without intention: inadvertently *Star Wars* had been cast without a single black actor."[7] "Inadvertently?" As if Lucas hadn't noticed the ethnicity of the actors until casting was done? Salewicz makes no further comment on the issue, but Lucas's comments cited above seem to indicate that Lucas had the option of casting non-white actors in key roles and made a conscious decision not to.

There are two ways to consider Vader, neither of which are particularly flattering. The first is that Vader literally embodies the presence of an absence — by being who he is, and voiced by one of the best known black actors in Hollywood, Vader serves as reminder that there are no other people of color in this film. There are no people of African descent playing Rebels, none in the Imperial hierarchy, none even in the cantina which has dozens of species. Vader is the present absence — he is the Black Man who is not there, except as a disembodied voice. The actor who plays Vader's body is white. The character under the mask is white (as we subsequently see in *Jedi* and the second trilogy). Only the voice of a black man, whose presence is masked and hidden under black armor, is present in the film, reminding the audience of what is absent.

The other way of considering Vader is that he is the only "black" presence in the film, and he is evil. He kills the Rebel Blockade Runner captain, several Rebel pilots, and Ben Kenobi. He tortures Leia. He is part of a group that destroys planets. He is violent, angry, and destructive. Kenobi tells him that he is "a master of evil." Vader was "seduced by the Dark Side of the Force," which made him "hunt down and destroy the Jedi Knights." He betrayed and murder Luke's father (at least that is what Obi-Wan tells Luke — we subsequently learn that Vader is Luke's father).

Vader is not only evil, he is dangerous and emasculating to white men. He chokes the Rebel Blockade Runner Captain and Admiral Motti. He "kills" Ben. In *Empire* he then cuts off Luke's hand. He is sexually threatening to Leia when he enters her cell and announces, "And now, your highness, we will discuss the location of your hidden rebel base." He is followed by what the screenplay calls, "a black torture robot," which begs the question, why is it black?[8] The camera focuses in on the large hypodermic needle coming off the side of the device. The implied threat to Leia is that she, who is dressed in virginal white and is a princess, is left alone in a cell with the large black figure of Vader and the penetrating "black torture robot." Cinematically, this scene echoes numerous serials, films, and other media in which the virginal white woman is menaced by the large black man, going all the way back to *Birth of a Nation*.

Homi K. Bhabha argues that Fanon sees "the phobic image of the Negro, the native, the colonized deeply woven into the psychic pattern of the West."[9] In other words, the white man fears the black man: fears his power, strength, Otherness and his sexuality. Vader is the phobic black image. As noted in previous chapters, there is something inherently Freudian about the lightsaber battles in the two trilogies. Vader uses a lightsaber to kill and emasculate white men. Vader uses a black torture robot to penetrate and torment virginal white women. Vader is morally evil and sexually dangerous.

Richard A. Maynard, after Lawrence Reddick, identifies nineteen basic stereotypes of blacks in American society, some of which can be combined in a single individual.[10] Vader occupies the categories of "the corrupt politician," "the vicious criminal," and "the razor and knife toter." Vader is powerful, both politically (as Lord of the Sith and second to the Emperor) and metaphysical (as noted in Chapter 1, he can kill with his mind by using the Force). Vader was once part of the Jedi, but he was corrupted (in every sense of the word). He is also dangerous, not only is he a lightsaber toter, but, again, he can kill with his mind through the Force. He is a criminal who has been given authority. In the course of three films, Vader kills several people, including many Rebels attacking the Death Star in *A New Hope* (Gold Two, Gold Five, Gold Leader, Red Twelve, Red Ten, Red Leader, and Biggs, Luke's childhood friend and pilot of one of the rebel X-wings), Admiral Ozzel, and General Needa. He tortures Leia in *A New Hope* and Han Solo in *Empire*. He chokes Admiral Motti to prove a point and is willing to oversee the destruction of entire planets. He plans to convert his own son to the Dark Side or kill him. Vader is a dangerous, corrupt, vicious monster.

Sadly, even as a threatening, dangerous, sexual monster, Vader is not the greatest threat in the galaxy. That privilege is reserved for an old white man. Vader ultimately must bow before the Emperor, as he does literally in both *Empire* and *Jedi*. He calls the Emperor "my master." "Darth Vader" is not even his real name — it is his "Sith name" (his "slave name," perhaps?) as all Sith must take the name "Darth." His birth name is Anakin

Skywalker, but he must leave that name behind. "Anakin Skywalker," by all accounts, is dead. Even the Emperor speaks of him in the third person, calling Luke "the son of Skywalker" in *Empire*. Vader, for all his power and danger is a tool for his evil white master to use as he pleases and then cast aside. The Emperor even plans to kill Vader, whom he is growing to fear, apparently, and replace him with Luke.

And yet the films revolve around his character, especially with the advent of the second trilogy. Anakin Skywalker becomes Vader in the new trilogy, which means the old trilogy is essentially about how Luke Skywalker makes Vader become Anakin Skywalker again. Vader is his father and Luke rescues him by refusing to be like him. Vader saves Luke from a torturous death at the hands of the Emperor. He rejects the Dark Side and embraces the Good Side of the Force. Vader then removes his mask and is revealed to be an old white man. When Vader is no longer bad, he is no longer black. His voice changes. It is not James Earl Jones inside the costume. For that matter, it is not even David Prowse, who had played Vader throughout the saga. Sebastian Shaw plays Vader in these final scenes, with a different voice, a different face, and different everything.

As Daniel Leonard Bernardi writes, "[O]nce Vader returns to the force, to the side of good, he literally turns white."[11] The absence is now complete — there is no more Vader, even that reminder of the absence of blacks is completely erased. He has been replaced, however, by Lando Calrissian as the significant character of color in the saga. Although Lando, as Bernardi observes in his analysis of ethnicity in *Star Trek*, falls into the same category Sulu and Uhura: "background color in a time when humans were almost all white."[12] As will be argued in the next section, Lando Calrissian seemed like a simple solution to the lack of people of color in the *Star Wars* universe, yet his presence is a complex coding of ethnicity in space that is as troubling as Vader's in terms of sexuality, negative characterization, along with the added problem, as just noted, of not having a huge amount to do for much of the two films he is in.

"The First Interstellar Mack Ever Spotted on Screen"[13]

The Empire Strikes Back introduced the first major character of color to the *Star Wars* universe: Lando Calrissian, played by Billy Dee Williams. Williams is a romantic lead, first coming to prominence in *Lady Sings the Blues* (1972) and then rising to stardom in *Mahogany* (1975). He plays charming characters with a bit of the wild side. Lucasfilm trumpeted both the casting and his performance as the amiable rogue Lando. Elvis Mitchell, however, even while praising Williams in an essay on the character, still points out the flaws in the character, admitting "Lando is a kind of roué cliché," at best a token, at worst a stereotype.[14]

Elvis Mitchell also sees the casting of Williams in *Empire* as "generosity," which is problematic.[15] Granted, it allows Williams to be a part of a huge franchise and raises his recognizability. As with all the featured performers in the saga, he is now inextricably linked with his character. "Generosity," for these reasons, however, applies not just to Williams, but to everyone in the cast. One must wonder why Williams is singled out. Lando, however, like Chewbacca, is destined for sidekick status.

One might see Lando as Han's old friend as echoing a then-current cycle of interracial "buddy films," such as the Rocky series, in which Apollo Creed (Carl Weathers) moves from worthy opponent to Rocky's friend and coach, the *Lethal Weapon* series, in which Danny Glover gives meaning and stability to Mel Gibson, and *Nighthawks*. As Donald Bogle points out, in between *Empire* and *Jedi* Billy Dee Williams was Sylvester Stallone's sidekick in *Nighthawks*, and none of the three "gave him much to do."[16]

Not only is Lando a sidekick, he is also an amiable rogue. Han's first description of Lando to Leia in *Empire* is not promising: "He's a cardplayer, gambler, scoundrel. You'd like him." When asked how Lando came to be the administrator for Bespin, Han replies, "Lando conned somebody out of it." Leia asks Han if he trusts Lando, to which Han responds, "No." Later, after Lando has been introduced and given "the first interstellar mack," he comments on the difficulties and challenges on being an administrator. Han states that Lando sounds "responsible," and "Who'd have thought that?"

Lando's being a scoundrel, irresponsible, and an all-around shady character ordinarily would not be a problem. After all, Han Solo is disreputable, selfish, a smuggler, and an associate of very shady characters like Greedo and Jabba. We expect Han's associates and friends to be low lifes. The reason why Lando's being disreputable and Han speaking ill of him for much of the film is problematic is that Lando is the only African-American presence on screen (James Earl Jones is present in voice only). At least Han is countered by Luke and Ben. Where is the positive African-American counterpart to Lando?

Further problematizing his presence is the fact that Lando, in addition to being a scoundrel, is also known as a betrayer. In the British television series *Spaced* (2001), when one character allows police into the flat, his roommate, an avid *Star Wars* fan, accuses him, "You Lando!"[17]

Like Vader, Lando is also a sexual presence. This section title, "the first interstellar mack ever spotted on screen," is a quotation from Elvis

Mitchell's "Works Every Time" in *A Galaxy Not So Far Away*, referring to Lando's "what have we here" line in response to seeing Leia for the first time (77). Mitchell argues that Lando's character is an intertext with Billy Dee Williams's own persona and the other roles that he has played as a charming, sexy, slightly dangerous, streetwise black man known for his skills with the ladies. Lando ignores C3PO and only throws a quick greeting to Chewbacca, but Leia gets all of his attention. Lando is a sexual presence — a roguish, charming, but ultimately dangerous one.

Like Vader, Lando is ultimately transformed by his encounters with the Rebellion. Vader leaves the dark side and becomes white. Lando joins the Rebellion and becomes ineffective. He loses any power that that interstellar mack may have indicated. In *Jedi*, for example, Lando is one of the most ineffective members of the rescue team. While Leia is strangling Jabba, Artoo is preparing the escape from the sail barge and sending Luke his lightsaber, Luke fights off a dozen opponents armed with laser rifles at once, and Han and Chewie are fighting the guards on their skiff, Lando is knocked overboard and is threatened by the tentacles of the Sarlacc. Blind Han Solo must then rescue Lando — one of his ostensible rescuers — by shooting the tentacle holding Lando. "No, wait! I thought you were blind!" cries Calrissian as Solo aims the gun in his direction while hanging upside down from a listing sail barge, held at the ankles by Chewbacca.

"It's all right! Trust me! Don't move!" responds Solo.

"A little higher! Just a little higher!" Lando pleads as a blind man hanging upside down from a tilting barge in the middle of a battle is attempting to shoot a tentacle three inches thick that is also wrapped around Lando's leg. As the screenplay notes, "[T]he fuzzy-eyed pirate fires at the tentacle. Direct hit."[18] In other words, Lando, part of the infiltration team sent to help rescue Solo does nothing in Jabba's palace to help the other characters. He then, during the one part of the rescue when he could have proven himself useful, falls off the skiff at the first blast from a laser which did not even hit him (remember, this is an "old scoundrel" and pirate himself who was skilled enough at the Battle of Taanab to get himself the rank of General and command of the squad attacking the Death Star!). For all practical purposes, Lando serves no real use in the rescue. He then needs to be rescued himself by the blinded and barely functional Han Solo. The rescuee must become a rescuer. Why did Han not fall from the same blast that shook the skiff? He's blind. He's got "hibernation sickness" when he comes out of the carbonite, shaking and barely in control of his body. When on the skiff he is "feeling better" as "instead of a big dark blur, I see a big light blur." And yet this blind, shaking, sick, exhausted man is more effective during his own rescue than Lando. It is not too out of line to suggest that the film seems to be stating that even under these most adverse conditions, Han is better and more effective than Lando.

Lando also indicates the larger issue of blackness in the *Star Wars* universe. Lando is never not black. Neither is Billy Dee Williams. Han Solo and Luke Skywalker are not defined by their whiteness. Neither are Harrison Ford and Mark Hamill. Whiteness is not a defining aspect. Blackness is. Lando is the "black character." Billy Dee Williams is the "black actor" cast as Lando Calrissian. In this case, we see the catch 22 of casting Billy Dee Williams: by raising the presence of blackness in the *Star Wars* films, the character and the actor are defined by their ethnicity.

Dale Pollock reports that Lucas was "still smarting from criticism that *Star Wars* was racist," so he "conceived of Lando as a suave, dashing black man in his thirties."[19] The irony is that Billy Dee Williams was interested in the role precisely because the character wasn't specifically black — there is nothing inherent in the script that makes Lando a person of color, other than the fact that specified in the script is that half the residents of Bespin are black. Of course in the final version, only two or three of the residents of Bespin are black.

The creators of *Empire* thought they had a simple solution to the problem of the perception of exclusion of people of color from the *Star Wars* universe. Lando was loudly trumpeted as an example of the inclusionary nature of the saga, which brought about new charges of racial exclusion on the part of Lucas. He remarks:

> In a press release I had described Billy Dee Williams as a black actor to illustrate the fact that the cast is becoming even more varied. I hadn't meant to set him apart, but Billy felt it did. He is a fine, sensitive actor and a serious minded man. But past usage of this word has made him sensitive to it. Yet, in this instance, "black" has been used to express an interesting distinction.[20]

The saga has since been continually plagued by accusations of racism and Lucas himself certainly seems uncomfortable with race. He believes calling Billy Dee Williams "black" makes it an "interesting distinction," yet Lando the character is problematic. Similarly, as will be argued below, the characters of color in the *Star Wars* universe are either evil or are given nothing useful to do. Vader is evil; Mace Windu is passive to the point of being inert for most of the second trilogy.

Billy Dee Williams rejects the idea that black actors can only play "black characters":

> I'm bored with the race problem. My hope is to be recognized interna-

tionally as a leading actor.... It bothers me to be part of a limiting concept of being black. What is this phenomenon of color prejudice?[21]

And yet Williams also stated that part of his own development as a performer moving from child actor to adult actor in a culture undergoing transitions about race was connecting to his own ethnic and cultural origins: "Suddenly it was hard and I was looking around for roots. But the culture around me was based on European Western culture, and if you're really not a part of that, you feel uneasy."[22]

According to Bourzereau, Lando was not even black until the second draft of the script.[23] In response to criticism of the lack of persons of color in *A New Hope*, Lando was cast using a black performer. Chris Salewicz argues that Billy Dee was cast because, "given the subliminal history of how James Earl Jones came to be hired for the voice of Darth Vader, you might feel that here a certain amount of political correctness was being exercised."[24] By employing the term "political correctness," Salewicz implies that Billy Dee Williams was cast not because of his strength or talent as an actor but his ethnicity— he was only cast because he was black, which means that the character is only defined in terms of ethnicity. One might also ask what is the "subliminal" history of casting— Lucas has been clear on how casting occurred in *A New Hope* and why he chose not to cast actors of color. Salewicz is making excuses for Lucas.

Once Lando was cast, the character is further problematized, as noted above, by his initial Machiavellian behavior, and then by the absence of any worthy contribution. The destruction of the second Death Star is presented as secondary to the other objectives of the Rebels in *Jedi*. Furthermore, Lando is separated out from the other main characters. Han, Leia, Chewbacca, and the droids are on the moon of Endor. Luke fights Vader in front of the Emperor. Lando is off by himself with another new character, Nien Nunb, who serves as his co-pilot. Like Chewbacca, Nien Nunb does not speak Galactic Standard (he does, however, use some words of Wolof, an African language!) but his own language which, of course, Lando understands. Whereas the film cuts back and forth between the group on the moon and Luke, Lando is only shown occasionally. Lando is present in the Rebel briefing room. He then is not seen again until the beginning of the battle, after the landing team has passed the security checkpoint, killed the speeder scouts, and enlisted the aid of the Ewoks. Luke then leaves to go meet Vader. Once the characters split up and the battle begins, the three plot threads— Leia and Han's assault on the shield generator, Lando's assault on the Death Star, and Luke's fighting with/for Vader — are given equal time. But until the beginning of the battle, Lando has effectively vanished. The people Lando is surrounded with — Admiral Ackbar, Nien Nunb, and Wedge — are either new or minor to insignificant. Lando joins the second string team, so to speak, while the main characters actively fight the Empire. Lando has but a single job — to blow up the Death Star. It is presented as much easier than Luke's destruction of the first Death Star in *A New Hope*. Lando and company then race the expanding explosion, attempting to outrun certain destruction.

Poor Lando, everybody wants to kill him. Bourzereau reports that Lawrence Kasdan wanted Lando to die in the Sarlaac pit, as "it would have been a real surprise to the audience," and only Lucas's desire that only villains perish in the Sarlacc scene saved Lando.[25] Later, in another version of the film, Lando does not survive the attack on the Death Star, dying when the Millennium Falcon explodes which was foreshadowed by Han's line "I just got a funny feeling. Like I'm not gonna see her again." This version was shown to preview audiences, which overwhelmingly rejected this plot twist. As John Baxter reports, "After poor reactions during preview screenings, probably more at the loss of the well-loved Falcon than Lando's underdrawn character, both were allowed to survive."[26] Thus, not only do fans like a ship more than the only significant character of color in the first trilogy, perhaps the only thing that kept him alive was the fact that there was no good way to kill him without destroying the more-appreciated ship he was piloting.

In fairness, Kasdan also thought it would be an interesting plot twist to have Luke die by Vader's hand and Leia step up and accept the Skywalker mantle as the real chosen one, who will bring about the return of the Jedi. Lucas refused to allow that death either.[27] None of the three main characters (Luke, Han, and Leia) could be allowed to die, and the droids, both of which were abused and occasionally destroyed, could be repaired, and Ben and Yoda did not so much die as "become more powerful than ever" by becoming one with the Force. They are still presences in the real world and can communicate with those still alive. In short, Lando seems to be the only character among the "good guys" who can be killed.

Following Lawrence Riddick's list of black stereotypes on film, Lando occupies the role of "the corrupt politician," who sells out his friends to keep his power. He is also, as suggested by the subtitle of this section, "the sexual superman," the only character in the *Star Wars* saga to display genuine sexuality, intertextually mixed with William's other roles as a "sexual superman." Lastly, he is "the petty thief" and "the irresponsible citizen" — before administering Bespin he was a scoundrel, a card player, a con-man and a criminal. He used to own the Millennium Falcon until Han Solo won it from him.

Lando is also presented as an ultimate failure as a politician and citizen of Bespin. He betrays his friends in a deal to "keep the Empire out of here forever," and then is surprised when Vader betrays him and reneges on the deal. Upon turning Bespin over to the Empire, he encourages his people to become refugees: "The Empire has taken control of the city. I advise everyone to leave before more Imperial troops arrive." No other group in the entire saga are made refugees by the Empire or by the failure of their leaders to protect them. Not the Naboo (although the Gungun also flee their cities when the Trade Federation comes), but Amidala returns to defeat the Trade Federation. The Hutts rule Tatooine and despite their criminality, no one flees the planet. The Ewoks do not need to flee the Empire. Lando alone leads his people into refugee status.

Lando Calrissian is not quite "a positive black role model in the realm of science fiction/fantasy," as Holden asserts. The fault, however, is not Williams'. Lando has been written as a stereotypical character without much to do once he gets past his charming amorality.

Nothing to Do: Mace Windu

By the time *Phantom Menace* was released, almost two decades after *Jedi*, the lack of people of color in the *Star Wars* universe had become a joke. Dale Pollock, in the revised edition of *Skywalking*, subtitled *The Life and Films of George Lucas*, wrote "Samuel Jackson [is] playing the obligatory single black character in a *Star Wars* story."[28] Like Lando in *Jedi*, Mace Windu is a character in search of a purpose. Like Lando in *Jedi*, he is also sidelined from the main action in *Phantom* and all but the last twenty minutes of *Clones*. He is one of the leaders of the Jedi Council, but most of his scenes are with a computer generated Yoda. Whereas Liam Neeson, Ewan McGregor, Jake Lloyd, and Natalie Portman also worked with the computer generated Jar Jar, they also had each other to react to— Samuel L. Jackson follows Lando in *Jedi*— the characters he is surrounded by are secondary. He interacts briefly with the main characters, but his role in the narrative is minimal, bordering on the insignificant, at least for *Phantom* and much of *Clones*.

In his discussion of the work of Samuel L. Jackson, Donald Bogle argues of *Phantom Menace*, "[H]e had so little to do that it almost looked like he were being used as a contrast to the caricatured antics of Jar Jar Binks."[29] Whereas Jar Jar, whose presence in the films will be analyzed in depth below, is a buffoon figure, Mace Windu is the serious, powerful Jedi, meant to be taken seriously. Not a scoundrel like Lando, nor a villain like

Vader, nor a clown like Jar Jar, Mace Windu possibly can be seen as a positive black role model in the realm of science-fiction/fantasy. The only problem being, he doesn't do anything and he is sidekick to Yoda, who gets the final fight in *Clones*. Windu may kill Jango Fett, but Yoda's fight with Count Dooku is the one that is celebrated and the one that ends the film. Yoda must rescue Windu and the other Jedi, bringing the clone army. After that, Windu disappears from the battle, emerging again only back on Coruscant to question the emergence of Darth Tyranus and the Clone Army of the Republic. A few seconds of lightsaber battle and Windu returns to doing nothing. Bogle concludes that his inclusion in the new trilogy is "another case of tokenism," despite the fact that Jackson had "presence and assurance."[30]

Sith, the climax of the prequel trilogy, should have given Windu more to do. He sits as head of the Jedi Council, but his primary role seems to be adversary to Anakin. He allows Anakin to join the Council at Palpatine's request, but does not grant him the rank of "Master." No reason is given. When Anakin informs Mace Windu that Palpatine is the Sith Lord that has been the source of all his grief (something that a Jedi Master like Windu should have figured out decades before), Windu moves to arrest Palpatine, who immediately slaughters the other three Jedi with Windu.

Mace Windu can barely hold his own against Palpatine, but manages to defeat him as Anakin arrives. In a rather strange moment, Mace faces the same temptation Anakin faced in the opening sequence with Count Dooku: an unarmed man is at his mercy. Anakin, under pressure from Palpatine, kills Dooku, although he observes that "it's not the Jedi way." Mace Windu, however, argues that he must kill Palpatine — the Senate and the courts are unreliable and under Palpatine's control. The only way to ensure safety and security is for Windu to be judge, jury and executioner all in one. This time, Anakin argues that Mace Windu must obey the Jedi code and not strike down an unarmed man. One must wonder either why Mace Windu hesitates and has the conversation with Anakin — he has never been seen as indecisive before — or why he needs to be lectured on the Jedi way by a young Jedi Knight who is already working his way down the path to the Dark Side.

When Mace Windu decides to kill Palpatine, Anakin easily parries his blow and then cuts Mace's lightsaber hand off. In other words, Anakin easily defeats Mace Windu, the nominal head of the Jedi Council. Palpatine then sends him flying out the window to his death. While the scene is a tribute to the strength of the Dark Side and the abilities of both Palpatine and Anakin, Mace Windu has been left as an easily defeated victim who closes out his life of not much to do by being blown out a window.

Jackson has appeared in dozens of films, including several genre films such as *Exorcist III* (1990), *Jurassic Park* (1993), *Sphere* (1998), and *Deep Blue Sea* (1999), and is a highly regarded actor. He is an outstanding actor, recognized as having great talent and being a major box office draw. Yet he is not used to his capacity in any of the films. Mace Windu, Jedi Master, is a powerful character but a more or less inactive one. It might not be mere tokenism, but it certainly is not an active black presence either.

Other Persons of Color in the *Star Wars* Universe

Other than the voice of James Earl Jones, the original film featured only one actor of color — an extra in two scenes is barely seen in the background at the Rebel base. In the famed cantina scene, all humans are white. There are no people of color in the Empire, it seems, as there are none among the command crew on the Death Star. It is only at the hidden Rebel base on the fourth moon of Yavin that a person of color is visible in *A New Hope*, and even then, he is simply an extra in the background. No named characters nor featured extras who are black appear in this film.

In *Empire*, we are introduced to the first and only major, visible black presence in the original trilogy: Lando, as discussed above. Bespin was originally intended to have a much larger population of color. In the second draft of the screenplay, "half the citizens" of Bespin "are black."[31] By the time of the actual filming of *Empire*, however, this number is reduced down to two black men clearly visible in Lando's initial guard detachment. These two men show up again as part of the detail that rescues Leia and Chewbacca from the stormtroopers. The black presence on Bespin goes from "half the population" to two extras.

Still, that is two more than on Hoth, where the entire rebel army is white. Two more than in the imperial fleet, where all visible faces are white. Two more than the rebel fleet to which Luke, Leia, Lando, and Chewbacca return at the end of the film. Interestingly, while significantly raising the black presence in the *Star Wars* universe, *Empire* still manages to promote the idea that while humans are everywhere in the galaxy, the vast majority of them are white.

Return of the Jedi marked the return of Lando—first disguised as a guard in Jabba's palace and then as the general leading the rebel attack on the new Death Star. The only other person of color (in the first half) in *Jedi* is another guard in Jabba's palace, visible only in two scenes. He is in the background when Leia, disguised as Boushh the Bounty Hunter, enters the palace, and then he is one of the guards who grabs Luke and brings him before Jabba after Luke has killed the Rancor.

The guard carries a spear, wears a metallic chest plate over a bare chest, seems to have dreadlocks, and is arguably the only human not from the principle cast in the palace scenes. The only other human is the Rancor keeper, an overweight Euro-male whose crying at the death of the Rancor is intended to be amusing. All other characters in Jabba's palace are aliens, except for this one guard of color, dressed in what seems to be a costume suggestive of traditional cinema savage-wear.

The other characters of color in *Jedi* are simply extras in the rebellion scenes. In the briefing scene in the Rebel war room, a man of color sits next to Leia before the briefing. Lando enters and takes his place standing next to Chewbacca, who is sitting next to Han, who is sitting next to Leia — thus the heroes are bookended by apparently the only two black men in the Rebellion. With the exception of General Calrissian, the entire command staff of the Rebellion is white — three men and two women, and Mon Calamari. In fact, there are more Mon Calamari than humans of color in the Rebellion, despite the hundreds of humans present. In the screenplay, the description notes, "Hundreds of Rebel commanders of all races and forms are assembling in the war room."[32] It would seem that mere tokenism applies only to humans of color.

In subsequent scenes, only two more black extras are visible: one over Han's shoulder when he asks Lando to take care of the Falcon and one of the Rebel commandoes with Han's team on the forest moon of Endor. One must look carefully to see either as both are in the background of their respective shots. All three films in the original trilogy make people of color a true minority — they exist only in the distant background, have no names, and do nothing of significance in any of the films. The only strong black presences, Lando and Vader, are a scoundrel and the villain, respectively.

The Phantom Menace effectively quadrupled the presentation of people of color in the *Star Wars* universe. Two members of the Jedi Council, Mace Windu and Adi Gallia were played by actors of African descent. Samuel L. Jackson played Mace Windu and Gin (aka Gin Clarke), a catwalk model discovered in the early nineties by French designer Jean-Paul Gaultier and best known for her shaved head, played Adi Gallia, who had no lines and can only be seen in widescreen in one Jedi Council scene. Gin can also be seen in a small role in *The Fifth Element* and repeated the role of Adi Gallia, again lineless, in *Attack of the Clones*.

Joining them in the new trilogy were two Naboo of color, Captain Panaka, played by British actor Hugh Quarshie, and "Bravo Three," one of the pilots under Ric Olié in the attack on the Trade Federation's space station above Naboo. Panaka is the other significant role featuring an actor of color, and Quarshie is a presence in it. He is the head of Naboo's Royal Security Forces, which means he personally provides directly for security for the queen and apparently also has authority over the Naboo military. He does more than Mace Windu, simply by virtue of being a sidekick to the Queen, and therefore in many of the same situations as her, although he does disappear for the most part when they reach Tatooine. On the other hand, it can be argued that he is the most positive black role model in the *Star Wars* series: he is confident, honorable, disciplined, and active. He is listened to by the queen, even if she does not take his advice. He opposes the return to Naboo for fear the Trade Federation will force the queen to sign the treaty. Yet when she announces that she wants to take back the planet, even if only with the twelve people on board her ship, he leads the planning. He also thinks that victory is impossible, but joins in the attack and leads Amidala's group to the throne room. Though he expresses doubts about their chances of success, Panaka is an active force in retaking Naboo from the Trade Federation.

Captain Panaka is a sensible, forceful, thoughtful character who plays an active role in the narrative. Hugh Quarshie, who was born in Ghana and is a British actor, has a strong background in stage acting, as well as many film and television roles, including several genre roles, such as in Clive Barker's *Nightbreed*. The role is one of the smaller in the film, but it is a significant one in terms of positive characters of color. As Billy Dee Williams had hoped, Captain Panaka is a role that is not rooted in the ethnicity of the character, and yet remains a powerful black presence in the film. Sadly, it is arguably one of the only ones in the entire series.

"Bravo Three," played by Clarence Smith, had only two lines in the final cut of the film. The first was, "Roger, Bravo Leader" in response to Ric Olié's command to begin the attack on the station. Then, after Anakin destroyed the station from within, flying his craft out of the hangar bay at the last possible second, "Bravo Three" sees him, saying, "Look! One of ours! Out of the main hold!" These two lines are the sole appearance of this character and the only lines spoken by a character of color other than Mace or Panaka. In the entire rest of the cast of *Phantom*, there are only three black men and one (silent) black woman, which also begs the question, after discussing Vader, Lando, Windu, and Panaka: where are the women of color in the *Star Wars* universe? In their essay "Fifty Reasons Why *Jedi* Sucks," Dan Vebber and Dana Gould mock Admiral Ackbar and the Mon Calamari, but also note that "there are more fish people in *Jedi* than there are black people or female people."[33] If one puts the two together, then one realizes that "black women people" don't exist or are only seen silent in the distance in a galaxy far, far away.

Ahmed Best, who plays Jar Jar Binks, shows up out of make-up in the cantina scene of *Clones* where he serves as a bit of an in-joke in two cut-away reaction shots to Anakin and Obi-Wan. Anthony Daniels (C3PO) is also present in the bar "out of character." *Sith* also has a few Jedi and Senators of color, but none with lines or any real presence.

Given the absence of people of color, it is remarkable that the *Star Wars* films are as popular in the African-American community as they are. In particular, the films have shaped and given source material to hip hop and rap music. As Harry Allen points out, *Star Wars* and hip-hop are roughly the same age.[34] References to the original trilogy abound within the hip-hop world, from 2 Live Crew's Luther Campbell referring to himself as "Luke Skywalker" to songs by Kool Moe Dee, Redman, Lords of the Underground, The Roots, House of Pain, Lewis Parker, Heltah Skeltah, Fugees, Busta Rhymes, Wu Tang Clan, Killarmy, Q-Tip, Kool Keith, DJ Stoic, the Walkmen, and DJ Q-Bert.[35] The names of the characters, the concepts, the planets, and the technology fill hip hop songs (and rock music as well, for that matter). There is perhaps an irony in how much influence the *Star Wars* saga has had on hip hop, considering how little these films engage the community or represent the members of the community that produced it.

Jar Jar Binks: Interstellar Stepin Fetchit in a Naboo Coon Show

In the next chapter I will argue that non-whites are represented in the saga through aliens. A large black presence in the new trilogy can be argued under the same logic. Many critics and scholars have seen a representation of people of color in the Gungun in *Phantom* and *Clones*, and specifically the greatest cause both of accusations of racism and of fan anger at Lucas in the new trilogy is arguably the character of Jar Jar Binks. The initial reviews of *Phantom*, after months of hype and publicity, were lukewarm, and were also downright hostile to the character of Jar Jar which, as will be argued below, echoed Hollywood stereotypes of blacks.

John Leo (*Washington Times*), Andy Seiler (*USA Today*), J. Hoberman (*Village Voice*), Joe Morgenstern (*Wall Street Journal*), David Ansen (*Newsweek*) and the *Toronto Star*, to name but a few of dozens of national and international reviewers, found Jar Jar to be a stereotypical if not outright racist portrayal. Elvis Mitchell refers to Jar Jar as "the Mantan Moreland of space."[36] He has also been compared with Stepin Fetchit, Willie Best, and Butterfly McQueen, all known for their exaggerated and stereotypical performances in old Hollywood films. Brent Staples, in an editorial in *The New York Times*, criticizes Lucas for Jar Jar. He observes, correctly, that Jar Jar "is by far the stupidest person in the film."[37]

Most argue that Lucas is not "the product of active bigotry," as the *Toronto Star* puts it, but rather from "plain ignorance."[38] Staples, however, places the blame on the creative process of Lucasfilm:

> Binks did not spring fully blown from the forehead of the universe. The filmmakers drafted a dancer from the show "Stomp." They then instructed him on how to speak and move in a way they found amusing. Finally, they replaced the human dancer with a digital version of an amphibian creature they had created from scratch.[39]

Staples further dismisses the "it's just a fantasy" defense by arguing that so were the black characters in *Birth of a Nation*, but that didn't make them any less racist or stereotypical.

As Staples notes, the process of creation of Jar Jar involved hiring a young black performer named Ahmed Best to play Jar Jar and give voice to the character that would eventually be digitally created. Best is a dancer who was performing in *Stomp* when "discovered" by *Phantom* casting director Robin Gurland. Best had only one film to his credit when cast, but had a good deal of stage experience moving and dancing. He wore a Jar Jar mask on top of his head to give the other actors a sense of where the digital creature's face would eventually be. In short, for the second time in the saga, an actor of color provides the voice for a character that he does not really play. Unlike Vader, however, Jar Jar comes across as a stereotype, not least because of his lines and delivery of them.

Jar Jar's lines are even written in dialect reflective of the dialect of blacks found in nineteenth century minstrel shows and in more recent representations of blacks such as the various manifestations of *Amos and Andy* and *Gone with the Wind*:

> JAR JAR: Mesa yous humbule servaunt.
> QUI-GON: That won't be necessary.
> JAR JAR: Oh boot tis! Tis demanded byda guds. Tis a live debett, tis. Mesa culled Ja Ja Binkss.
> QUI-GON: I have no time for this now...[40]

By this exchange, Jar Jar is simple, superstitious, and wastes the time of the heroes. Jar Jar automatically assumes the role of servant and must now serve Qui-Gon because it is demanded by the gods. He is also incapable of speaking comprehensibly.

Star Wars Episode I: The Visual Dictionary states of Jar Jar that he "speaks a pidgin Gungun dialect of Galactic Basic. Few Gunguns speak the pure Gungun language."[41] In other words, Jar Jar not only cannot speak the language that everyone else speaks (or at least understands) fluently, he and his people cannot speak their own language well! If, as Staples observes above, Jar Jar is the "stupidest person in the film," then the Gungun are the stupidest species in the film — they invented a language not even they can speak so they must speak a pidgin form of Galactic Basic. J. Hoberman, in his review of *Phantom Menace* in the *Village Voice*, argues that Jar Jar's "pidgin English degenerates from Caribbean patois to Teletubby gurgle."[42]

If we compare Jar Jar with the characters with which he is surrounded — the clipped British accents of Qui-Gon Jinn, Obi-Wan Kenobi, and Captain Panaka, the faux British accent of Queen Amidala, even eight-year-old Anakin Skywalker — Jar Jar comes across as an exceedingly unintelligent individual. The child speaks better and more comprehensibly than he does.

Much of what is presented on the screen seems to echo Caribbean culture. Several reviewers compare Jar Jar's ears to dreadlocks. His manner of speaking falls into stereotypical dialect for Caribbean characters. The justification is that Jar Jar is intended as comic relief, yet his entire community speaks the same manner. The leader of the community has the title "Boss." When we first meet him, he displays an inferiority complex towards the Naboo. He is represented as short-sighted and self-important. He has he same dialect as Jar Jar:

> Boss Nass: Wesa no like da Naboo! Un dey no like uss-ens. Da Naboo tink dey so smarty den uss-ens. Dey tink day brains so big.
> Qui-Gon: After those droids take control the surface, they will come here and take control of you.
> Boss Nass: No, mesa no tink so. Mesa scant talkie witda Naboo, and no nutten talkie wit outlaunders. Dos mackineeks no comen here! Dey not know of uss-en.[43]

As leader of the Gungun, Boss Nass is the voice of the community as well as its representative being. Yet he also speaks in the same patois as Jar Jar. The entire Gungun community is presented as insular, backwards and primitive. And it is identified in large part in reviews of *Phantom* as being indicative of Caribbean cultures.

Gungun are presented as primitive and swamp-dwelling. In their battle against the Trade Federation droids in *Phantom Menace*, they face laser canons, tanks, ships, and a robot army with slings, catapults, kaadu (horse-like, bipedal lizard mounts), shields, and an energy shield generated by a pack on the backs of a pair of Fambaas, which resemble domesticated dinosaurs. Their sole use of technology is in the form of the energy shield (which is ineffective as soon as the droids walk through the curtain of energy) and in "boomers"— the small globes of energy which the slings and catapults launch at the droids. No other projectiles, firearms, or hand-to-hand weapons are employed — no swords, spears, bows, etc. The *Star Wars Episode I: The Visual Dictionary* states that this is because the Gungun "have a close affinity with the natural world" and prefer animals and organic materials to technology.[44]

Jar Jar and the Gungun are what Hal Foster terms "exclusionary stereotypes," an effective way to turn the Other into "a pure object, spectacle [or] clown."[45] In the first trilogy, Vader excludes blacks by proving to be evil and Lando by proving to be a corrupt politician. In the second trilogy, blacks are reduced to the clown figure of Jar Jar, the servant Panaka, and the purposeless Mace Windu. In Reddick's formulation, Jar Jar is "the mental inferior" "the happy slave," and "the irresponsible citizen." Jar Jar was exiled from the Gungun city for accidentally flooding one of the living quarters. He is clumsy, a coward, and simple-minded, but devoted to Qui-Gon, Anakin, and Amidala as a happy slave would be.

Maynard also notes the stereotype of the black as comic relief in a white-driven narrative: "He is the clown, but seldom a magnificent clown; a buffoon; the butt of jokes, not the projector of them, except against himself."[46] The character is clearly intended as comic relief and meant to be laughed at. Sadly, as a stand-in for people of color, Jar Jar serves as an exclusionary stereotype — a clown that is an effective way to reinforce the idea of non-whites as both inferior and Other. Jar Jar as clown becomes an alien Stepin Fetchit.

Stepin Fetchit (1902–1985) appeared in many films for Fox and other studios. Donald Bogle argues that Fetchit is the manifestation of the stereotype of "the coon," which first made its appearance in cinema in the 1905 film *Wooing and Wedding of a Coon*, despite of its having been a mainstay in the minstrel show tradition in the theatre for almost a century.[47] Bogle defines a "coon" as "the Negro as amusement object and black buffoon," and posits it as "the most blatantly degrading of all black stereotypes."[48]

Defining characteristics of this stereotype include that he is "unreliable" and "lazy," he "butcher[s] the English language," he displays cowardice, simplicity, stupidity, and superstition, and that he exists solely as the counterpoint to the (often white) hero and to serve as comic relief for the audience to laugh at, not with.[49] Bogle also offers this physical description of Stepin Fetchit, who was very tall, very skinny, and shaved his head:

"His grin was always very wide, his teeth very white, his eyes very widened, his feet very large, his walk very slow, his dialect very broken."[50] Fetchit was in the film to be laughed at: his behavior, his appearance, the manner in which other characters interacted with him were all designed at the most benign to make an audience laugh and at the most malevolent to hold him in contemptuous scorn as an example of the worst qualities of his race.

Lastly, Fetchit always played characters that were redeemable and could be reformed. These characters would never be as intelligent, brave, or resourceful as the whites with whom they interacted, but they could become productive members of society. Fetchit's own phrase for his character type is "a lazy man with a soul."[51] This concept could also be applied to Jar Jar — not only is he redeemed at the Battle of Naboo, he is made into a Senator from Naboo. He clearly redeems himself, despite being exiled by his community in *Phantom*, and despite the facts that all Gungun clearly see Jar Jar's inadvertent heroism at the battle. One must wonder why Jar Jar is selected as the first Gungun senator. He is not brave, or intelligent, or resourceful. He is, in fact, the accidental hero.

Compare, for example, Jar Jar's inadvertent heroism in the Battle of Naboo, which is intercut with Qui-Gon and Obi-Wan's genuine warrior prowess against Darth Maul and Anakin's inadvertent, but effortless heroism against the Neimoidian fleet. As the screenplay for *Phantom Menace* records,

> JAR JAR's clumsiness works for him in the battle. He gets caught up in the wiring of a blasted droid, dragging the torso around with him, the droid's gun firing randomly, accidentally blasting SEVERAL DROIDS in the process.[52]

Remember, Jar Jar is a general in the Gungun army—for his role in bringing the Naboo and the Gungun together, Jar Jar has been given a high military appointment. He is one of the leaders of the Gungun army in what is arguably its first interstellar battle. Yet he does nothing to actually fight the droids, he attempts to flee and ends up destroying the enemy, not intentionally but comically and unthinkingly.

Later in the same battle, Jar Jar initially hides under a wagon. Then, while attempting to retreat from the battle in mindless panic, he accidentally unhooks the back gate of the wagon holding the energy ball weapons that the Gungun have employed against the droids. The balls roll out of the wagon, down a hill, and explode against several destroyer droids. As the screenplay notes, "JAR JAR's bumbling destroys several more BATTLE DROIDS."[53] Jar Jar then lands on a tank and, when thrown a "boomer," as the Gungun call them (small energy ball weapons), clumsily juggles it like a hot potato, then accidentally tosses it on the droid solider who has emerged from the tank to kill him. The destruction of this pilot droid allows the tank to crash into other droids. Jar Jar has single handedly defeated more of the enemy than any other character on screen, but it all has been not only accidental and inadvertent but directly because of his "bumbling." When they are then surrounded by droids in the next sequence, the other Gungun general states, "We should think of something." Jar Jar raises his hands, turns to the droids, and states plainly, "I give up."

In contrast, Anakin, placed in a Naboo fighter for safekeeping by Qui-Gon, learns how to activate the controls, fire the laser canon to destroy the droids shooting at Amidala and the Jedi, and then flies the fighter to the space battle raging above the planet because the ship is on autopilot. He keeps his cool, noting, "This is tense," and asking R2-D2 to turn off the autopilot, "before it gets us both killed." He flies his ship better than the experienced pilots and safely crash-lands in the landing bay of the enemy ship. He fires his torpedoes down a long hall, destroying the generators which power the droid army on the surface (reminiscent of Luke destroying the Death Star in *New Hope*) and then flies out of the exploding ship to safety.

Anakin's heroism is fortunate, but it is neither comical nor due to his bumbling as Jar Jar's is. He keeps his head and his dignity. Anakin's heroism is not as inadvertent as Jar Jar's, as his is effortless and assured—not born of panic or accident. Jar Jar surrenders, Anakin destroys not only the Neimoidian space station, his actions win the ground battle as well by robbing the droids of power. Anakin did not know this would be the result of his action; he naturally knows he must fire his torpedoes and race out again. His intentions are correct, even if he does not know the effect they will have. Jar Jar does not have any intentions—he only tries to escape danger and in doing so inadvertently destroys the enemy. Even this effect is mitigated, however, by the fact that the droid army defeats the Gungun. It is Anakin's actions that ultimately save them. Jar Jar's heroism is not only inadvertent, it is ineffectual and ultimately inconsequential. His accidental engagement of the enemy has saved only him, and not had any real impact on his enemy or on victory.

In further contrast, the climactic duel between Darth Maul and the two Jedi rages at the same time. "An intense display of swordsmanship" is how the screenplay describes it.[54] In the power generator pit of Theed, the capitol of Naboo, the three characters fight an intense and fierce battle across catwalks and with force shields raising up and closing off corridors every few minutes. Darth Maul kills Qui-Gon and nearly defeats Obi-Wan, forcing him into a pit and kicking his lightsaber down the seemingly bottomless shaft. Obi-Wan then uses the force to draw Qui-Gon's light-saber to him and cuts Maul in half. The battle is violent, energetic, and demonstrative of great martial prowess on the part of all three characters involved. The death of Qui-Gon is particularly poignant as he has been the protagonist and the voice of wisdom and comfort throughout the film. His death weighs more heavily than the deaths of all the Gungun, Naboo pilots and soldiers, and battle droids put together.

The fourth narrative line intercut with these concerns the efforts of Amidala to find and capture the Viceroy, forcing Gunray to sign a new treaty in which the Neimoidians relinquish their claim to Naboo. They sneak into the palace, fight their way to the throne room, use Sabé dressed like the queen and accompanied by several troops as a decoy, and capture Nute Gunray and Rune Haako, effectively ending the Trade Federation's control of Naboo. Thus, Amidala, Anakin, and Obi-Wan are presented as heroic because their actions end the threat to Naboo. Jar Jar, on the other hand, is comically inept at best, dangerous at worst, and his heroics are a mere simulacrum of the others.

The message sent by these intercut battle sequences is that a white woman and white child are more heroic and effective than the Gungun and that white men are the most heroic of them all. The death of a single white male far outweighs the deaths of dozens if not hundreds of aliens whom most critics agree are based on a stereotype of people of color. Jar Jar is one of "Stepin's Step-Chillun," as Bogle refers to them, and consisting of a number of actors who specialized in playing Coon characters: Willie Best aka "Sleep 'n Eat"(?—1962) and Mantan Moreland (1902–1973), who always played "a coward who was never there when the heroes needed him."[55] Jar Jar is a coward whose bumbling allows him to save himself long enough for the whites to really save the planet. In short, Jar Jar is a racist construction that echoes historic stereotypical characters.

Apologists for the film and the character attempt to turn the interpretation of Jar Jar as a racist construction back on the viewer. Steven A. Galipeau argues that Jar Jar

> becomes a "hook" for people's projections of their own unconscious racial stereotypes. Such attitudes are not only offensive to the meaning of the character's part in the story but also to the African-American actor who was given much latitude in voicing and creating the character.[56]

Others, such as Clarence Page, Paul Craig Roberts, and Christian Toto (all columnists writing in the *Washington Times*), separately defend Lucas against the charge of stereotypes (with Roberts going so far as to blame the critics as well: "All this says more about how liberals see ... blacks than about how Mr. Lucas sees them.")[57]

Ironically, Galipeau, a Jungian analyst and *Star Wars* fan, posits Lando as Han Solo's shadow side, observing that Lando ignores C3PO, making him "more 'mechanical' than the droid."[58] Galipeau further argues that

> In our culture people of color (especially African Americans) are espe-
> cially susceptible to shadow projections from Caucasians. Dream figures
> portraying people of color generally represent important qualities that the
> dreamer has lost connection with or disowned as negation.[59]

This reading is remarkably Eurocentric. Whose culture is "our culture?" People of color in Caucasian dreams are "shadow projections," but what are people of color in the dreams of people of color? Galipeau is assuming a white dreamer. Lando is Han's shadow side and not the reverse because whites are the center in the *Star Wars* universe. Black is defined in terms of white in the saga.

Why is Jar Jar the projection of Lucas and not the viewer? Quite simply because the characters are created by Lucas, very carefully constructed and specifically developed. The whites are in the center and other than Captain Panaka, all other characters of color are evil, inactive and ineffective, or stupid and unintentionally heroic at best. There are no positive roles for people of color in the films. The films also echo a century of racist and stereotypical representations of blacks. The blacks in *Birth of a Nation* are not a projection by "liberals," they genuinely are a stereotypical construction, as is Jar Jar.

I argued in the introduction that films such as the *Star Wars* saga are a form of education. John Leo, in his analysis of *Phantom Menace*, argues that Jar Jar is, for that very reason, not just offensive, but a very real danger: "If blacks talk and act like this movie says they do, how can they possibly expect equal treatment?"[60] Given that the films are aimed at a young audience, the danger is apparent. To white audiences (especially children), the lesson is that blacks are evil and inferior. To black audiences (especially children), the lesson is that they are evil and inferior. Deborah Wyrick states that popular culture "force[s] the black child to identify with white heroes and reject the black-hearted, dim-witted, often dark-skinned enemies."[61] The two trilogies certainly prove that argument.

As Jar Jar has proven, the non-whites of the Lucas universe are as likely to be represented as literally alien others. In the next chapter I consider the referencing of non–Euro peoples in the *Star Wars* films through the use of aliens. Not only are blacks constructed and represented through alien beings such as the Gungun, other non–Euros are also represented as aliens. Just as Asian culture has been appropriated and placed in the hands of non–Asians, the absence of real Asians and other ethnicities is made present in the form of alien beings.

To return to Hooper X and *Chasing Amy*, Kevin Smith's "amusing" take on an Afrocentric reading of the "Holy trilogy" is, at heart, Fanonian. It is also not entirely inaccurate. The black characters in the two trilogies are inactive, evil, or comic relief. In *Black Skin, White Masks*, Fanon asks, after Freud, "What does a black man want?" Fanon also supplies the answer: "The black man wants to be white!"[62]

CHAPTER 5

"Bridge on the Planet Naboo": Asians (and Others) as Aliens

See, you think every time you do one of those demeaning roles, the only thing lost is your dignity. That the only person who has to pay is you. Don't you see that every time you do that millions of people in movie theaters will see it. Believe it. Every time you do any old stereotypic role just to pay the bills, someone has to pay for it.
— Bradley Yamahita to Vincent Chang, *Yankee Dawg You Die*, Philip Kan Gotanda[1]

The above epigram is from Philip Kan Gotanda's *Yankee Dawg You Die*, an indictment of how Hollywood and the American stage have treated Asian actors and Asian characters. Bradley Yamahita, a young Japanese actor, befriends Vincent Chang, an older Asian actor who feels forced to play stereotypical roles. With interludes that reflect popular culture portraits of Asia and Asians from Charlie Chan to Godzilla, the play explores the compromises that Asian actors must make in order to work and how one may fight these reductivist and offensive representation.

Bradley's larger objection about these representations, as noted above, is that not only are they stereotypical and offensive, they reinforce those stereotypes in the minds of the audience, and the Asian and Asian-American community, individually and collectively, "pay for it." The play deals with the different roles for Asian actors that are prevalent even to this day: houseboy, waiter, martial-arts using gang member, drug dealers, hookers, and soldier — Viet Cong, ancient Chinese, samurai, ninja, or World War II

Japanese. In fact, the play's title comes from the "Jap Soldier" character that Vincent played in a war movie. As the plays begins, the audience is shown a sequence from the film in which Vincent wears "Thick Coke-bottle glasses, holding a gun. Acts in an exaggerated, stereotypic — almost cartoonish manner."[2] Playing "Sergeant Moto," he pretends to sleep while the American G.I.s he guards attempt to escape: "The snake-like lids of his slanty eyes drooping into a feigned slumber."[3] He awakens and curses the Americans, threatening the Americans. He graduated from U.C.L.A. in 1934 he reveals, and he "speakee" English. Later in the play, mocking the Moto character, Vincent begins responding to all statements to him with, "Yankee Dawg You Die!"[4]

It is this image of the evil Asian, the cinematic heritage of both World War II and the orientalist tendencies of the Victorian stage that sadly dominates much of the Star Wars films. In the Star Wars films, Fanon's colonial alienation becomes a colonial alien nation, or a colonial alienization. Tom Carson correctly observes that in the Star Wars films white people are human beings and everybody else is Other, in what is an "old fashioned racial schema."[5] In fairness to the filmmakers of the twentieth century, however, the Othering of non–Westerners is not unique to cinema and the modern era. Asia was the land of aliens, monsters, and non-humans for the West since the classical era. Western understanding of Asia has always had an element of fantasy (both negative and positive) to it. As Sheridan Prasro writes, "The 'Orient' has always meant lands far away, full of opulence and sensuality, danger, depravity and opportunity."[6]

Homer's epics, The Iliad and The Odyssey, report on the Orient and the strange monsters and monstrous races of men that live in the area around the Mediterranean. In Book III and Book IV of Histories, Herodotus gives the first recorded reports of India and Indian culture in the West — the farthest East that the West could conceive. In his article "Marvels of the East: A Study in the History of Monsters," Rudolf Wittkower analyzes a history of the representation of Asia, primarily India, in the narratives of the classical, medieval and early modern West. Wittkower argues "compound beings"—creatures that are mixtures of human and animal such as satyrs, centaurs, sirens, and harpies— are not only part of Greek mythology, but also take a non-religious form as a means of perceiving Indians and others as monstrous races, or monster men.[7] Travelers' narratives, natural sciences, geographies, and other texts from the Greeks on saw in a culture and people far, far away monster men and compound beings easily the equal of all the characters in Jabba's palace or the Mos Eisley cantina.

In the fourth century B.C.E. Ktesias of Kridos, a court physician in Persia, wrote what became considered one of the definitive texts about India in the ancient world, only fragments of which are still available. Ktesias reports that living in India are pygmies, *scapodes* (men with a single large foot), *cynocephali* (dog-headed men), headless men with faces between their shoulders, 8-fingered, 8-toed, long-eared people, giants, men with tails, and monstrous animals.[8] Subsequent Greek and Roman authors increased the monstrosity of the East. While Wittkower argues that some of the stories of monster men originated in Indian narratives (an argument that has merit as the *Mahabharata* and the *Ramayana* and Indian folk stories also contain fantastic and monstrous beasts and men as well), it seems that the subsequent tales are rooted in the idea of making and keeping the foreign not only Other, but also inhuman and alien.[9]

This trend of monsterizing the non–West continued through the Middle Ages and the Renaissance, even occurring in the theatre. In Shakespeare's *Othello*, the Moor of Venice, himself an outsider, an Other, a non–Westerner, and a person of color, reports of his travels to the wild lands of Africa and Asia:

> It was my hint to speak — such was my process —
> And of the Cannibals that each [other] eat,
> The Anthropophagi, and men whose heads
> [Do grow] beneath their shoulders [I.iii.142–145].[10]

Othello is a hero and Desdemona loves him because he has faced the monstrous Other. Ziauddin Sardar observes that this tradition continues through the *Star Wars* saga:

> The imaginative aliens of "a galaxy far, far away" have their inception
> in the anthropophagi, troglodytes, the dog-headed people, and the beings
> with no feet but appendages so profuse they can function as sunshades
> when they lie on their backs.[11]

The two trilogies follow the Western tradition of making the Other truly monstrous and alien, in both its definition as "foreign" and "strange or unnatural." They are rooted in Western constructions of Easterners as nonhuman and truly alien. In doing so, the films become part of imperialist literature. As noted in Chapter 1, Edward Said wrote of imperialist literature that it concerns itself

> with far-flung and sometimes unknown spaces, with eccentric or unac-
> ceptable human beings, with fortune enhancing or fantasized activities
> like emigration, money making, and sexual adventure.[12]

What are aliens other than "eccentric or unacceptable human beings?"

This summary of imperialist literature could just as easily be a summary of the *Star Wars* films.

Elaine L. Graham writes about "the political nature of monstrosity," that by studying what is normalized and acceptable and what is not we understand what is acceptable and not acceptable to society.[13] Graham calls monsters "the gatekeepers to the acceptable."[14] In the case of the *Star Wars* saga this will ultimately mean which aliens are considered good and friendly (such as Wookiees, Ewoks, and Yoda, for example) and which are evil, monstrous, and dangerous (Neimoidians, Jabba, and Darth Maul, for example).

As noted in Chapter 1, early science fiction writers such as Edgar Rice Burroughs used monster men and aliens as plot devices and characters in his novels of Barsoom and Tarzan. Tarzan faced the Ant Men, the Leopard Men, the Lion Man, and an entire variety of other aliens and animal men. On Barsoom, John Carter battled against manlike creatures with green, yellow, or black skin to win the hand of red-skinned Dejah Thoris. Science fiction and science fantasy have a tradition of the alien Other. Historically, the cinema, being a primarily visual medium, has maintained a tradition of the monstrous alien that also reads as having real world corollaries.

For example, Eric Greene has argued that the *Planet of the Apes* series uses the monstrous alien Other to posit an allegory for contemporary race relations in America.[15] *Escape from the Planet of the Apes* (1971), *Conquest of the Planet of the Apes* (1972), and *Battle for the Planet of the Apes* (1973) function as "allegories about racial conflict" by presenting white humans in conflict with black, brown, and orange apes (gorillas, chimpanzees, and orangutans). The apes are meant to stand for people of African descent in the United States, a point made very clear in the last two films as Caesar (Roddy McDowell) keeps reminding MacDonald (Hari Rhodes), an African-American and assistant to the governor who hates apes, that "You, above everyone else should understand," as apes have replaced blacks as the slave class in America. MacDonald is presented as identifying more with an intelligent chimpanzee than with other humans if they are of European descent. The films, argues Greene, invert the racist inscription of blacks as lesser primates by putting the lesser primates in the same position as African-Americans and showing them rebelling as well.[16] In doing so, the films both distance that struggle and yet make it more sympathetic — we are clearly meant to side with Caesar and not with the specieist (racist?) governor in *Conquest of the Planet of the Apes*. We are meant to side with the human/ape coalition and not the gorillas or mutant humans of *Battle for the Planet of the Apes*. Not so the *Star Wars* films, where the good guys are almost all white males and the bad guys aliens who stand in for other Earth ethnicities.

Science fiction and science fantasy cinema has had a history of seeing the Asian as alien and the alien as Asian. What is Ming the Merciless from Mongo, if not alliterative Asianness? "Mongo" simply a shortened version of Mongolia. "Ming" is the name of a Chinese dynasty. Ming the Merciless is one in a fairly long line of Asian aliens and monsters.

One might also consider Fu Manchu as the spiritual and cinematic father of the Neimoidians in the second trilogy, particularly in *The Phantom Menace*. Sax Rohmer, the pseudonym of British popular adventure and thriller writer Arthur Sarsfield Ward (1883–1959) created the character of Fu Manchu in the second decade of the twentieth century, capitalizing on the British fears of the Chinese at the time in the wake of the Boxer Rebellion and later Chinese uprisings against the British. Fu Manchu represents one of the great villains who embodies the "Yellow Peril"— the threat that Asians really wanted to take over the world and were doing so via immigration without assimilation among other means. As Jachinson Chan reports in his own analysis of the Fu Manchu figure: "The Dr. Fu Manchu character perpetuates the myth that the Chinese, and by extension, Asians, are trying to take over the Western world."[17]

Fu Manchu is an evil genius, a doctor, a scientist, and the head of a secret Chinese organization whose goal was world conquest and domination. The horror, as in H.G. Wells's *War of the World* seemingly comes from the idea of an Asian trying to do to the United Kingdom and the West what the United Kingdom and the West were trying to do to the rest of the world. Fu Manchu plans to colonize the Occident, which is terrifying to the West. In *Phantom Menace*, the Neimoidians plan to colonize the Naboo. Both sets of material involve the effort of white characters to contain and even destroy the "yellow peril."

Through a series of fourteen novels which then became the basis for a variety of incarnations in film, Fu Manchu schemed to take over the world through a variety of fiendish plots, but was always eventually (if temporarily) defeated by a small group of British agents, policemen, and scientists. With titles such as *The Mystery of Dr. Fu Manchu, The Drums of Fu Manchu, The Insidious Dr. Fu Manchu,* and *The Mask of Fu Manchu,* these occult science fiction thrillers represented the Chinese as dangerous villains, and Dr. Fu Manchu himself as almost alien in his thought process and evil genius. The cinema used these novels as raw material in order to create films which further represented the Asian as a dangerous monster with almost superhuman powers who needed to be stopped at all costs.[18]

Fu Manchu began cinematic life in silent serials starring Harry Agar

Lyons as the fiendish doctor. *The Mystery of Fu Manchu* in 1923 and *The Further Mysteries of Fu Manchu* the following year presented an extended story of Fu's plot to take over the world and its foiling by Sir Dennis Nayland Smith of Scotland Yard, his archnemesis. The very name of the Briton who would fight and defeat Fu Manchu embodied Britishness— he was titled with some sort of order of the British Empire, at least a knighthood ("Sir Dennis") and worked for Scotland Yard, the British police force founded by Colonel Charles Rowan and Sir Richard Mayne at the direction of Home Secretary Robert Peele and self-described greatest and oldest modern police force in the world.

The first talkie based on Rohmer's creation, *The Mysterious Dr. Fu Manchu*, was produced in 1929 with Warner Oland, better known as Charlie Chan, in the title role. Oland, himself of Swedish descent, made a career of playing Asian characters. He continued as Fu Manchu in a few more serials, following the same basic plotlines and the same exact representations of Asians.

In 1932, producer Irving Thalberg brought *The Mask of Fu Manchu* to the silver screen in a full-length feature. Boris Karloff, who had risen to acclaim the year before playing the monster in *Frankenstein*, now played what was perceived as yet another monster role: the Chinese Fu Manchu. In this film, the Asian villain seeks the mask and sword of Genghis Khan, so that he might rally the nations of Asia to rise up and attack the west. Not content with political intrigue, Fu Manchu also uses monstrous tarantulas, zombies, and a death ray. Peter Nicholls and John Brosnan see this film as a forerunner of *Raiders of the Lost Ark*, yet another Lucas-produced film, and one that sought to capture the feel of pre-war pulp and adventure movies.[19]

Henry Brandon, another Euro-American, then took on the role of Fu Manchu for *The Drums of Fu Manchu*, produced by Republic pictures in 1939 and released in 1940 after the start of the Second World War. Although the attack on Pearl Harbor had not yet occurred, the film in some ways represents the concern over the war already raging in Asia, and anxiety over the loss of colonial dominance in Asia by European powers. The Japanese threat to British and American colonies in the Pacific and Asia is present in the film, even if covertly. Furthermore, it echoes the standard adventure film with exotic locations and dangerous foreign villains. The plot, echoing *Mask*, involves the search for the "sacred scepter of Genghis Kahn," which Fu Manchu plans to use "to unite the tribes of the Orient" and drive out "the foreign devils."

In the postwar period, Fu Manchu found his way to television, played on NBC in 1952 by John Carradine in *The Zayat Kiss*. This adaptation of a Sax Rohmer tale was followed in 1955 by a television series, *The Adventures of Fu Manchu*, with Glen Gordon in the title role. Again, Republic Pictures produced the film. Although the series ended in 1956 after a single season, it brought the Asian villain to a wider audience. One might also note that both television versions followed the start of the Korean War. Again, anxiety over Asia in the West results in a fantasy narrative that posits a superhuman (nonhuman?) Asian as the villain.

In 1965, the British producer Harry Alan Towers began a new series of films based on the character with *The Face of Fu Manchu*. Perhaps after the defeat of Japan in the Second World War, the rise of Communist China and the war that had raged in Korea and the one just starting in Vietnam, the cinema was again ready to cater to public fear of (warlike?) Asians by embodying the most feared qualities in the Chinese master villain. Christopher Lee, already well known for his work with Hammer Studios and who would go on to play Count Dooku/Darth Tyranus in *Clones* and *Sith*, played the Asian who wanted to dominate the world, only to see his plans foiled at the last minute by Sir Dennis Smith. Over the next three years, four more films in the series would follow: *Brides of Fu Manchu*, *Vengeance of Fu Manchu*, *Castle of Fu Manchu* and *Blood of Fu Manchu*, with Christopher Lee as the title character in them all. All were fairly formulaic, taking inspiration from the novels, earlier series, and old movie series. All employed special effects, weapons, monstrous creatures and "oriental armies" as tools to either conquer or destroy the West.

Finally, in 1980, three years after *A New Hope*, *The Fiendish Plot of Fu Manchu* saw noted comic actor Peter Sellers take over both the role of Fu Manchu as well as his nemesis, Sir Dennis. The plot and representation of Asians in this film are overtly racist and much of the humor is derived from stereotypes about Asians and about Chinese in particular. The tagline for the film read, "See this movie! An hour later you'll want to see it again!" Sellers also makes a great deal of Fu Manchu's inability to speak English correctly, overemphasizing his accent.

What all of the Fu Manchu films have in common is the fact that Fu Manchu was always played by a Western actor — Harry Agar Lyons, Warner Oland, Boris Karloff (real name William Henry Pratt), Henry Brandon, John Carradine, Glen Gordon, Christopher Lee, and Peter Sellers. Fu Manchu inevitably has a thick accent. He threatens violence. He uses a number of other Asian characters, often flunkies, servants, or assassins, played by Asian actors to do his evil bidding. He is not only a stereotype — he is an archetype.

The Neimoidians in *Phantom Menace*, and in particular Nute Gunray, share some qualities with Fu Manchu: a plot to take over a world, the use of ingenious devices and an army of followers, and the desire to colonize the land of white humans. The Neimoidians have thick accents that echo the tradition of cinematic Asian villains. Both the Fu Manchu movies, books, and television shows and *The Phantom Menace* vilify Asians to maintain the supremacy of Europeans—the evil Asians must be defeated by the good white characters. The characters of European descent work for the forces of good and order, whereas the Asians represent chaos and destruction, as well as, in the case of *Phantom Menace*, aggressive business and corporations. In both sets of films, the Asian villains are played by Western actors.

It is in their aggressive and rapacious capitalism, the Neimoidians echo Fu Manchu—they literally seek world domination. The Trade Federation is emblematic of Western cinema's fears of Asian businesses, not unlike Michael Crichton's *Rising Sun*. Throughout the eighties Japanese corporations bought American companies, businesses and real estate. The xenophobic concern over the Japanese economy was made manifest in films that showed Asians, and in particular Japanese, as dangerously aggressive in their acquisition of American property. Asian business and investment was seen as invasion, much as in nineteenth century America Asian immigration was also seen as invasion. In *Phantom Menace* the "yellow peril" of the United States is replaced with the "grey peril" of Neimoidians.

In one of the "official" LucasBooks publications, *Star Wars Episode I: The Visual Dictionary*, aspects of Neimoidian biology and society are presented that are not discussed in the film. They are a "status-driven society" that lives in "communal hives."[20] They are "known for their exceptional organizing abilities" and "have built the largest commercial corporation in the galaxy."[21] These are also qualities stereotypically associated with the Japanese: status-driven, communally-oriented, highly-organized, and devoted to business. Likewise, the Neimoidians, like Fu Manchu, are "dangerous, mysterious, and inscrutable."[22]

Species displaying the same characteristics are cast in positive and negative light depending on the race or species of the possessor. In the Fu Manchu novels, intelligence is comparatively good or evil depending on the ethnicity of the character. Dr. Fu Manchu is a genius, a brilliant scientist, and a scientist. Yet the books focus on the difference between "British intelligence" and "Chinese cunning."[23] The Western characters are "intelligent" and "clever," whereas the Asian characters are "cunning," or "tricky." Amidala's tricking of Nute Gunray, forcing him to sign a treaty, is presented as a clever ruse that allows her to triumph over an evil adversary, whereas Nute Gunray's attempts to make Amidala sign a treaty are presented as examples of his Machiavellian manipulation. She is clever, he is deceitful. She is resourceful, he is insidious. She is shrewd, he is sneaky.

In representing Asians, such narratives posit that actions do not define the ethics of the character, the ethnicity of the character defines the ethics of the actions. Yet there is a greater danger in the manner in which the *Star Wars* films present Asians than the mere recycling of stereotypes. The saga inverts Asian identity, appropriating it in the form of the Jedi, all played by Western actors.

The previous chapter outlined the role (or lack thereof) of people of African descent. The third chapter outlined how much Asian culture has shaped the films and how Lucas has constructed a science fantasy world rooted in the visual culture of Asia. The dark side, however, is seductive and deceptive, and so is Lucas's construction. He has, like so many before him, appropriated Asian culture with nary an actual Asian in sight. As in the Charlie Chan and Fu Manchu movies, the characters with Asian names and representing Asian qualities are played by European actors. Obi-Wan Kenobi is played by Sir Alec Guinness in the original trilogy (whose very title "Sir" ironically suggests Empire) and by Ewan McGregor in the prequel trilogy. As noted above, Kurosawa favorite Mifune Toshiro was initially considered to play the role of Obi-Wan in *New Hope*. Qui-Gon Jinn is played by Liam Neeson, also a British actor. Yoda is a puppet, given life by American Frank Oz. Despite Asian names and Asian culture, European, (specifically, British) actors play the Jedi. Luke Skywalker, who brings balance to the Force, is played by All-American Boy Mark Hamill. At one point, Lucas even considered having Luke and Leia be Asian, but, in Lucas's words "when there are four main characters, it seemed better to have them all be the same race."[24] Thus, Obi-Wan, Luke, Leia, and Han all remained Westerners, despite their names. European and European-American actors ultimately represent the Asian culture that is privileged visually and philosophically.

That Lucas is subverting the anti-colonial narrative in the films manifests itself more than simply by the casting of European actors as the Asian characters in both the original trilogy and the prequel trilogy. The forces that act to protect the interests of the Empire are demonstrated to be Western in the original trilogy, in which Lord Vader and Grand Moff Tarkin (played by British actor Peter Cushing), and the Emperor are clearly Western in name, in dress, and in action. Yet, in *The Phantom Menace*, Lucas superficially presents the evil characters as Western in nature, but in actuality they represent the Asian Other. Other than Darth Sidious (the future Emperor), the two major nemeses of the Jedi are Darth Maul and the members of the Neimoidian Trade Federation, in particular Viceroy Nute Gunray and his assistant Rune Haako, all three of whom are non-human alien characters. All three characters, who, it should be noted, have Western names, suggest the stereotypical Asian Other through their behavior, costumes, and speech patterns. If the original trilogy has the films of Kurosawa Akira as their predecessors, then, as will be shown below, *The Phantom Menace* has as its predecessor *The Bridge on the River Kwai* and World War II films in which the Japanese are presented as the insidious and dangerous adversary.

The major active nemesis of the Jedi in *The Phantom Menace* is Darth Maul, who, while initially seemingly Western-derived is actually an Asian-inspired character. According to George Lucas in an interview with Bill Moyers for *Time*, "We went back into representations of evil," in order to find a way to visually represent Darth Maul.[25] Moyers himself is reminded by Maul of *Paradise Lost* or *Inferno*; however, the physical description of Satan in these two works does not match Darth Maul's visage, which seems to be much closer to the stylized makeup of Asian theatre.[26]

In *Paradise Lost*, Satan is described as having "horrid hair" (II:710), as being winged and very ugly (IV:118). Zephon (another fallen demon) tells him "thou resmbl'st now / Thy sin and place of doom obscure and foul" (IV:118–9). Yet Satan can also appear innocent and friendly by "practis'd falsehood under saintly show" (IV:122). Thus, according to Milton, Satan is either foul, winged and hairy or saintly looking, neither of which describes Darth Maul, who is wingless, bald, crowned with small nubby horns, and has a tattooed red and black face. He appears malevolent, not saintly.

Inferno's depiction of Satan is even less suggestive of Maul. Dante and Virgil descend to the final circle of hell to find Satan encased in a frozen lake. Satan has three faces:

> ...one — in front — blood red;
> and then another two that, just above
> the midpoint of each shoulder, joined the first;
> and at the crown, all three were reattached;
> the right looked somewhat yellow, somewhat white;
> the left in its appearance was like those
> who come from where the Nile, descending, flows [XXXIV:39–45].

Out of these three faces sprout six bat-like wings which fan a frozen wind, and all six eyes of Satan weep constantly as his three mouths chew Judas, Brutus, and Cassius, respectively, for eternity. Perhaps Moyer was envisioning the Doré illustrations of other demons in both *Inferno* and *Paradise Lost*, but neither of these literary works invoke anything resembling Maul.

Rather than a representation of a Western devil, Darth Maul suggests

Gustav Doré's illustration of Satan from Milton's *Paradise Lost,* one of the supposed sources of the design of Darth Maul. Yet Maul looks nothing like this. Instead, compare Maul with images from traditional Chinese and Japanese theatre, specifically *Jingju* and *Kabuki,* respectively (photograph courtesy of Special Collections and Archives, Oviatt Library, California State University, Northridge).

the *kumadori,* or stylized makeup of *aragoto* roles in Kabuki theatre. *Aragoto* roles are heroes and villains who are played in a "highly exaggerated, bravura style."[27] Kabuki expert James Brandon notes that this acting style began in 1673 when Ichikawa Danjro I "playing the role of the superhuman Kintoki" entered the Edo stage "wearing bold 'black and red makeup,' rampaged up the side of a mountain and single-handedly demolished a number of opponents."[28] This description also suggests Darth Maul, larger than life, in bold makeup, stunningly defeating Qui-Gon Jinn. In *Kumadori* code, red (*beni*) can also stand for anger, forcefulness, rage, or cruelty (although the truly evil wear blue). Black (*sumi*) is used to suggest fear or terror. Horns are found in the makeup for *oni*— demons— which also use a complete red base (as opposed to red stripes over white) to indicate their supernaturalness as well as their fearsomeness. The black lines on Maul's face suggest *Kumadori*, the horns suggest the *kijin* masks of noh, masks with horns for playing demon-gods such as *oni*.

Darth Maul's appearance also has antecedents in Beijing opera, in which one of the four principle categories of roles are called *Jing*, "painted face roles." A.C. Scott claims that the highly colored abstract pattern makeup of *Jing* roles "suggests power," and is worn by "men of action, warriors, swashbuckling outlaws ... as well as gods and supernatural beings."[29] Not only is Darth Maul's face similar in appearance to the makeup of *Jing* roles, but his movement and action have more in common which the Beijing opera characters than with the Western devil. *Jing* roles require acrobatics and martial arts. The characters fight, tumble, and twirl. The lightsaber duel is clearly derived from Asian forms of combat. Few, if any, accounts of a Western devil depict such a physically active, martially combative creature. In short, a martial artist, made up to resemble a kabuki or Beijing opera character, using Asian fighting techniques, represents the greatest challenge to a Jedi's skills, as well as the embodiment of "the Dark Side." Darth Maul is more Asian villain than Western devil; a "kung fu fighter" with a Western name and an Eastern pedigree who represents evil.

Therein, of course, lies the "Dark Side" of the *Star Wars* saga, whose worst offender is the *Phantom Menace*. Having appropriated Asian culture for both heroes and villains, and having constructed a colonialist model in which the evil Western Trade Federation and later the Empire attempt to manipulate and conquer the peaceful, cultured East, Lucas casts European (Caucasian) actors in the heroic roles and reduces the evil characters to literally alien Others.

Bridge on the Planet Naboo: *Phantom Menace* as Prisoner of War Movie

First and foremost, *The Phantom Menace* is a war movie, but it is also a movie about an occupation and, to a lesser extent, a prisoner of war movie. *Phantom Menace* continues the use of Fanonian metaphor by dealing with one group attacking, conquering and occupying the territory of another in the form of the Trade Federation (headed by the Neimoidians) invading the planet Naboo with a droid army and attempting to force Queen Amidala to sign a treaty which will guarantee the Trade Federation both monopolistic trading rights and virtual control over the planet. The Neimoidians are non-human aliens with large heads with green eyes with thin slits for pupils. They speak thickly accented English.

The original *Star Wars* echoed the dogfight films of the Second World War in its depiction of the attack on the Death Star. *Phantom Menace* is more of an echo of ground battle and occupation films. The invading force consists of a blockade followed by an invasion and occupation. The Trade Federation uses huge battle ships run by battle droids to place a blockade around the planet Naboo until the Queen agrees to a trade treaty. Nute Gunray and Rune Haako both have utterly alien countenances that remain inscrutable and devoid of emotion throughout the film. Their robes and headgear suggest both the ceremonial garb of Shinto priests and the costume of Chinese scholar-officials at the Imperial Court. In short, the Neimoidian Trade Federation is represented as technologically-driven, economically-driven group of inhuman aliens. Throughout the entire film, Gunray, Haako, and the other Neimoidians have spoken slow, broken English with slurred accents, suggesting Asian speakers, specifically Japanese. As will be explored below, Nute Gunray and Rune Haako suggest the Japanese antagonists of *The Bridge on the River Kwai*, as well as other American films about the Second World War, such as *Bataan, Back to Bataan, The Purple Heart, Three Came Home, Halls of Montezuma*, and *The Sands of Iwo Jima*, all of which feature (even if only briefly) Japanese characters who speak broken English with slurred accents.

As Jeanine Basinger observes in her survey of combat films of World War II, the war with Germany was an ideological war, whereas the war with Japan was a "race war": "When we disliked the Germans, it was the Nazis we meant. When we disliked the Japanese, it was all of them."[30] In the *Star Wars* films, there are good and bad humans—the audience is encouraged to "like" the Jedi and "dislike" the Sith and the Imperials. Yet all Neimoidians are meant to be disliked. There is not a single Neimoidian presented in a positive light in either *Phantom* or *Clones*. A survey of American citizens in the forties, just as the war began, described the Japanese as "ungodly, subhuman, beastly, sneaky, and treacherous."[31] In other words, in the wake of the Second World War, the dehumanizing of the Asian had already begun in American cinema, reinforcing a stereotype of Asian as alien, distant Other.

Eugene Franklin Wong locates the origin of use of dehumanizing stereotypes against the Japanese as enemy (as opposed to Asian stereotypes in general, which have been around since the origin of films) in 1942's *Wake Island*, which he calls "the prototypical anti–Japanese film":

> The otherwise inhuman characteristics of early Asians in America were integrated into the Asian *enemy*, the competitor, the unfair and degrading threat to white labor, the culturally peculiar **alien** who whose low standard of living paralleled their own low value on human life, and the secretive Japanese farmer who was under his coveralls a barbaric samurai, ready at a moment's notice to spearhead an invasion of white, Christian America [*bold emphasis added*].[32]

The Asian in American cinema in the forties was an "alien" whose culture placed "low value on human life." The enemy of white Americans was an Asian alien, one who threatens to invade and attack the home of the white characters, not unlike the Neimoidians invading the Naboo.

The army of the Neimoidians— droids— are presented as a faceless, mindless, horde that exists mostly to threaten the Gungun and the Naboo and be killed and destroyed by the Jedi and other "good guys." These droids have replaced the stormtroopers as the faceless, unified enemies. Basinger writes of *Bataan* (1943) and *Guadalcanal Diary* (1943), both about jungle wars against the Japanese, that "The Japanese are seen as an impersonal, faceless enemy. They are a mindless group, as opposed to our collection of strongly delineated individuals."[33] The battle droids of the Neimoidians are the same impersonal faceless enemy. Even "our" droids— R2-D2 and C3PO have personalities and distinctiveness. The battle droids of *Phantom* are the Japanese soldiers of the World War II combat films: no will of their own, they live to serve (and die for) their imperial masters, and they keep coming in identical, faceless masses until we kill every last one of them.

The use of pronouns is deliberate: the *Star Wars* films posit the Jedi and the Naboo as being "us," whereas the Neimoidians are clearly "them." Just as in the World War II combat film the American platoon, or company, or unit is clearly "us," and the Japanese clearly "them." As *Phantom* is also a prisoner of war/occupation movie as well as a war movie, I would like to explore how the first film in the second trilogy echoes the Academy Award–winning *The Bridge on the River Kwai*.

The Bridge on the River Kwai, based on the 1954 novel by Pierre Boulle, who is also the author of *Planet of the Apes*, was produced by Sam Spiegel and directed by David Lean and released in 1957. It was both a critical and popular success upon release, winning seven Academy Awards, including Best Picture, Best Director, Best Adapted Screenplay, and Best Actor (for Alec Guinness). Its theme song, the "Colonel Bogey March" is one of the more recognizable movie tunes, much like John Williams' *Star Wars Theme* or *Imperial March* and became a worldwide hit. It is the quintessential World War II movie set in the Pacific. It also featured many Japanese actors.

Sessue Hayakawa, who plays Colonel Saito (and who also was nominated for, but did not win, the Best Supporting Actor Oscar), had long been active in Hollywood. Though born in Japan, in Chiba, he attended the University of Chicago, earning a degree in political science before moving to Los Angeles and becoming a film actor. He made his screen debut in *The Hateful God* in 1913. His first talking role, in fact, was in a Fu Manchu film: *Daughter of the Dragon*. In this 1931 movie, Fu Manchu was played by Warner Oland. Hayakawa plays Ah Kee, a Chinese investigator for Scotland Yard who has a relationship with Fu Manchu's daughter while he seeks to stop Fu Manchu. Hayakawa might be seen as a model for Vincent Chang in the above-mentioned *Yankee Dawg You Die*: an educated and intelligent actor forced by Hollywood to play stereotypical characters because of his ethnicity.

The film is can be divided into two halves. The first half is a contest of wills between Colonel Nicholson and Colonel Saito. The second half is occupied by the attempt by Shears (played by William Holden) and his fellow commandoes to destroy the bridge Nicholson has built for Saito. I must state categorically that in no way does the plot of *Phantom* imitate or follow that of *The Bridge on the River Kwai*. Rather, the latter finds its elements as a prisoner of war movie and its character types reflected in the former. I use *River Kwai* solely as a comparative and do not argue that Lucas attempts in anyway to incorporate or appropriate the earlier film into his work.

At the beginning of the film, Colonel Nicholson's men have been captured by the Japanese and are escorted into a Japanese POW camp in Rangoon. When we first see Colonel Saito, he is kneeling Japanese-style in full kimono. He is presented from the very beginning as outwardly "Asian." While Nicholson's men march into camp whistling the famous "Colonel Bogey March," Saito changes into a military uniform. He informs the British prisoners that they will work to build the titular bridge across the river Kwai for the Japanese Bangkok–Rangoon railway.

Nicholson will allow his men to work, but refuses to allow his officers to engage in manual labor, as per the Geneva Convention. As Saito does not recognize the Geneva Convention, only the code of Bushido, Nicholson "considers [himself] absolved of [his] duty to obey." Saito responds that Nicholson will change his mind after he is forced to sit in an "oven," corrugated iron boxes which are left out in the midday sun until the prisoners inside die from the heat and dehydration. Saito threatens to machinegun the officers unless they work. Lastly, Saito threatens to close the prisoner's hospital and cut off food and care for the sick and injured. "Many will die and he will be responsible," Saito proclaims. Saito clearly is using a standard element in prisoner of war movies—forcing the leader to acquiesce by punishing those under him or her and then blaming the leader for their suffering.

In *Phantom*, after committing a sneak attack on Naboo, the Neimoidians take over the planet and set up prison camps. When informed that the Queen has been captured, Gunray states, "Ah. Victory." He immediately moves to confront her. The exchange between Gunray and the Queen suggests the relationship between Colonel Nicholson and Colonel Saito. Similarly, when Queen Amidala refuses to sign the treaty with the Neimoidians, Gunray tells her, "In time, the suffering of your people will persuade you to see our point of view." The "sneak attack" and threatening of torture for the Naboo in prison camps has its antecedents in the anti–Japanese movies of the World War II era and the Neimoidians are the Japanese.

Another echo occurs when Sio Bibble, the Governor of Naboo, is escorted to Nute Gunray in his walking chair, resembling a palanquin:

> NUTE: Your queen is lost, your people are starving, and you, Governor, are going to die much sooner than your people, I'm afraid.
> BIBBLE: This invasion will gain you nothing. We're a democracy. The people have decided.
> NUTE: Take him away.

Nute Gunray's dismissal of Sio Bibble and his later frustration at Amidala ("Your little insurrection is at an end, Your Highness. Time for you to sign the treaty...") echo the hatred of Saito for the British: They "are defeated but have no shame" and are "too stubborn." It also echoes Saito's repeated insistence that Nicholson will eventually have to give in to the Japanese and stop resisting the call for labor.

In *The Bridge on the River Kwai*, Nicholson does not give in to the Japanese because of a threat of violence against himself or his men. He ultimately begins working for the Japanese both to organize the battalion so as to improve morale and also as a matter of pride — he believes the British can and will engineer a much better bridge than the Japanese ("Let's teach these barbarians a lesson in western methods and efficiency that will put them to shame!"). He chooses a new location for the bridge, and sets about organizing the design and labor of the building. His pride in the bridge is so great that he has a wooden plaque created to hang on the bridge indicating who built it.

It is at this point that the American prisoner, Shears, who has escaped from the camp, returns to it as a member of a British commando team. Shears, who has disguised himself as an officer to avoid manual labor in the camp, is revealed to be an enlisted man and more or less blackmailed to lead the British back to the camp. A decision has been made to destroy the bridge. The call for help in this film is echoed in *Phantom* when Sio Bibble secretly contacts Amidala, telling her that "The death toll is catastrophic. We must bow to their wishes. You must contact me." Amidala, after pleading her case in the Senate, returns to Naboo with the Jedi in order to defeat the invasion.

Furthermore, in *River Kwai*, the audience learns Saito's motivation: if the bridge is not completed he will be forced to commit ritual suicide. This threat motivates him to threaten Nicholson further: "If I am to die, others will die before me." Likewise, in *Phantom*, Gunray must have the treaty signed or Darth Sidious will have him executed. Gunray speaks and acts similarly to Saito, and their behaviors are remarkably similar.

Like the Jedi and Jar Jar, Shears and the commandoes must travel through a swamp and jungle to get to their objective. Both films feature small teams attacking the occupying force and sacrificing themselves in order to destroy the enemy's ability to occupy. Qui-Gon Jinn is killed by Darth Maul while fighting on behalf of the Naboo. Maul is then killed by Obi-Wan Kenobi. Both Nicholson and Shears are killed by the Japanese, and Lt. Joyce, the young British commando played by Geoffrey Horne, kills Saito. With his last act, Shears blows up the bridge, as Anakin Skywalker blows up the Neimoidian flagship. In each film, the explosion signals the end of the both the villain's seeming victory and the film itself.

Colonel Nicholson and Amidala and the Jedi are ultimately dupes. Nicholson builds the bridge for the Japanese. Amidala and the Jedi, by fighting with the Neimoidians and Separatists, are ultimately serving the purposes of Darth Sidious, allowing for the creation of the Empire. When Darth Tyranus returns to Coruscant, he tells Sidious, "Good news, my master. War has begun." The whole purpose of the invasion of Naboo and the creation of the Separatists is to generate a reason for Sidious to become Emperor and rule the galaxy in the name of the Dark Side. The whole purpose behind building a bridge over the River Kwai is to allow the Japanese to move troops and supply to fight the allies. At the end of *Bridge on the River Kwai* Nicholson realizes that the bridge he has taken such pride in will really serve his enemy, helping kill his fellow countrymen.

The Neimoidians and Nute Gunray return in *Clones*. They have joined the Separatists in attempting to leave the Republic. Gunray is still referred to by his title of "Viceroy," though clearly he is not only not the Viceroy of Naboo anymore, he is almost living in exile on Geonosis. Yet he remains the alien (and Asian) villain. He delights, in the same manner as Ming the Merciless or Fu Manchu, the impending demise of his nemesis, Amidala, in the arena on Geonosis. He is shown to take sadistic pleasure in her being injured by an animal in the arena, laughing with delight and pumping his arms as she screams in pain. He takes no such interest in Anakin or Obi-Wan, who are also fighting in the arena. When Amidala frees herself and the Jedi defeat the animal attacking her, Nute Gunray's response is astonished denial, which the audience is supposed to find amusing: "This is not the way it is supposed to go." He then demands Jango Fett to "kill her." Again, note that his sole interest is in defeating the person whom he perceives as having defeated him.

In *Clones*, Nute Gunray continues to play the role assigned to him: sadistic, powerful, yet cowardly enemy. He is a stand-in for any one of a number of Japanese, Chinese, or Vietnamese torturers who want to hurt their American prisoners, but ultimately prove cowardly when faced on equal terms. Nute Gunray follows in the footsteps of Asian characters in films such as *Rambo, Rambo III, Lethal Weapon,* and *Missing in Action.* Asians in these movies get sadistic pleasure out of the torture of their American enemies, but are ultimately defeated and their cowardice is revealed as they flee from the prisoner's rescuers (who are oftentimes the former prisoners themselves, come back for revenge). Defeated at Naboo and again at Geonosis, the Neimoidians flee once more, allowing their droids to fight while they escape.

The similarity between films argued above is not to suggest that Lucas is appropriating *The Bridge on the River Kwai*, but rather he is presenting a very similar situation (the "Other" villain must break the will of his captives in order to achieve a desired goal in order to avoid punishment) and has an alien character in Asian-inspired costuming speaking in an accent which sounds Oriental to American ears. While the Europeans play the Asian-derived "good" characters, the villains are ethnic Asians in alien faces. All that remains in *Phantom* is for Nute Gunray to ask the Naboo if they are surprised that he speaks such good galactic standard and announce that he studied at Yale, U.C.L.A., Harvard, or in Hawaii before returning to fight for the Emperor. Lucas has returned to good old-fashioned orientalism. The Neimoidians represent a kind of exclusionary stereotype that Others Asians.

What Is Watto? People of the Middle East in *Star Wars*

The Middle East is an exotic and sinister place in American cinema. In the *Star Wars* films, Tunisia in North Africa was the location that served as the model of Tatooine — a desert nation with a predominantly Muslim culture. Reversing the location with what it represents, however, one might argue that Tatooine in many ways is also a stand-in for the Middle East and North Africa. In popular culture, North Africa and the Middle East become conflated. There are 22 Arab states. Only 12 percent of the world's Muslims are Arab, but Hollywood (and the media and popular American imagination) conflate the two, and also conflate all Muslim nations into "The Middle East."

Laurence Michalak argues that since the 1920s, "Hollywood's Middle East has become a more sinister place," one full of murder, slavery, theft, abduction, and corruption.[34] Arabs, write Allen L. Woll and Randall M. Miller, "have appeared as lustful, criminal, and exotic villains or foils to Western heroes or heroines."[35] Tatooine shows up in four of the five films to date. It is always portrayed negatively, as a sinister and dangerous place filled with lustful, exotic, and criminal villains. In *New Hope*, Obi-Wan remarks that Mos Eisley is a "wretched hive of scum and villainy." In *Phantom*, Captain Panaka objects to stopping at Tatooine. While Qui-Gon appreciates that it is "remote" and "far beyond the reach of the Trade Federation," Panaka calls the planet "dangerous," worried that the Hutts who control the planet are "an alliance of gangs."

The variety of desert-dwellers on Tatooine are echoes of Hollywood stereotypes of Middle Easterners, Muslims, and Arabs.[36] Jabba, Watto, Jawas, and Tusken Raiders, also called "Sand People," are among the Tatooine characters that echo earlier Hollywood portraits of Arabs, Jews, and other Middle Easterners and North Africans. Tusken Raiders, for example, can be read as Arab nomads. In *The Star Wars Encyclopedia*, Stephen J. Sansweet defines them as: "A nomadic and often violent species, the Sand People of the planet Tatooine are as fierce and discomforting as their harsh environment."[37] Another "official" publication, *Star Wars Episode I: The Visual Dictionary*, states that humans on Tatooine are "settlers," but that Sand People and Jawas are indigenous.[38]

Tusken Raiders are nomads who ride Banthas, much like oversized camels. Their bodies are completely wrapped in cloth, as are their faces. We never see what they look like as their faces are never uncovered. They wield a particular weapon, the gaderffi stick, as well as laser rifles. They are exotic; they are dangerous. They represent a threat to the human colonists, attacking those who wander out by themselves in the wastes, as Luke does in *New Hope*, shooting at the podracers in *Phantom Menace*, and kidnap Shmi Skywalker in *Clones*. They exist in the films solely to be dangerous adversaries for Luke and Anakin. They echo the savage nomadic Arabs of the Indiana Jones movies, of *The Mummy* and *The Mummy Returns*, and of *Hidalgo*.

The Jawas on the other hand are desert traders. They are scavengers and merchants. They sell scavenged droids to the settlers of Tatooine. They are not above selling defective merchandise, as we see in *A New Hope*, when the first R2 unit sold to Owen Lars has a "bad motivator." They also are not above selling stolen merchandise — they capture C3PO and R2-D2. Later, after witnessing part of Leia's message, Luke thinks "these droids may be stolen." "Jawas can offer real bargains in the junk that they repair, but are notoriously tricky and will swindle the unwary buyer," writes David West Reynolds in *Star Wars: The Visual Dictionary*. "When a Jawa sandcrawler arrives to sell and trade at the edge of a town, the droids hide, and people watch their speeders extra closely. Things tend to disappear when Jawas are around," he concludes.[39] Although their names seemingly echo "Jews," and they can be seen as embodying some of the stereotypes associated with Jewish people, the Jawas might more readily be seen to echo the cinema's Arab traders and merchants. The Tusken Raiders and Jawas serve as the lustful Arab and the greedy Arab of movie serials and early films which are then more obviously echoed by Jabba and Watto.

Jabba is described in the screenplay of *Jedi* as "a repulsively fat, sultanlike monster."[40] It is this term "sultanlike" that indicates the echo which *Jedi* is aiming for and indicates that Jabba should be read as part of the history of cinematic Arabs. If further proof were needed, in a recent documentary a technician for *Jedi* shared that one inspiration for Jabba was Sydney Greenstreet in *Casablanca*. At one point in the design process, a fez, like that worn by Greenstreet to indicate his "Moroccanness," was considered for Jabba.

As Laurence Michalak argues in *Cruel and Unusual: Negative Images of Arabs in American Popular Culture*, American movies have a history of presenting Arabs as violent and lusty, particularly obsessed with possessing white women.[41] One might argue that this is certainly reflected in the kidnapping of Shmi Skywalker in *Clones* by Tusken Raiders who do not kill her but keep her alive long enough for Anakin to arrive, talk with her, witness her death, and take revenge by killing all the Sand People in their village, including the females and children. Though this is meant to signal to the audience the dark potential within Anakin towards violence, anger, and the Dark Side, clearly the Tusken Raiders are meant to be understood as keeping her prisoner for nefarious, if not blatantly sexual purposes. Anakin is seeking revenge for his mother being turned into a sex slave of the Sand People, having already been a slave for Watto. Anakin does not necessarily object to the slavery, it is the sexual slavery of the Tusken Raiders that is objectionable. They represent a sexual threat. They like violence and they kidnap white women.

Much more blatant, however, is Jabba the Hutt as a violent and sexually dangerous Arab. Jabba is modeled after the cinematic sultans and sheiks of the twenties and thirties. In *The Sheik* (1921), Rudolph Valentino plays "the lusty abductor of white women," a role he reprised in *Son of the Sheik* (1926).[42] In these, as in other movies that feature Arabs as the villain, the main villain is a powerful local ruler of a desert community, surrounded by guards and sycophants, who abducts a white woman to serve as his slave and, most likely, sex slave. She is forced to dress provocatively, remains under guard if not chained up, and must eventually be rescued by the (white) hero, who as often as not, will kill the villain for daring to abduct the white woman.

For example, in *A Café in Cairo* (1924), Kali, a desert bandit, kills a British couple and only spares their beautiful daughter on the condition that when she is old enough she will marry him. Barry Braxton, who plays the hero, is captured and bound by Kali, who throws him into a crocodile-filled Nile. But Braxton escapes, defeats and kills Kali, and rescues the daughter who falls in love with him.

This narrative is echoed not once but twice within *Jedi*. Jabba is presented from the very beginning as a lusty, decadent sultan-like creature. He reclines on a throne, eats decadent food, and is surrounded by guards and sycophants. The screenplay for the special edition describes the scene:

> The court of Jabba the Hutt is in the midst of a drunken, raucous party. Sloppy, smelly monsters cheer and make rude noises as Oola and a large six-breasted female dancer perform in front of Jabba's throne. Jabba's alien band plays a wildly rhythmic tune on reeds, drums, and other exotic instruments. The Hutt rocks and swings in time with the music and toys with Oola's leash.[43]

Why is it necessary to specify that the monsters are "smelly" in a cinematic screenplay, unless the film will be presented in smell-o-vision? The scene of depravity and iniquity reveals Jabba to be a hedonist in the tradition of cinematic sheiks. When Oola resists Jabba's advances, he feeds her to the Rancor.

In the next scene, Leia, sent to rescue Han at Jabba's desert palace, is instead captured and put into a slave girl outfit that accentuates her sexuality. Her position indicates her subjugation to Jabba. The screenplay reads, "Leia is now dressed in the skimpy costume of a dancing girl; a chain runs from a manacle/necklace at her throat to her new master, Jabba the Hutt."[44] Until this point in the series, Leia's sexuality has been deemphasized. In *A New Hope*, she wears a floor-length white dress which covered her entirely, leaving only face and hands visible. In *Empire* she wears cold weather clothing on Hoth, again leaving her completely covered except for face and hands. On Bespin she changes into another outfit, but again, everything is covered and her sexuality is deemphasized by the costume. It is not until she is Jabba's prisoner that Leia is dressed provocatively. The implied threat is that Leia is now Jabba's sex slave.

Luke arrives to rescue the entire company, and, like Braxton in *A Café in Cairo*, is thrown to wild animals: he is dropped in the Rancor pit, the same one in which the audience has just seen Oola perish. He manages to defeat the Rancor, angering Jabba all the further, who decides that Han, Luke, and Chewbacca will be taken to "The Dune Sea," to be thrown into the "Pit of Carkoon," which is "the nesting place of the all-powerful Sarlacc." Echoing Braxton, bound and thrown in the Nile to be eaten by crocodiles, Luke is to be bound and thrown into a pit where he will be eaten by the Sarlacc. Like Braxton, however, Luke escapes this fate and frees his friends. Leia, using the very chain that ties her to Jabba, chokes him to death. He is justly killed by his own lusty appetites, the film seems to indicate. His barge and all who sail on it are destroyed when Luke rescues Leia and fires the cannon at the deck as he swings, with her in his arms, to the waiting rescue ship.

The entire opening sequence of *Jedi* is an echo of desert adventure films in which the white woman must be rescued from the lusty and violent Arab ruler. Every trope is present and for the first time in the saga Leia is sexualized, elevating the threat. Furthermore, the film denies the larger issues of ethics. The film leaves unquestioned the assumption of the rightness of the rescue of Han and the deaths (murders?) of Jabba and those on the sail barge.

Han owed Jabba money — quite a bit, as established in *New Hope*. Jabba has hired several bounty hunters to bring Solo to him. These bounty hunters are doubly employed when the Empire hires them to find the rebels as well, and Boba Fett locates them on Bespin. He thus gets to bring Jabba Han frozen in carbonite and claim the reward. Jabba's death is seemingly warranted in the film because audiences like Han Solo, because he is one of the good guys, because Jabba is a criminal, because Jabba hires bounty hunters. Yet none of this changes the fact that Han, too, is a criminal, Han did, in fact, do the things for which Jabba demands payment and Han has failed to live up to his contractual obligations. At the end of *New Hope*, Han is taking his "reward" to pay off Jabba. One might ask, why didn't he? Why did Han not simply return to Tatooine after the Battle of Yavin and pay Jabba? No bounty hunters would have been employed. Boba Fett would not have followed the rebels to Bespin. There would have been no need to rescue Han, nor would there have been a need to kill hundreds in order to rescue one.

What crime have those on the sail barge committed that earns them the death sentence, other than the guilt by association by being with Jabba and that they are different — aliens? By what authority does Luke orchestrate this complex rescue, which will most likely end in the deaths of many people? Jabba is a racially different, inferior enemy, surrounded by other racially different, inferior beings, which is what makes it acceptable to kill them all and enjoy the spectacle of it.

Given the above argument about Jabba, one might ask how Watto, a fairly asexual being, echoes cinematic Arabs. As Allen L. Woll and Randall M. Miller point out, "Modern movie Arabs seemed more interested in the Westerner's money than their women."[45] Jabba echoes the cinematic Arab of the serials and old Hollywood; Watto echoes the modern Arab — the money-obsessed trader. As he tells Qui-Gon, "I'm a Toydarian. Mind tricks don'ta work on me — only money. No money, no parts!" And, in fact, it is his love of money and his desire to get more that allows the Jedi to get the engine parts they need and free Anakin. Watto fronts the fee for the race, but bets against Anakin in favor of Sebulba. Qui-Gon wagers for the boy's freedom if he wins. Watto is furious when Anakin wins, as Watto has lost money, the parts, and his slave. Watto is less interested in white women (though his only other slave than Anakin that we know of is Shmi Skywalker, so his slaves are women and children) than in money.

Many reviewers responded to *Phantom Menace* by critiquing Watto, among other characters, as another racial stereotype. Andy Seiler in *USA Today* sees him as "vaguely Semitic," as he is a "hook-nosed, money grubbing slaveholder."[46] Watto is thus either Jewish or Arabic. Gilbert Adair in London's *The Independent* sees the character as having "come straight from the Nazi's anti–Semitic stock barrel."[47] John Leo, consulting law professor Patricia Williams, argues that "Watto looks strikingly like an anti–Jewish caricature published in Vienna at the turn of the century — round-bellied, big-nosed with spindly arms, wings sprouting from his shoulders and a scroll that says, 'Anything for money.'"[48] Watto, Leo concludes, "is a conventional, crooked Middle Eastern merchant. This is a generic anti–Semitic image, Jewish if you want him to be, Arab if you don't."[49] Leo's summation argues the point: Watto can be seen as either an anti–Semitic caricature of a Jew or an anti–Semitic caricature of an Arab. The audience members' point of view can shape which stereotype one chooses to see. But either way, a Middle Eastern stereotype is being embraced and presented as an alien.

The same holds true for Jawas, as noted above — who might be read as Arab merchants who cheat the Westerners and steal their goods, or who might be read as Jewish merchants who live in clans and try to sell defective, scavenged goods to the human settlers. Either way, Jawas are constructed as Middle Eastern stereotypes. In the four films in which Tatooine is presented, aliens echoing the stereotypes of Arabs and other Middle Eastern peoples from early Western cinema are featured. Tatooine is the Egypt of Indiana Jones, the *Mummy* films, and the Middle East and North Africa of countless movie serials. As with Asians, Middle Easterners are presented in the saga through constructed aliens, and the images are always negative. There are no positive Hutts, Toyndarians, or Tusken Raiders in the *Star Wars* movies.

"Primitives" in a Technological Universe

It is safe to say that the two trilogies are technocentric — not only is the universe of *Star Wars* centered around advanced technology — space ships, laser weapons, the Death Star, faster than light travel — even the traditional weapons of the Jedi, lightsabers, are technologically based — but also the films themselves are known for their technological advances in filmmaking. A new *Star Wars* film usually means state-of-the art special effects, so much so that one reviewer called *Clones*, "a demo reel heralding the latest advances in digital filmmaking."[50] Yet, conversely, primitives are also present, and even embraced, celebrated and privileged in film after film: Wookiees, Ewoks, Gungun, and the insects of Geonosis. And as with Asians and Middle Easterners, the primitive races of *Star Wars* often have real world or reel world echoes. Lucas, quoted in Pye and Myles, states that *A New Hope* needed "strange savages and bizarre things in an exotic land," as that is the basis for myth.[51]

In *Jedi*, the Ewoks are presented as a particularly primitive race. In the documentary *From Star Wars to Jedi: The Making of a Saga* the Ewoks are repeatedly called "primitive," their society is "primitive," whereas Chewbacca hails from a "relatively sophisticated" society. They carry stone age spears: wood topped with flint tied with animal hide thongs. They have a tribal social structure ruled by a chief (Chirpa) and a shaman (Logray, called a "Medicine Man" in the screenplay).[52] They decorate themselves with jewelry made from the teeth and claws of animals and wear headdresses made of animal skulls and feathers. They eat people — or at least threaten to have Han Solo as "the main course at a banquet in [Threepio's] honor," believing the droid (arguably the lowest of the Rebels) to be a god. They play drums at all important tribal functions and storytelling is the chief form of entertainment. The drum music which underscores the final scene in the Special Edition of *Jedi* could be taken from any one of a number of jungle movies set in Africa from the thirties to the fifties. Lastly, as in many narratives of the Great White Hunter who knows the jungle better than the indigenous, the heroes (Luke, Leia, Chewbacca, Han, R2-D2 and C-3PO) are accepted as members of the tribe because of their bravery.

In his analysis of the films as myth, Steven A. Galipeau calls the Ewoks meeting of C3PO "a tribe in the midst of new religious experience."[53] Galipeau further cites his eight-year-old son, who sees Ewoks as "animal Indians," meaning Native Americans.[54] In other words, the primitive peoples of Endor are seen, even by an eight-year-old child, as Native Americans. The real world equivalencies are comprehended by an eight year old.

Cinematic Native Americans have already been referenced in the first film, when Luke returns home to find the buildings burning and the bodies of Uncle Owen and Aunt Beru lie on the ground before them. The scene is a reconstruction of John Ford's *The Searchers* in which the hero returns home to find his parents massacred by Native Americans. Yet the killers are not primitives, but members of the Imperial Army.

The films tend to take a Victorian or Romantic view of the primitive species—they live untouched in a more natural environment. Ewoks are the embodiment of Montaigne's "noble savage." Hal Foster writes in *Recodings* that the primitive is both "a spectacle of savagery" and "a state of grace."[55] The Ewoks are both savage and existing in a state of grace. They accept the Rebels and fight the Empire alongside them. They would eat Han Solo to honor C3PO, but they also offer Leia shelter. They know no evil, no sense of politics, or conventional morality. They are presented as simple and happy.

As Marianna Torgovnick writes of primitives in her fine study *Gone Primitive*:

> They exist for us in a cherished series of dichotomies: by turns gentle, in tune with nature, paradisal, ideal — or violent, in need of control; what we should emulate or, alternately, what we should fear; noble savages or cannibals.[56]

The Ewoks are gentle and in tune with nature. Yet they are also savage and although not cannibalistic in the sense that we never see them eating other Ewoks, they are cannibalistic in the sense that they will eat humans, which is the true horror of cannibalism to the Western mind.

The Ewoks are also the reason why the Rebel force is able to defeat the Empire. Through primitive weapons—vines, logs, use of the landscape, and rocks, the technological resources of the Empire are defeated. It is almost because of their natural purity that the Ewoks are allowed to defeat the technologically advanced Empire. The Empire does not expect a guerrilla war waged with primitive booby traps. A blaster is no good against logs rolling down a hill.

The sinister side of the encounter between the technological and the "primitive" is missing from *Jedi*, but real world models suggest a not so happy future for the Ewoks. The rebels, after all, employ the same technology as the Empire. The rebels embrace the same basic culture as the Empire. The Rebels are now a presence on Endor. As Kenneth M. Cameron observes of *The African Queen*, the unquestioned assumption is that the English and the Germans have a right to fight over ownership of an African lake.[57] Likewise, the unquestioned assumption in *Jedi* is that the Rebels are right to fight on Endor.

As during the Cold War, when the United States and the Soviet Union would fight wars through proxies in third world countries in Africa, Asia, and Latin America, the Rebellion and the Empire fight their battles in places where the indigenous are not involved in the battle. The Ewoks are brought into the fight against the Empire when the Empire has not attempted to conquer or engage them at all. One might argue that the Rebellion uses the Ewoks to fight for them. Tatooine, Bespin, Yavin — none of them have an Imperial presence until the Rebellion brings it there. The primitive places are made the battleground over which the battles are fought.

In a related argument, not all critics see Ewoks as Native Americans. Tom Carson argues that the Ewoks are "the oddest cinematic tribute the Viet Cong are ever likely to get."[58] Richard Keller Simon argues that both *Empire* and *Jedi* are full of "obvious" references to Vietnam, especially *Jedi*, "where primitive Jungle people defend their homeland against the attack of an advanced technological empire."[59]

Before the Ewoks, Chewbacca was the dominant primitive in the *Star Wars* universe. Lucas states that "Chewbacca [is] nonhuman and non-white. I realize it seems rather obscure and abstract, but it was intended to be a statement."[60] As this chapter has argued, it is neither obscure nor abstract that aliens are read as non-whites (it is interesting that Lucas puts "nonhuman" before "non-white"). This statement, however, does reflect an understanding on Lucas's part that aliens are read as substitutions for non-Westerners. Lucas also never clarifies what statement was intended, but Chewbacca is a sidekick, not a Self. Only Han (and presumably other Wookiees) can understand him. He is devoted to Han. He repairs the ship and serves as co-pilot. Whereas everyone else in the Rebellion is given a rank ("Captain Solo," "General Calrissian," "Senator Leia," even "Admiral

Akbar"), Chewbacca remains rankless— it is never "Captain Chewbacca," "General Chewbacca" or even "Private Chewbacca."

Chewbacca's savagery is also used to comic effect in *A New Hope.* "It's not wise to upset a Wookiee," Solo tells the droids. "Droids don't pull people's arms out of their sockets when they lose. Wookiees are known to do that," he warns as Chewbacca smugly places his arms behind his head. Later, in the Death Star, Luke and Han disguise themselves as stormtroopers and Chewbacca pretends to be their prisoner. They are met by the prison officer who asks, "Where are you taking this ... thing.?" Chewbacca then breaks free and begins smashing the guards. Lastly, after being freed, but disappointed in the lack of organization in her rescue, Leia asks, "Will somebody get this big, walking carpet out of my way?" If Chewbacca is meant to be "non-white" as Lucas suggests, how should the audience read the fact that he is dismissed as a violent savage, a "thing," a "big walking carpet," and that he is Han's sidekick. At the end of the film, Luke and Han are given medals. Chewbacca, also in the Millennium Falcon and risking his life as much as Han, does not get a medal — he is simply allowed to roar at the crowd after walking in behind Luke and Han.

Like the Ewoks, Chewbacca is perceived by some critics as being representative of Native Americans, starting with Lucas. Lucas, quoted in Paul Scanlon, states that "The Wookiees are more like the Indians, more like noble savages."[61] Don Rubey sees echoes of the Native American characters in *Last of the Mohicans* and Jim in *The Adventures of Huckleberry Finn* in Chewbacca: he is the Other who accompanies the central white male who may walk between worlds.[62] He is the "non-competitive, non-sexual" sidekick, utterly devoted to the hero.[63]

Chewbacca is seen as having a special bond with Ewoks, perhaps because they are both hairy and "primitive." He is presented as the "older brother" of the Ewoks. The films collectively present primitive peoples relating to one another. Yet Chewbacca is a resident of the technological world as well — he flies the Millennium Falcon, he uses a blaster (albeit a specific one called a "bowcaster," which resembles a crossbow, further distinguishing him from the humans), he repairs C3PO in Empire. Chewbacca is the "civilized savage," the indigenous person who has embraced the technology and the culture of "civilization."

In *Sith*, the audience is finally given a glimpse of Kashyyyk, the Wookiee homeworld. They wear no clothes, live in tree houses, braid things into their hair and attack an approaching droid army straight on. Yet they have blaster technology, aircraft and space ships, and numerous other examples of technology. In *Star Wars: Revenge of the Sith: The Visual Dictionary*, it is revealed that the technology was not developed by the Wookiees, but instead gleaned through trade with other worlds: "Wookiees fuse nature with offworld technology."[64] In other words, Wookiees are very much like Native Americans, who did not develop firearm technology, but fully integrated it within their own cultures upon encounters with the Europeans. Wookiees are presented as different than Ewoks in that they are technologically savvy and involved in inter-species trade, communication and interaction. Wookiees are involved in the Republic — they are clearly represented in the Senate in *Phantom* and Yoda remarks that he has positive relationships with the Wookiees for many years in *Sith*. In being seen in this manner, Chewbacca is the Tonto of *Star Wars*.

The danger, of course, in positing Chewbacca and Ewoks as "noble savages" and "primitive rebels" as Patrick Brantlinger, after Marianna Torgovnick, argues is that "even in positive conceptions of 'primitive societies,' imperialist and racist forms of othering that entail ideological temptations exist."[65] Celebrations of "primitive people" often express a "sentimental racism," for example the presentation of Native Americans in the writings of James Fenimore Cooper.[66] Ewok culture and religion are things to be manipulated — C3PO demonstrates his "magic" to get the Ewoks to release Luke and the others — in order to achieve the ends of the Rebellion. The Ewoks themselves are slightly aggressive teddy bears using stone age weapons — they are cute. The audience is meant to look down upon them, enjoying their appearance and behavior, but never seeing them as equals or worthy contributors to the Rebellion. If an eight year old can read Native Americans in the Ewoks, and Ewoks are not equal to the human members of the Rebellion, then the conclusion of the syllogism has more than sentimental racism directed at the indigenous peoples of North America.

Masses of Others

The bad guys in the *Star Wars* movies are depersonalized: stormtroopers, battle droids, and the inhabitants of Geonosis are all faceless and unindividuated. One might compare the masses of enemies that the Rebels must fight and defeat, perhaps even slaughter, as echoes of the alien Other in other imperial films, such as the Zulu in *Zulu* or the Native Americans in John Wayne films.

As a result, the battles are cost free. Despite millions being killed statistically (with the destruction of Alderaan and two Death Stars) and hundreds of on-screen deaths, the only "real" battle deaths in the entire saga are Obi-Wan, Qui-Gon Jinn, Grand Moff Tarkin, Darth Maul, and the X-Wing pilots in *A New Hope* whom we come to know only briefly: Biggs and Porkins are the only named ones, the others are all merely numbers: Red Ten, Red Seven, Red Eleven, and so forth. No other major characters are killed. The deaths of Obi-Wan and Qui-Gon are major tragedies. The vast majority of deaths in the saga are of stormtroopers and battle droids. We are not meant to feel any emotion at their deaths. Non-humans can die in numbers without regret. Non-whites can die in numbers without regret.

Numerous reviewers of *Phantom Menace* take issue with the fact that the film reduces war and its cost in lives to a video game. Droids are blown up left and right. An eight-year-old boy blows up an entire fleet of alien ships and the only death that the audience is really made to feel is Qui-Gon Jinn's. There is thus no cost to battle — when faceless, undifferentiated beings are killed, there is no real cause for regret. As Leif Furhammar and Folke Isakson write,

> The cliché for Asiatics is based on the treatment of the Japanese in World War II films or the Chinese and the Koreans during the Korean War. They are quite anonymous and therefore cannot arouse empathy. We rarely see their faces.[67]

The stormtroopers and battle droids are Native Americans in Westerns, African warriors in films such as *Zulu* and *Zulu Dawn*, and Asians in war movies. Their deaths mean nothing. In fact, they exist to be slaughtered by the heroes. Their purpose is to be cannon fodder to prove the heroism of the human characters, much as the Zulu of *Zulu* are all undifferentiated — they exist to be slaughtered by the British.

Asians, Aliens and Stereotypes

Aliens in the *Star Wars* films are both literally and figuratively constructs. They are made using latex, foam, hair, and other appliances in order to make the human into the alien — in order to make the familiar into the unfamiliar. They are made in a computer using CGI — "computer generated images" — pixels are digitally generated and the eye perceives them as a creature or ship or monster. They are made up by George Lucas and his collaborators in make up, digital and special effects, and production design. Aliens are constructions in the world of *Star Wars*.

Aliens are constructed in the real world as well. James Moy reports the constructed image of the Chinese in mid to late nineteenth century California — the Chinese are an "invasion" of "deceitful" and "dangerous" foreigners.[68] The Chinese would be represented in newspaper illustrations and political cartoons as reptilian, with bat wings, fangs, pointed ears, scaly tails, and claws. They would literally be represented as monstrous or alien.

The Media Action Network for Asian Americans has published an open "Memo to Hollywood" on its website.[69] The organization notes that for much of the twentieth century, the image of the Asian has been defined world wide by American popular culture. "Too often," the memo reads, "an Asian face or accent is presented as a shorthand symbol for anything antithetical to American or Western culture." This analysis can also be applied to the Neimoidians in *Phantom Menace* and *Clones*. Interestingly, many of the items in MANAA's list of restrictive portrayals of Asians and Asian Americans in the media can be applied into how the Neimoidians are presented in these films as well.

By presenting Asians as aliens, *Phantom Menace* literalizes the image of "Asian Americans as foreigners who cannot be assimilated." Neimoidians are not only racially and culturally distinctive from the other characters, their differences with even other alien beings are highlighted. Wookiees, Ewoks, and even Gungun are shown as working well with humans and adapting to their ways, although that is attributable to their "primitive" nature, which makes them pliable. Even as part of the Senate, however, Neimoidians are different, distant, and sinister.

Two more "restrictive portrayals" follow off of this idea: "Asian cultures [are] inherently predatory" and Asians are inherently sinister. The Neimoidians use the debate over taxation of trade routes to justify an invasion, occupation and colonization of the Naboo. Meanwhile the Viceroy will force the Queen to sign a treaty to legitimize the occupation. Lott Dod, the Trade Federation senator, uses his position to head off a censure from the Senate by demanding that an investigation be carried out to determine the accuracy of Amidala's accusation that the Trade Federation has invaded Naboo. He does not actually lie — he does not deny the invasion, he simply objects to Amidala's remarks, states that "there is no proof," and that a commission should be formed "to ascertain the truth." In fact, he knows the truth, but uses the system to gain advantage over the (white) Naboo. After their defeat, the Neimoidians join up with the Separatists in the building up of a droid army to fight the Republic and allow for free market, predatory capitalism. There is no problem with having Asian villains, the danger is that the villainy is attributed to their ethnicity and that there is no corresponding Asian heroes.

Even seemingly positive attributions can ultimately prove restrictive. As argued in the third chapter, the Jedi are a construct rooted in Asian culture. MANAA calls attention to the fact that "Asianness [often serves] as an 'explanation' for the magical or supernatural." Especially in genre films such as *Big Trouble in Little China, The Shadow,* or the Fu Manchu movies, the fact that something is Asian is offered as the reason why it is supernatural or has special powers. "Ancient Chinese secret" is a line from an old detergent commercial that can also be used to explain how Asians are able to do seemingly impossible things. "Granted," allows MANAA, "Asian magic can sometimes be portrayed positively in fiction," and certainly that would include the Jedi. Nevertheless it does not change the fact that the assertion of magic powers inherent in "Asianness" continues to produce a misleading, mystifying, and inaccurate stereotype.

Furthermore, as argued in the third chapter, Yoda, Obi-Wan Kenobi, and Qui-Gon Jinn are Asian names for Asian-derived characters. As argued in this chapter, the greater problem is that these characters are played by Western actors. As MANAA contends, "Asians [are] relegated to supporting roles in projects with Asian or Asian-American contexts." In films such as *The Last Samurai, Big Trouble in Little China, Shogun, The Killing Fields* and *Seven Years in Tibet,* the setting is Asian, the subject matter is Asian, but the main character is a Western male. The white protagonist serves as the bridge through which the Asian narrative is related. In the case of the *Star Wars* films, the Asians are actually played by Western actors. As noted above, Qui-Gon Jinn, Obi-Wan Kenobi, and Yoda are played by Western actors. The *Star Wars* saga owes a great deal to Asian culture, and has repaid it by removing the Asian heroes, replacing them with Western actors, and given the alien villains Asian aspects.

Numerous reviews of *The Phantom Menace* critiqued the film for its seemingly blatant use of what Brent Staples in an editorial in *The New York Times* called "Hollywood's most offensive racial stereotypes."[70] Acknowledging that science fiction authors and producers had embraced multicultural, multiethnic works decades before the rest of America, Staples criticizes Lucasfilm for the construction of the Neimoidians and Jar Jar Binks, dismissing the argument that the saga is only "a fantasy" by pointing out "Lucasfilm built this fantasy plank by plank and nail by nail." Gilbert Adair calls Lucas "the real menace" in a review in the (London) *Independent,* citing the echo of Willie Best in Jar Jar and noting that the charge of racism "can't be shrugged off as political correctness run rampant."[71]

Even conservative columnist John Leo, writing in the conservative paper the *Washington Times,* agrees that the characters in *Phantom Menace* are "awful" racial stereotypes. "A stereotype on this level is more than an insult," he correctly notes. "It is a teaching instrument and a powerful, nonverbal argument saying that racial equality is a hopeless cause."[72] Leo is correct when he asserts, as has been argued in this study, that the characters of the *Star Wars* saga are part of a larger cultural education.

As a result of this across-the-board criticism, there was also a back-lash in the press against the accusations of racism or stereotypical portraits in *Phantom Menace*. Three writers in the *Washington Times*, Christian Toto, Clarence Page, and Paul Craig Roberts, all individually came to Lucas's defense in their respective columns.[73] Roberts blamed "liberals," whom he claims "writhe under the black and white clarity of the *Star Wars* struggle between good and evil," who replace stereotyping minorities with "vicious stereotyping of the White Male," and who "hate" Mr. Lucas because he made "big unaccountable government, which liberals worship" as the evil enemy.[74] Page, an African-American commentator, claims that "the racism charge is a bum rap against Mr. Lucas," and that he "wasn't offended as an African-American."[75] That Page was not offended does not make the film's constructions of Jar Jar any less racist, nor the lack of actors of color any less apparent. Roberts borders on the ludicrous, as he attempts to dismiss criticism of the film as knee-jerk liberal response to a conservative film. John Leo, certainly no liberal, sees the very things that Roberts claims only liberals will see.

Interestingly, one of the strongest arguments that minorities have been either absent or stereotyped in the films is the fact that in response to all the media criticism of the portrayal of ethnicity in *Phantom Menace*, it was reported in *Variety* and several other industry sources that the casting directors of *Clones* were looking for Native American, Indian, Hispanic, and Asian actors.[76] That same week, the Canadian press reported that Native American, Hispanic, and Asian actors were being sought to play specific new characters. Native American actors Graham Greene and Tantoo Cardinal were singled out as "buzzing around Hollywood" for roles in the next film.[77] Nevertheless, neither actor ultimately appeared in *Clones*. Yet the point remains that the very fact that Lucasfilm promised to create a more ethnically diverse cast is an indirect admission of a lack of previous diversity. Similarly, an expressed desire for more sensitivity would seem to be an admission of a lack of same.

These newspaper reports confirm that Lucasfilm was concerned with the appearance of stereotyping or inadvertent racism in the films. Interestingly, in the *Variety* article, Jonathan Bing states at the time it is "not clear whether the next episode will sidestep ethnic stereotypes or merely add new ones."[78] In the end, however, the answer was a bit less than the earlier casting publicity seemed to indicate. A few more non–Western actors were seen in *Clones*. The actors playing Jango and Boba Fett (Temuera Morrison and Daniel Logan, respectively) were both from New Zealand and part Maori. The new queen of Naboo was Indian (played by Ayesha Dharker, an actress from Bombay). There is also a single Asian woman among the Jedi at the arena on Geonosis who is seen in the background as part of the fight in *Clones*. Yet, as argued in previous chapters and above, the ethnic stereotypes as embodied in Nute Gunray, Watto, and Jar Jar Binks are still present in *Clones* and Gunray and Binks are seen in *Clones* as well. In fact, the Neimoidians continue to be featured in speaking roles in *Sith*, whereas Jar Jar has been reduced to two close-ups and a few background shots.

Lucasfilm cannot claim either ignorance or fantasy in defense. In Dale Pollock's *Skywalking*, Lucas claims aliens and droids are used in the first trilogy to demonstrate discrimination.[79] In the cantina scene in *New Hope*, the bartender tells Luke, "Hey, we don't serve their kind here! ... Your droids. They'll have to wait outside." Yet the response to this discrimination in the film is to give in to it. Luke tells the droids, "Why don't you wait out by the speeder? We don't want any trouble." From his privileged position as a non-droid, Luke may stay within the cantina. In order to avoid "trouble," the droids are told to go outside. Discrimination is certainly demonstrated, but it is not resisted.

By constructing aliens that echo earlier cinematic portraits of Asians, Africans, Arabs, and Native Americans, the saga defines its heroes in opposition to the Other, and defines the Other in opposition to the heroes. Jabba threatening to kill Han is a bad thing. Leia actually killing Jabba is a good thing. We define Amidala as being everything the Neimoidians and Nute Gunray are not, and conversely they are as unheroic and oppressive as she is heroic and freedom-loving. As Ziauddin Sardar observes: "Aliens demonstrate what is not human the better to exemplify what it is to be human. Difference and otherness are the essence of aliens."[80] By having aliens with such recognizable real world antecedents, the saga Others the people upon whom those aliens are based. Native Americans are savage. Asians are treacherous. Arabs are obsessed with money and white women. Aliens perpetuate our stereotypes.

Edward Said notes that Orientalism is "a Western style for dominating, restructuring, and having authority over the Orient," and "because of Orientalism, the Orient was not (and is not) a free subject of thought and action."[81] In the *Star Wars* films, nonwesterners (nonwhites) are literally dominated and restructured and brought under authority by being constructed as alien Other. As such, Asians, Native Americans, Africans, and Arabs are not a free subject of thought and action in these movies. They are instead products of the American Imperial gaze — the Empire triumphs by subjugating the Other. The racist history of Hollywood echoes through the two trilogies. The nostalgia they invoke also evokes less diverse, more ethnocentric and racist constructions of the Other.

The Empire Triumphant:
Cultural Appropriation
and Postcolonial Discourse

The studio system is dead.... The power is with the people now. The workers have the means of production.
— George Lucas, 1969, after seeing *Easy Rider*[1]

As of this writing, the final installation in the new trilogy has just been released. With the advent of the final film in the second trilogy, *Episode III: Revenge of the Sith*, the series will have achieved a sense of closure, as it had when *Return of the Jedi* was released, but with more finality. Advertisements for *Sith* contained the tag line "The Saga Is Complete," which would seem to indicate no further episodes will be produced. There was at one time conjecture that Lucas would film Episodes VII, VIII, and IX upon completion of the prequel trilogy, but Lucas has announced that he is done with the narrative (except, of course, for re-releasing all six films as 3-D IMAX versions and creating a few television specials about the Clone Wars—but then he will be well and truly done. Really.).

Lucas has stated in an interview that the entire series is ultimately about redemption.[1] Interestingly, the story has been told backwards: episodes four through six, the end of the narrative, were told first, and then the first three episodes were presented. This fact makes the new trilogy almost like a Greek tragic trilogy from fifth century Athens: the conclusion of the story is already known. Thus, what is important is how the story is told and what happens to lead the audience to the foregone conclusion. We,

184

the audience, know from the moment Anakin appears in *Episode I* that he will become Darth Vader. In fact, one of the more popular posters for sale was of a young Anakin casting the shadow of Darth Vader. The future fall is inevitable. It only remains to be played out in *Revenge of the Sith*. We know he becomes Vader. Now the question is how.

In this image, however, we also find a metaphor for the cultural challenge of the *Star Wars* films. In the innocence of childhood are the seeds for a dark future of Othering, oppression, appropriation and imperialism. The films are aimed at a young audience, and that audience has the potential to grow up and embrace the dark side of human relations because of stereotypes and models of oppression built into popular culture. The dangers of the films are that the films *are* educational. Race, religion and rebellion are the subjects and the intertextual themes of the films. Young audiences can be seduced by the dark side of negative representations that then carry over into the real world. The audience can and might grow up to oppress, to be Vader themselves. It is not direct, and it is not overt or apparent, but like the shadow of Vader behind young Anakin, it is subtly there, reminding those who can see it of what the future holds.

Lucas "takes seriously the notion that entertainers have an obligation to promote positive moral values in their works."[2] Certainly the *Star Wars* films carry many positive moral messages, from the assertion of the importance of spirituality to the value of the individual. Yet the films also contain messages that white people are the center of the galaxy and are heroic, people of color belong on the margins, as they are not quite human anyway. Lucas also feels free to engage in cultural appropriation. The attempt to capture the good parts of the Saturday morning serial experience also recreates the more problematic ones: ethnic stereotypes, reductivism and oversimplification of complex real-world situations, marginalizing the Other and women, and the assertion of the West as the center of the universe.

John Seabrook calls Lucas "the first of the great content robber barons," explaining that he is "the first wholesale appropriator of world culture, which he [then] sold back to the world as *Star Wars*."[3] Seabrook is wrong in a sense — the history of culture is the history of appropriation and feedback, it went on long before Lucas and will continue long after him. Seabrook, however, is really saying not that Lucas was the first to appropriate, but rather he was merely the first to appropriate at the scale in which he did — taking from so many different cultures and from so many different media, including now himself, that one cannot begin to list all of the sources, even in a book of this length.

The original trilogy has been re-released yet again, this time on DVD, with more changes to the canonical films and several hours of additional features, documentaries, behind-the-scenes, etc. Lucas continues to remake his own films. No doubt the collection will also remain a bestseller for a while, ensuring more money coming to Lucasfilm. *Revenge of the Sith* has been through the theatres but it will subsequently appear on home viewing media such as DVD, VHS, and cable after this book has been released. It is not only possible but likely that Lucasfilm will subsequently reissue the second trilogy as a complete set. It is also not out of the bounds of possibility that when the complete set is issued it will again be re-edited.

On the one hand, one can view this constant reworking of the films as the attempt to maintain a living mythology. As time passes (and technology improves), the creator is able to reenter the creation and continue to adjust, change and "fix" it. Which ultimately means that the films themselves are unstable as meaning makers as the content changes with each new release. Not substantially, but enough to change meanings in some small, and some large, cases.

One can also more cynically view the reworking of the films as a capitalist technique to continue making money off of the same exact product by continually re-releasing it in slight variations with different packaging. Tremendous amounts of money can be made by selling the same thing over and over and over. It costs hundreds of millions to make a new *Star Wars* film, but only a few million to release an "Extra Special" version with a few more minutes of added footage.

In addition, the release of the original trilogy on DVD serves as an advertisement for the next film to be released, just as the "Special Editions" were advertisement for *Phantom*, released a year and a half later. The films have become their own marketing just as the marketing has become the films. Already the internet is humming with information about the next film. The plot, new characters, new technologies and new worlds will already be known to many in the audience before they have seen one frame of footage. The hype shapes the experience, and will be packaged and repackaged. If, as noted in the first chapter, that colonization is the occupation of another's property for material benefit, the *Star Wars* franchise might be seen as the ultimate in colonization. One of the defenders of *Phantom*'s racial constructions, Christian Toto, writing in the *Washington Times*, argues that "Mr. Lucas isn't looking to change the world, just fill your little cousin's bedroom with Yoda bed sheets."[4] Yet by filling the bedrooms of the little cousins of the world with bed sheets (not to mention action figures, video games, clothing, candy, plush toys, masks, and hundred of other licensed merchandise), Lucas is changing the world. Especially if that cousin with the Yoda bed sheets now understands the world in terms of the models provided to him or her by the films and their merchandise.

Lucas "criticizes himself for the scene played for laughs in *Raiders of the Lost Ark* where Indiana Jones drops his bullwhip and casually guns down an Arab swordsman."[5] There has been a recognition on his part of the Othering of Arabs in that film and how it serves as a message about the film's ideology and position on non–Westerners. It is harder to criticize one-self for Jar Jar Binks unless one also recognizes the indirect construction of an ethnic Other in the form of an alien. As Patrick Brantlinger states, "At least it is good to express the vision of a non-exploitive, non-imperialist world," and Lucas's admission of self criticism indicates that there is reflexive thought on the world represented on celluloid.[6]

As stated in the introduction, I am a fan, and remain one despite the negative aspects of the series. I must agree with Kenneth von Gunden, "George Lucas *is* a brilliant filmmaker."[7] I do not deny the man's genius as an artist, a visionary and especially as a businessman. Nor do I believe I have asserted anything about the man personally, only about the artist, the filmmaker, the corporation. My final concern is how the *Star Wars* universe, controlled as it is by one single individual, echoes itself.

As Sally Klein writes in the introduction to her book of interviews with Lucas, "Even at the height of his wealth and domination, Lucas's anti-establishment attitude belies his position as the ultimate symbol of that establishment."[8] The danger with rebellions is that those who carry them out tend to replace the empires they overthrow. Jonathan Rosenbaum sees *Phantom* as being "more American" than many of the blockbusters exported around the world from Hollywood, as it does not emerge from the studio system, but rather is the product of "an American individual" with "more power and independence" than any other filmmaker in America.[9] Film-making is very much a collective art — unlike painting, writing or other visual and performance arts, film cannot be created by itself. Under the American way of making movies, thousands of individuals are involved in the creation of a single movie. Yet only a single name is associated with the *Star Wars* series as the sole proprietor and creator. The republic that is filmmaking has become an empire.

As the title of this book suggests, I must ultimately agree with John Seabrook when he writes that Lucas has become the conservative busi-nessman his father wanted him to be, which he had rebelled against by going to school to become a filmmaker, rather than taking over the family store. Lucas has become an Emperor of his own private empire, the *Star Wars* universe. This, Seabrook states, is "the real lesson of *Star Wars*: In the end, the empire wins."[10]

Chapter Notes

Introduction

1. Arthur Asa Berger, *Manufacturing Desire: Media, Popular Culture and Everyday Life* (New Brunswick: Transaction, 1996) 4.

2. Quoted in Jack G. Shaheen, *Reel Bad Arabs: How Hollywood Vilifies a People* (New York: Olive Branch, 2001) 5.

3. Richard Keller Simon, *Trash Culture: Popular Culture and the Great Tradition* (Berkeley: U California P, 1999) 29.

4. Quoted in Tom Roston, "Holy Sith!" *Premiere* 18.8 (May 2005): 55.

5. Will Brooker, *Using the Force: Creativity, Community and Star Wars Fans* (New York: Continuum, 2002) xv.

6. Nick Clooney, *The Movies That Changed Us* (New York: Atria, 2002) 35.

7. See Brooker.

8. I use the term and definition after Charlene Dellinger-Pate, a communications professor at Southern Connecticut State University, who was discussing the role of *The Simpsons* in creating communities in Bob Baker, "The Real First Family" (*Los Angeles Times*, 16 February 2003) E34. The phenomenon of symbolic relational culture can be seen with a number of popular cultural phenomena — *Star Trek*, the writings of J.R.R. Tolkien, *X-Files*, graphic novels, and *Doctor Who*, to name but a few.

9. Brooker xv.

10. Krysten Crawford, "The 'Star Wars' Blitzkrieg" CNN.com <http://money.cnn. com/2005/05/13/news/newsmakers/star-wars/index.htm>. 13 May 2005.

11. Kenneth Turan, "It *Looks* Hot ..." *Los Angeles Times*. 16 May 2005: E5.

12. Clooney 41.

13. Although certainly some of the fans' and critics' objections to the new trilogy is that it seemed more aimed at children than containing elements that would appeal to both young and old, certainly *Phantom* is the worst culprit in this area, with an eight year old Anakin Skywalker and Jar Jar Binks. On the other hand, Lucas seemed to go out of his way to make *Sith* reverse this trend, becoming the first film in the franchise to receive a PG-13 rating, primarily for extended scenes of violence.

14. Quoted in Stephen Zito, "George Lucas Goes Far Out" in Sally Klein, ed., *George Lucas: Interviews* (Jackson: U Mississippi P, 1999) 47.

15. Interestingly, even though *Sith* was rated PG-13, and thus presumably children under 13 would not see it, a huge number of toys aimed at the under ten set was released before the film was. Several Wal-Marts had overnight hours when *Star Wars* toys were released, a phenomenon only shared in this era with the release of a new Harry Potter book. In fact, the most popular toy in the United States for ages four and up in the month before the film was a plastic lightsaber. Brian Golden, who oversees the US line of toys for Hasbro argued that, "Even if they can't go to the movie,

they can be a part of it" (quoted in Geoff
Boucher, "Gone to the Dark Side," *Los
Angeles Times*, 10 May 2005, E10). In other
words, even if one can't see the film, one
can participate in the culture of marketing
that surrounds it. On the other hand, the
makers of the merchandise also know that
the toys will be purchased by teenagers and
up as well. The author must confess to having a line of action figures looking down
upon him as he writes this.

16. Eric Greene, *Planet of the Apes as
American Myth: Race, Politics, and Popular
Culture* (Hanover: UP of New England,
1998) xiv.

17. Statistics given in John Seabrook,
"Why Is the Force Still with Us?" *The New
Yorker* LXXII.41 (6 January 1997): 40.

18. Fredric Jameson, "Postmodernism
and Consumer Society." *The Anti-Aesthetic.*
Ed. Hal Foster (Port Townsend: Bay Press,
1983) 116.

19. Jameson 116.

20. Peter Biskind. *Easy Riders, Raging
Bulls.* New York: Simon and Schuster, 1998.

21. Quoted in Ted Edwards, *The Unauthorized Star Wars Compendium* (Boston:
Little, Brown, and Company, 1999) 155.

22. John Baxter, *Mythmaker: The Life
and Work of George Lucas* (New York: Avon,
1999), Dale Pollock, *Skywalking: The Life
and Films of George Lucas* (Rev. ed., New
York: DaCapo Press, 1999), Garry Jenkins,
*Empire Building: The Remarkable, Real-Life
Story of Star Wars* (Seacacus: Citadel, 1999).
See also Maxford 1999, Salewicz, Champlin
1992, Von Gunden 1991, Klein 1999, and
Arnold 1980. The number of these books
that were released in 1999, corresponding
to the release of *Episode I: The Phantom
Menace* also indicates that the marketing of
the new trilogy is connected to celebrating
the old while paying tribute to Lucas the
visionary who created it all.

23. Henry Jenkins, *Textual Poachers: Television Fans and Participatory Culture* (New
York: Routledge, 1992) 30–31.

24. Lucas, quoted in Aljean Harmetz,
"Burden of Dreams: George Lucas" in Sally
Klein, ed., *George Lucas: Interviews* (Jack-
son: U Mississippi P, 1999) 143.

25. Stuart Hall, "The Whites of Their
Eyes: Racist Ideologies and the Media" in
*Silver Linings: Some Strategies for the Eight-
ies, eds. George Bridges and Rosalind Brunt
(London: Lawrence and Wisehart, 1981)
37–8.

26. Henry A. Giroux, *Channel Surfing*
(New York: St. Martins, 1997) 56.

27. Ursula K. Le Guin, *Dancing at the Edge
of the World: Thoughts on Words, Women,
Places* (New York: Grove, 1989) 198–9.

28. Kenneth von Gunden, *Postmodern
Auteurs: Coppola, Lucas, DePalma, Spielberg, and Scorsese* (Jefferson: McFarland,
1991) 56.

29. Although, since the Jawas "speak" a
form of kiSwahili, a language with which I
am familiar, one might make the argument
that I do—but kiSwahili was not learned
because of *Star Wars*, it was learned as I was
a student of African theatre and wanted to
engage the plays in their original language.

30. Brooker xiii.

31. Jeffery H. Mills, "*Star Trek IV*: The
Good, The Bad, and the Unquenched Thirst"
The Best of Trek #15. Eds. Walter Irwin and
G.B. Love (New York: ROC, 1990) 126.

32. Robin Wood, *Hollywood from Vietnam to Reagan* (New York: Columbia UP,
1986) 163.

33. Henry A. Giroux, *Living Dangerously*
(New York: Peter Lang, 1996) 26.

34. John Seabrook, *Nobrow: The Culture
of Marketing, the Marketing of Culture* (New
York: Alfred A. Knopf, 2000) 142.

35. Seabrook, *Nobrow* 142.

Chapter 1

1. Edward Said, "Blind Imperial Arrogance," *Los Angeles Times* (20 July 2003)
M5.

2. Said, "Blind" M5.

3. Martin Green, *Dreams of Adventure,
Deeds of Empire* (New York: Basic Books,
1979) 4.

4. Ariel Dorfman and Armand Matte-
lart, *How to Read Donald Duck: Imperialist
Ideology in the Disney Comic*, translated by
David Kunzle (New York: International
General, 1971, rev. ed. 1991) 11.

5. Basil Davidson, *The African Genius*
(Boston: Little, Brown and Company, 1969)
39.

6. Edward Said, *Culture and Imperialism* (New York: Alfred A. Knopf, 1994) xii.

7. Said, *Culture* 64.

8. Edward Said, *Orientalism* (New York: Vintage, 1979) 55.

9. Patrick Brantlinger, *Rule of Darkness, British Literature and Imperialism, 1830–1914* (Ithaca: Cornell UP, 1988) 229.

10. Brantliner, *Rule of Darkness* 233.

11. Brantlinger, *Rule of Darkness* 230.

12. Edward James, "Yellow, Black, Metallic and Tentacled: The Race Question in American Science Fiction," *Science Fiction, Social Conflict, and War,* Ed. Philip John Davies (Manchester: Manchester UP, 1990) 28.

13. Baxter 69.

14. Green 3.

15. Walter James Miller, "Afterword," *20,000 Leagues Under the Sea.* Jules Verne. Trans. Mendor T. Brunetti (New York: Signet, 2001) 448–9.

16. Miller 450.

17. John J. Pierce, *Foundations of Science Fiction: A Study in Imagination and Evolution* (Westport: Greenwood, 1987) 59.

18. Edward James, "Violent Revolution in Modern American Science Fiction," in *Science Fiction, Social Conflict, and War,* edited by Philip John Davies (Manchester: Manchester UP, 1990) 98.

19. James 105.

20. Michael Okuda, Denise Okuda, and Debbie Mirek, *The Star Trek Encyclopedia* (New York: Pocket Books, 1994) 261.

21. In one episode in the original series, "Bread and Circuses," Captain Kirk even argued that the culture based on the model of ancient Rome which developed as a result of the crash of the survey vessel S.S. *Beagle,* resulting in an imperial government, gladiator games, and slavery, has a right to full Prime Directive protection. Even societies that developed as a result of earlier cultural "contamination" are afforded protection to continue to develop. Of course, this argument is later undercut in the episode when Kirk aids a slave uprising and encourages the planet to develop a more open and free society based on UFP values (which were the values of the United States during the Vietnam War).

22. Mark Nash, et al., "Filmmakers' Dialogue" *The Fact of Blackness: Frantz Fanon*

and Visual Representations. Ed. Alan Read (Seattle: Bay Press) 168.

23. Nash 168.

24. Maxford 47.

25. Jenkins, *Empire* 94.

26. Jenkins, *Empire* 94.

27. Quoted in Jenkins, *Empire* 97.

28. Arnold 55.

29. These sources have been acknowledged by Lucas and others. See Howard Maxford, *George Lucas Companion* (London: BT Batsford, 1999), Garry Jenkins, *Empire Building,* rev. ed. (Secaucus: Citadel, 1999), Martin M. Winkler, "*Star Wars* and the Roman Empire," *Classical Myth and Culture in the Cinema,* ed. Martini M. Winkler (Oxford: Oxford UP, 2001), Sally Klein, ed., *George Lucas: Interviews* (Jackson: U Mississippi P, 1999), and John Baxter, *Mythmaker: The Life and Work of George Lucas* (New York: Avon, 1999).

30. Quoted in Jeff Jensen, "What a Long Strange Trip It's Been," *Entertainment Weekly,* No. 820 (May 20, 2005): 26.

31. Kenneth von Gunden, *Postmodern Auteurs: Coppola, Lucas, DePalma, Spielberg, and Scorsese* (Jefferson: McFarland, 1991) 11.

32. Robin Wood, *Hollywood from Vietnam to Reagan* (New York: Columbia UP, 1986) 167.

33. Chris Tiffin and Alan Lawson, "Introduction: The Textuality of Empire" in *De-scribing Empire: Post Colonialism and Textuality,* edited by Chris Tiffin and Alan Lawson (London: Routledge, 1994) 3.

34. Peter Lev, *American Films of the 70s: Conflicting Visions* (Austin: U Texas P, 2000) 165.

35. For more on Fanon see Anthony C. Alessandrini, ed. *Frantz Fanon: Critical Perspectives* (London: Routledge, 1999), L.R. Gordon, T.D. Sharpley-White, and R.T. White, eds. *Fanon: A Critical Reader* (Cambridge: Blackwell, 1996), A. Read, ed. *The Fact of Blackness: Frantz Fanon and Visual Representation* (Seattle: Bay Press, 1996), Debra Wyrick, *Fanon for Beginners* (New York: Writers and Readers, 1998), and Fanon's own books: *Black Skin White Masks* (Trans. Charles Lam Markmann, New York: Grove Press, 1967), *A Dying Colonialism* (Trans. H. Chevalier, New York: Grove, 1967), *Toward the African Revolution* (Trans.

H. Chevalier, New York: Grove, 1988), and *The Wretched of the Earth* (Trans. Constance Farrington, New York: Grove, 1969).

36. Fanon, *Black Skin* 224.

37. Jean-Paul Sartre, "Preface," Fanon, *Wretched* 10.

38. Fanon, *Wretched* 64.

39. David West Reynolds, *Star Wars Episode I: The Visual Dictionary* (New York: DK Publishing/Lucas Books, 1999) 7.

40. Bill Ashcroft, Gareth Griffiths, and Helen Tiffin, *The Empire Writes Back: Theory and Practice in Post-Colonial Literature* (London: Routledge, 1989).

41. The names are given by their representatives at the separatists' meeting in *Clones* and confirmed on the official *Star Wars* website (http://www.starwars.com/databank).

42. Peter Farb, *Word Play: What Happens When People Talk* (New York: Vintage, 1993) 138.

43. Deborah Wyrick, *Fanon for Beginners* (London: Writers and Readers, 1998) 62.

44. Winkler 273.

45. Winkler 275, 277, 278.

46. Fanon, *Wretched* 61.

47. Fanon, *Wretched* 73.

48. Stephen J. Sansweet, *The Star Wars Encyclopedia* (New York: Ballentine, 1998) 90.

49. Sansweet 224.

50. Reynolds 51.

51. In *Star Wars: Revenge of the Sith: The Visual Dictionary*, James Luceno writes that Kashyyyk was attacked by "Trandoshan slavers" in league with the Separatists, who also provided a droid army (New York: Dorling Kindersley, 2005) 6. He also notes that Yoda is beloved by the Wookiees for helping to fight the Wookiee slave trade (57). Neither fact is mentioned in the film, however.

52. Kenneth M. Cameron, *Africa on Film: Beyond Black and White* (New York: Continuum, 1994) 12.

53. Quoted in Peter Krämer, "*Star Wars*," *The Movies as History*. Ed. David Ellwood (Trowbridge: Sutton, 2000) 50.

54. Michael Pye and Lynda Myles, *The Movie Brats: How the Film Generation Took Over Hollywood* (New York: Holt, Rinehart and Winston, 1979) 136.

55. Tom Carson, "Jedi Uber Alles." *A Galaxy Not So Far Away*. Ed. Glenn Kenny (New York: Henry Holt, 2002) 162.

56. Many have made this observation, including Carson 162.

57. Hal Colebatch, *The Return of the Heroes* (Perth: Australian Institute for Public Policy, 1990) 1.

58. Colebatch 38.

59. Mark Thornton, "*Star Wars* and Our Wars," *Ludwig von Mises Institute Website*, http://www.mises.org/fullarticle.asp?control=948 (3 May 2002), accessed 30 December 2002.

60. One could also easily argue that Thorton's premise is also fallacious, most unbiased historians acknowledge that the preservation of slavery was one of the key, if not the key motivators for the Civil War.

61. Mark Thornton, "*Star Wars* Revisited," *Ludwig von Mises Institute Website*, http://www.mises.org/fullarticle.asp?record=277&month11, (7 August 1999), accessed 25 February 2003.

62. David Germain, "Sci-Fi Themes Hit Closer to Home," *Los Angeles Times* (16 May 2005): E5.

63. Quoted in Germain E5.

64. J. W. Rinzler, *The Making of Star Wars Revenge of the Sith* (New York: Del Rey, 2005), 13.

65. Owen Glieberman, "Vader to Black," *Entertainment Weekly*, No. 821/822 (27 May 2005), 116.

66. Quoted in Maura Reynolds, "Senators Try for a Judicial Compromise," *Los Angeles Times* (20 May 2005), A18.

67. Joe Queenan, "Anakin Get Your Gun," *A Galaxy Not So Far Away*, Ed. Glenn Kenny (New York: Henry Holt, 2002) 115.

68. Queenan 115.

69. Richard Keller Simon, *Trash Culture: Popular Culture and the Great Tradition* (Berkeley: U California P, 1999) 35.

70. Queenan 119.

71. Dan Rubey, "Not So Far Away," *Jump Cut*, No. 18 (1978) 9.

72. Rubey 10.

73. Rubey 11.

74. Rubey 12.

75. Quoted in Alan Arnold, *Once Upon a Galaxy: A Journal of the Making of Empire Strikes Back* (New York: Del Rey, 1980) 15.

76. Jon Lewis, "*Return of the Jedi*," *Jump Cut*, No. 30 (1984) 3.

77. Peter Biskind, *Easy Riders, Raging Bulls* (New York: Simon and Shuster, 1998) 342.

78. Biskind 342.

79. Biskind 343.

80. J. Hoberman, "All Droid Up," *The Village Voice* 44.20 (25 May 1999) 125.

81. David Seed, *American Science Fiction and the Cold War* (Chicago, Fitzroy Dearborn, 1999) 189–190.

82. Michael Ryan and Douglas Kellner, *Camera Politica: The Politics and Ideology of Contemporary Hollywood Fiction* (Bloomington, Indiana UP, 1988) 228.

83. Ryan and Kellner 234.

84. Hoberman 125.

85. Fanon, *Wretched* 61.

86. Fanon, *Wretched* 40.

87. Bouzereau 35.

88. Frantz Fanon, *Wretched of the Earth*, (Trans. Constance Farrington. New York: Grove, 1963) 35

89. Fanon, *Wretched* 61.

90. Fanon, *Wretched* 86.

91. Lewis, *"Return"* 5.

92. Quoted in Arnold 15.

93. Cameron 74.

94. Ella Shohat, "Gender and Culture of Empire: Toward a Feminist Ethnography of the Cinema" in *Visions of the East: Orientalism in Film*, eds. Matthew Bernstein and Gaylyn Studlar (New Brunswick: Rutgers UP, 1997) 54.

95. Kenneth von Gunden, *Postmodern Auteurs: Coppola, Lucas, DePalma, Spielberg, and Scorsese* (Jefferson: McFarland, 1991) 67–8.

96. Wood 170.

97. Green 338.

98. Abdul R. Jan-Mohammed, "The Economy of Manichean Allegory: The Function of Racial Difference in Colonialist Literature" in *Race, Writing and Difference*, edited by Henry Louis Gates (Chicago: U Chicago P, 1985) 101.

99. Geoffrey Nunberg, "Them's Fightin' Words" *Los Angeles Times* (30 November 2003) M5.

Chapter 2

1. Kevin Smith, *Clerks and Chasing Amy: Two Screenplays* (New York: Hyperion, 1997)

53–4. The dialogue is from the screenplay for *Clerks*, but does not appear in the film.

2. Statistics taken from "Jedi 'Religion' Grows in Australia" from BBC News World Edition Online. <http://news.bbc.co.uk/2/hi/entertainment/2218456.stm>.Posted 27 August 2002. Accessed 13 April 2004.

3. Dean Kuipers, "Darth Shadows," *Los Angeles Times* (19 May 2005), E30.

4. Dale Pollock, *Skywalking: The Life and Films of George Lucas* (Rev. ed. New York: Da Capo Press, 1999) 139.

5. Peter Krämer, "*Star Wars*," *The Movies as History*. Ed. David Ellwood (Trowbridge: Sutton, 2000) 50.

6. Laurent Bouzereau, *Star Wars: The Annotated Screenplays* (New York: Del Rey, 1997) 35.

7. Quoted in Bill Moyers. "Of Myth and Men: An Interview with George Lucas." *Time*. April 26,1999. 92–3.

8. Frank Allnut, *The Force of Star Wars* (Van Nuys: Bible Voice, 1977) 26, 201.

9. Allnut 26.

10. Robert Jewett, *Saint Paul at the Movies: The Apostle's Dialogue with American Culture* (Louisville: Westminster / John Knox, 1993) 20.

11. Jewett 22.

12. Jewett 30.

13. Jim Windolf, "Star Wars: The Last Battle," *Vanity Fair*, no. 534 (February 2005), 117.

14. Chris Salewicz, *George Lucas Close Up* (New York: Thunder's Mouth, 1999) 46. See also Carlos Castaneda, *Tales of Power* (New York: Simon and Schuster, 1974).

15. Salewicz 79.

16. Richard Simon Keller, *Trash Culture: Popular Culture and the Great Tradition* (Berkeley: U California P, 1999) 35.

17. Moyers 92.

18. Fischer-Schreiber, Ingrid. *The Shambhala Dictionary of Taoism*. Trans. Werner Wünsche (Boston: Shambhala, 1996) 165.

19. Susan Mackey-Kallis, *The Hero and the Perennial Journey Home in American Film* (Philadelphia: U Pennsylvania, 2001) 213.

20. Quoted in Bouzereau 137.

21. Quoted in Bouzereau 188.

22. Pollock 140.

23. Quoted in Kuipers E30.

24. Stuart Voytilla, *Myth and the Movies* (Studio City: Michael Wiese, 1999) 273.

25. Quoted in Alan Arnold, *Once Upon a Galaxy: A Journal of the Making of the Empire Strikes Back* (New York: Del Rey, 1980) 188.

26. Quoted in Alan Arnold, *Once Upon a Galaxy: A Journal of the Making of Empire Strikes Back* (New York: Del Rey, 1980) 111.

27. Joseph Campbell and Bill Moyers, *The Power of Myth* (New York: Doubleday, 1988) 22.

28. Ernest Ferlita and John R. May, *Film Odyssey: The Art of Film as Search for Meaning* (New York: Paulist Press, 1976.

29. John Seabrook, "Why Is the Force Still with Us?" *The New Yorker* LXXII.41 (6 January 1997): 42.

30. Campbell and Moyers 18, 145–6, 166.

31. Mary Lefkowitz, *Greek Gods, Human Lives: What We Can Learn from Myths* (New Haven: Yale UP, 2003) 8.

32. Steven A. Galipeau, *The Journey of Luke Skywalker* (Chicago: Open Court, 2001) xi.

33. Galipeau 1–2.

34. Galipeau 19.

35. Galipeau 23, 29, 46, 142.

36. James F. Iaccino, *Jungian Reflections Within the Cinema* (Westport: Praeger, 1998). See chapter one, "The *Star Wars* Trilogy: The Space Father Archetype."

37. Voytilla viii.

38. Susan Mackey-Kallis, *The Hero and the Perennial Journey Home in American Film* (Philadelphia: U Pennsylvania, 2001).

39. Arthur Asa Berger, *Manufacturing Desire: Media, Popular Culture and Everyday Life* (New Brunswick, Transaction, 1996). See chapter 13 "*Star Wars* as Fairy Tale."

40. Bruno Bettelheim, "The Art of Moving Pictures," *Harpers*, 263.1577 (October 1981)82.

41. Bettelheim 82.

42. Bettelheim 82.

43. Bettelheim 82.

44. James Buhler, "*Star Wars*, Music and Myth" in *Music and Cinema*, Eds. James Buhler, Caryl Flinn, and David Neumeyer (Hanover: Wesleyan UP, 2000) 33.

45. Quoted in Buhler 34.

46. Hal Colebatch, *Return of the Heroes* (Perth: Australian Institute for Public Policy, 1990).

47. Lucas quoted in Michael Pye and Lynda Myles, *The Movie Brats* (New York: Holt, Rinehart and Winston, 1979) 133.

48. Ian Barbour, *Myths, Models, and Paradigms: A Comparative Study in Science and Religion* (New York: Harper, 1974) 24.

49. Tina Chen, "Dissecting the 'Devil Doctor': Stereotype and Sensationalism in Sax Rohmer's Fu Manchu" *Re/collecting Early Asian America: Essays in Cultural History*. Eds. Josephine Lee, Imogene L. Lim, and Yuko Matsukawa (Philadelphia: Temple UP, 2002) 221.

50. Roland Barthes, *Mythologies*, Trans. Annetta Lavers (New York: Hill and Wang, 1972) 109, 142.

51. Barthes 152.

52. David John, ed. *Star Wars: The Power of Myth* (New York: DK, 1999) 7–9.

53. John 11.

54. John 13.

55. John 32.

56. John 33.

57. John 33, 46.

58. Mary Henderson, *Star Wars: The Magic of Myth* (New York: Bantam, 1997) 3.

59. Henderson 47.

60. Henderson 54–55.

61. Henderson 96–97.

62. Henderson 11, 86–87.

63. Henderson 133.

64. Henderson 132.

65. For an analysis of Wong Fei Hung films, see Bey Logan, *Hong Kong Action Cinema* (Woodstock: Overlook, 1995).

66. Janice Rushing, "Evolution of 'The New Frontier' in *Alien* and *Aliens*: Patriarchal Co-optations of the Feminine Archetype" *Quarterly Journal of Speech*. 75 (1989): 21.

67. Joseph Campbell, *The Masks of God: Creative Mythology* (New York: Arkana, 1968) 6–7.

68. Campbell, *Creative Mythology* 609.

69. Campbell, *Creative Mythology* 611.

70. Campbell, *Creative Mythology* 621.

71. Campbell, *Creative Mythology* 623.

Chapter 3

1. Quoted in John Baxter, *Mythmaker: The Life and Work of George Lucas* (New York: Avon, 1999) 72.

2. James Goodwin. "Introduction." *Perspectives on Akira Kurosawa*. Ed. James Goodwin (New York: G.K. Hall, 1994) 8.

3. The sequence, called "Lucas on Kurosawa," is an eight-minute interview with Lucas that incorporates images and sequences from both Kurosawa's films and *Star Wars*. *The Hidden Fortress*, The Criterion Collection DVD, 2001.

4. Laurent Bouzereau, *Star Wars: The Annotated Screenplays* (New York: Del Rey, 1997) 9–10.

5. Baxter 72.

6. Baxter 74, 98.

7. See the chapter on *The Hidden Fortress* in Donald Richie, *The Films of Akira Kurosawa*. 3rd ed. (Berkeley: U California P, 1996) for a more detailed and lengthy analysis of Kurosawa's film.

8. Bouzereau 22.

9. Bouzereau 8.

10. This fact has been noted by several scholars and biographers of Lucas, most notably Garry Jenkins, *Empire Building*, rev. ed. (Secaucus: Citadel, 1999) 83.

11. Baxter 158.

12. For more on Kabuki *jidai*, see Leiter 1997 and Brandon 1992.

13. Charles Champlin, *George Lucas: The Creative Impulse* (New York: Harry N. Abrams, 1992) 42.

14. Quoted in Bouzereau 197.

15. Richie 135.

16. Lucas, in an interview with Mary Henderson at Skywalker Ranch on 27 September 1996. Quoted in Mary Henderson, *Star Wars: The Magic of Myth* (New York: Bantam, 1997) 133.

17. Baxter 72.

18. Quoted in Bouzereau 180.

19. Hal Colebatch, *Return of the Heroes* (Perth: Australian Institute for Public Policy, 1990) 36.

20. Bouzereau and Duncan 44.

21. Howard Maxford, *George Lucas Companion* (London: BT Batsford, 1999) 33.

22. David Chute, "Introduction" *Heroic Grace: The Chinese Martial Arts Film*. Eds. David Chute and Cheng-sim Lim (Los Angeles: UCLA Film and Television Archive, 2003) 6

23. Koo Siu-fung, "Philosophy and Tradition in the Swordplay Film." *A Study of the Hong Kong Swordplay Film (1945–1980)*.

Ed. Leong Mo-ling (Hong Kong: Urban Council of Hong Kong, 1981) 29.

24. David Desser, "The Martial Arts Film in the 1990s," *Film Genre 2000*, Ed. Wheeler Winston Dixon (Albany: State U of New York P, 2000) 88.

25. "Overview: 1985 — Hollywood's Banner Year for Martial Arts Movies" *Inside Kung Fu Presents the Best of Martial Arts Movies*, January 1985, 17.

26. The description of Yoda is taken directly from the screenplay (Bouzereau 187).

27. William O. Stephens, "Stoicism in the Stars: Yoda, The Emperor and the Force." *Star Wars and Philosophy*. Eds. Kevin S. Decker and Jason T. Eberl (Chicago: Open Court, 2005), 17.

28. See chapter four in Howard Reid and Michael Croucher's *The Fighting Arts* (New York: Simon and Schuster, 1983) for a history of the Shaolin Temple. For the history of *wuxia* films see Bey Logan, *Hong Kong Action Cinema* (Woodstock: Overlook, 1995), Lau Shing-hon, *A Study of the Hong Kong Martial Arts Film* (Hong Kong: Urban Council of Hong Kong, 1980), Leong Mo-ling, *A Study of the Hong Kong Swordplay Film (1945–1980)*, and Winnie Fu, ed., *The Making of Martial Arts Films as Told by Filmmakers and Stars* (Hong Kong: Hong Kong Film Archive, 1999).

29. The last two films are not so much about the training of a single hero (although inevitably one emerges) as the conflict between two schools. It is not unusual in *wuxia* films, especially those made by Bruce Lee, for the conflict to be between different schools of martial artists. It is not that much of a stretch to see the *Star Wars* saga as a conflict between two schools of martial artists: the Jedi and the Sith.

30. Chute 10.

31. Sam Ho, "From Page to Screen: A Brief History of *Wuxia* Fiction" in Chute and Lim, 15.

32. James J.Y. Liu, *The Chinese Knight Errant* (Chicago: U Chicago P, 1967) xii.

33. Joseph Campbell with Bill Moyers. *The Power of Myth*. (New York: Doubleday, 1988) 145.

34. Jeff A.R. Jones, "Jedi Master: An Interview with Nick Gillard." *The Fight Master*. 13.1(2000): 24.

35. Jones 25.

36. Jenkins, *Empire* 242.

37. From an interview with Ralph Mc-Quarrie by Mary Henderson, quoted in Henderson 186.

38. Baxter 196.

39. Erika Krouse also notes this similarity in "The Chrysanthemum and the Lightsaber" in *A Galaxy Not So Far Away*, ed. Glenn Kenny (New York: Henry Holt, 2002). Henderson also observes this fact, 189.

40. Henderson 189.

41. Quoted in Bouzereau 248.

42. Bob Woods, ed. Star Wars: Episode I: The Official Souvenir Magazine (New York: Topps, 1999) 43, 42.

43. Quoted in Woods 43.

44. Bouzereau and Duncan 62.

45. J. Hoberman, "All Droid Up," *The Village Voice* 44.20 (25 May 1999) 125.

46. Quoted in Laurent Bouzereau and Jody Duncan, *Star Wars: The Making of Episode I: The Phantom Menace* (New York, Del Rey, 1999) 25.

47. Bouzereau and Duncan 28.

48. Seiichi Makino and Michio Tsutsui, *A Dictionary of Basic Japanese Grammar* (Tokyo: Japan Times, 1989), 549. For a full analysis of the use of "yoda," see the complete entry, 547–552.

49. Walter Ritoku Robinson, "The Far East of Star Wars." *Star Wars and Philosophy*. Eds. Kevin S. Decker and Jason T. Eberl (Chicago: Open Court, 2005) 34.

50. Brian Crow with Chris Banfield, *An Introduction to Postcolonial Theatre* (Cambridge: Cambridge UP, 1996) x.

Chapter 4

1. *Clerks*, Smith's first film, featured an extended discussion of the role of private contractors in the building of the second Death Star. *Mallrats*, his second, featured several references, including Silent Bob (played by Smith) attempting to use "Jedi mind powers" to move a cigarette and get a video tape in a parallel to the Wampa cave sequence in *Empire Strikes Back*. *Chasing Amy*, the third film in the so-called "Jersey Trilogy" is discussed above. *Dogma* also featured brief references, mostly from Jay.

Mark Hamill played himself playing a villain in the film-within-the-film sequence from the obvious Lucas-inspired tribute film *Jay and Silent Bob Strike Back*. Kevin Smith himself also paid tribute to the films in an essay in *A Galaxy Not So Far Away*, edited by Glenn Kenny (New York: Henry Holt and Company, 2002), in which he discusses the parallels between *Clerks* and *Star Wars*, especially the parallel between C3PO and R2-D2 and Jay and Silent Bob as tangential characters who frame their respective stories. Smith argues that he used *Star Wars* references "to pander to a Gen X audience as nostalgic as we were" (72).

2. Kevin Smith, *Clerks and Chasing Amy: Two Screenplays* (New York: Hyperion, 1997) 184–186. There are slight differences between the version of the speech in the published screenplay and the one in the actual film.

3. Michael Pye and Lynda Myles, *The Movie Brats: How the Film Generation Took Over Hollywood* (New York: Holt, Rinehart and Winston, 1979) 136.

4. Pye and Myles 136.

5. Dale Pollock, *Skywalking: The Life and Films of George Lucas* (Rev. ed. New York: Da Capo Press, 1999) 151.

6. Quoted in Pollock 151.

7. Chris Salewicz, *George Lucas Close Up* (New York: Thunder's Mouth, 1999) 66.

8. Laurent Bouzereau, ed. *Star Wars: The Annotated Screenplays*. (New York: Del Rey, 1997) 40.

9. Homi K. Bhabha, "Remembering Fanon: Self, Psyche, and the Colonial Condition" in *Remaking Fanon* eds. Barbara Kruger and Phil Mariani (Seattle: Bay Press, 1989) 146.

10. The nineteen as designated by Reddick and summarized by Maynard are: "the savage African, the happy slave, the devoted servant, the corrupt politician, the irresponsible citizen, the petty thief, the social delinquent, the vicious criminal, the sexual superman, the superior athlete, the unhappy non-white, the natural-born cook, the natural-born musician, the perfect entertainer, the superstitious church-goer, the chicken and watermelon eater, the razor and knife toter, the uninhibited exhibitionist, and the mental inferior." Richard Maynard, "Editor's Introduction," in *The Black*

Man on Film: Racial Stereotyping, ed. Richard Maynard (Rochelle Park: Hayden Books Company, 1974) vi.

11. Daniel Leonard Bernardi, *Star Trek and History: Race-ing Toward a White Future* (New Brunswick: Rutgers UP, 1998) 80.

12. Bernardi 79.

13. Elvis Mitchell, "Works Every Time" *A Galaxy Not So Far Away*, ed. by Glenn Kenny (New York: Henry Holt and Company, 2002) 77.

14. Mitchell 80.

15. Mitchell 84.

16. Donald Bogle, *Toms, Coons, Mulattoes, Mammies, and Bucks: An Interpretive History of Blacks in American Films* (New York: Continuum, 2002) 275.

17. See Will Brooker, *Using the Force: Creativity, Community, and Star Wars Fans* (New York: Continuum, 2002) 80.

18. Bouzereau 261.

19. Pollock 213.

20. Quoted in Alan Arnold, *Once Upon a Galaxy: A Journal of the Making of The Empire Strikes Back* (New York: Del Rey, 1980) 60.

21. Quoted in Arnold 101.

22. Quoted in Arnold 97.

23. Bouzereau 196.

24. Salewicz 80.

25. Bouzereau 257.

26. John Baxter, *Mythmaker: The Life and Work of George Lucas* (New York: Avon, 1979) 327.

27. Reported in Bouzereau 314.

28. Pollock 286.

29. Bogle 422.

30. Bogle 423.

31. Bouzereau 196.

32. Bouzereau 271.

33. Dan Vebber and Dana Gould, "Fifty Reasons Why *Jedi* Sucks." *The Unauthorized Star Wars Compendium*. Ted Edwards (Boston: Little, Brown and Company, 1999) 221.

34. Harry Allen, "Planet Rock: *Star Wars* and Hip Hop." *A Galaxy Not So Far Away*. Ed. Glenn Kenny (New York: Henry Holt and Company, 2002) 153.

35. See Allen 156–157.

36. Mitchell 82.

37. Brent Staples, "Shuffling Through the *Star Wars*," *The New York Times* (20 June 1999) Sec. 4, 14.

38. "Lucas Blew It with Jar Jar," *Toronto Star* (11 June 1999).

39. Staples 14.

40. From the illustrated screenplay of *The Phantom Menace*, 16.

41. David West Reynolds, *Star Wars Episode I: The Visual Dictionary* (New York: DK Publishing/Lucas Books, 1999) 37.

42. J. Hoberman, "All Droid Up," *The Village Voice* 44.20 (25 May 1999) 125.

43. This text is not my transcription, but the actual lines as written in the screenplay (Bouzereau 20).

44. Reynolds 38.

45. Hal Foster, *Recodings: Art, Spectacle, Culture and Politics* (Port Townsend: Bay Press, 1985) 166.

46. Maynard 5.

47. Bogle 8.

48. Bogle 7–8.

49. Bogle 8.

50. Bogle 42.

51. Quoted in Bogle 42.

52. George Lucas, *Star Wars Episode I: The Phantom Menace: The Illustrated Screenplay* (New York: Del Rey, 1999) 125.

53. Lucas, *Episode I Screenplay* 128.

54. Lucas, *Episode I Screenplay* 126.

55. Bogle 71, 74.

56. Steven A. Galipeau, *The Journey of Luke Skywalker* (Chicago: Open Court, 2001) 266.

57. Clarence Page, "Phantom Menace: War of the Stereotypes," *Washington Times* (4 June 1999) A16, Paul Craig Roberts, "Designer Face of Designated Demons," *Washington Times* (14 July 1999) A16, Christian Toto, "*Star Wars*: The Political Battlefield," *Washington Times* (19 February 2000) D2.

58. Galipeau 143.

59. Galipeau 142.

60. John Leo, "Menace Stereotypes," *Washington Times* (11 July 1999) B3.

61. Deborah Wyrick, *Fanon for Beginners* (London: Writers and Readers, 1998) 45.

62. Frantz Fanon. *Black Skin White Masks*. (New York: Grove, 1967) 9.

Chapter 5

1. Philip Kan Gotanda, *Yankee Dawg You Die* (New York: Dramatists, 1991) 26.
2. Gotanda 6.
3. Gotanda 6.
4. Gotanda 29.
5. Tom Carson, "Jedi Uber Alles." *A Galaxy Not So Far Away.* Ed. Glenn Kenny (New York: Henry Holt, 2002) 168.
6. Sheridan Prasro, *The Asian Mystique* (New York: Public Affairs, 2005).
7. Rudolf Wittkower, "Marvels of the East: A Study in the History of Monsters," *Journal of the Warburg and Courtauld Institutes,* vol. 5 (1942), 159.
8. Wittkower 160.
9. Wittkower 164.
10. Reference from *Othello* is from *The Riverside Shakespeare*, edited by G. Blakemore Evans (Boston: Houghton Mifflin, 1974).
11. Ziauddin Sardar, "Introduction," *Aliens R Us: The Other in Science Fiction Cinema*, Eds. Sardar Ziauddin and Sean Cubitt (London: Pluto, 2002) 8–9.
12. Edward Said, *Culture and Imperialism* (New York: Alfred A. Knopf, 1994) 64.
13. Elaine L. Graham, *Representations of the Post/human: Monsters, Aliens, and Others in Popular Culture* (New Brunswick, Rutgers UP, 2002) 49.
14. Graham 53.
15. Eric Greene, *Planet of the Apes as American Myth: Race, Politics, and Popular Culture* (Hanover: UP of New England, 1998).
16. Greene 6.
17. Jachinson Chan, *Chinese American Masculinities: From Fu Manchu to Bruce Lee* (New York: Routledge, 2001) 27.
18. For some of the information on Fu Manchu on film and television I am in debt to the online Sax Rohmer database, *The Page of Fu Manchu*, edited by Dr. Lawrence Knapp and contributed to by Sax Rohmer scholars from around the world <http://www. njedge.net/~knapp/FuFrames.htm> Accessed 17 July 2004.
19. Peter Nicholls and John Brosnan, "*Mask of Fu Manchu*" *Encyclopedia of Science Fiction*, Eds. John Clute and Peter Nicholls (New York: St. Martins Press, 1993) 782.

20. David West Reynolds, *Star Wars Episode I: The Visual Dictionary* (New York: DK Publishing/LucasBooks, 1999) 16.
21. Reynolds, *Episode I* 16.
22. Chan 31.
23. This point is made by Tina Chen, "Dissecting the 'Devil Doctor': Stereotype and Sensationalism in Sax Rohmer's Fu Manchu" *Re/collecting Early Asian America: Essays in Cultural History.* Eds. Josephine Lee, Imogene L. Lim, and Yuko Matsukawa (Philadelphia: Temple UP, 2002) 220.
24. Quoted in Laurent Bourzereau, *Star Wars: The Annotated Screenplays* (New York: DelRey, 1997) 197.
25. Bill Moyers, "Of Myth and Men: An Interview with George Lucas." *Time* (April 26,1999) 90.
26. I am in debt to Professor Cynthia Turnbull and Erin Malone of Denison University who both independently pointed out to me the similarity between a Noh mask on my office wall and the picture of Darth Maul on my bulletin board, which had escaped my notice until then.
27. James Brandon, *Kabuki: Five Classic Plays* (Honolulu: U Hawaii P. 1992) 10.
28. Brandon 10.
29. A.C. Scott, "The Performance of Classical Theatre." *Chinese Theatre from Its Origin to the Present Day.* Ed. Colin Mackerras. (Honolulu: U Hawaii P, 1983) 125.
30. Jeanine Basinger, *The World War II Combat Films: Anatomy of a Genre* (New York: Columbia UP, 1986) 28.
31. Neil Sheehan, *A Bright Shining Lie: John Paul Vann and America in Vietnam* (London: Jonathan Cape, 1989) 154.
32. Eugene Franklin Wong, *On Visual Media Racism* (New York: Arno Press, 1978) 150.
33. Basinger 60.
34. Laurence Michalak, *Cruel and Unusual: Negative Images of Arabs in American Popular Culture* (Washington, D.C.: American-Arab Anti-Discrimination Committee, 1983) 30.
35. Allen L. Woll and Randall M. Miller, *Ethnic and Racial Images in American Film and Television.* (New York: Garland Publishing, 1987) 179.
36. Jack G. Shaheen, *Reel Bad Arabs: How Hollywood Vilifies a People* (New York: Olive Branch, 2001).

37. Stephen J. Sansweet, *The Star Wars Encyclopedia* (New York: Ballentine, 1998) 317.

38. Reynolds 59.

39. David West Reynolds, *Star Wars: The Visual Dictionary* (New York: DK Publishing, 1998) 55.

40. Bouzereau 242.

41. Michalak 16.

42. Michalak 15.

43. Bouzereau 242.

44. Bouzereau 249.

45. Woll and Miller 181.

46. Andy Seiler, "Something to Offend Everyone," *USA Today* (28 June 1999) 1D.

47. Gilbert Adair, "Cinema: It's Lucas Who's the Real Menace," *The Independent* (18 July 1999) 5. Adair confused the character, calling him "Sibulba," clearly conflating him with "Sebulba," a Dug pod racer and rival of young Anakin. Nevertheless, it is clear from Adair's description ("an elephantine slave-trader [with] hooked nose and oleaginous manners") that he is referencing Watto.

48. Quoted in John Leo, "Menace Stereotypes," *Washington Times* (11 July 1999) B3.

49. Leo B3.

50. A.O. Scott, "Kicking Up Cosmic Dust," *New York Times* (10 May 2002) E1.

51. Lucas quoted in Michael Pye and Lynda Myles, *The Movie Brats* (New York: Holt, Rinehart and Winston, 1979) 133.

52. Bouzereau 286.

53. Steven A. Galipeau, *The Journey of Luke Skywalker* (Chicago: Open Court, 2001) 217.

54. Galipeau 220.

55. Hal Foster, *Recodings: Art, Spectacle, Culture and Politics.* Port Townsend: Bay Press, 1985.

56. Marianna Torgovnick, *Gone Primitive: Savage Intellects, Modern Lives* (Chicago: U Chicago P, 1990) 3.

57. Kenneth M. Cameron, *Africa on Film: Beyond Black and White* (New York: Continuum, 1994) 72.

58. Carson 170.

59. Richard Keller Simon, *Trash Culture: Popular Culture and the Great Tradition* (Berkeley: U California P, 1999) 154.

60. Quoted in Dale Pollock, *Skywalking: The Life and Films of George Lucas*, rev. ed. (New York: DaCapo Press, 1999) 213.

61. Paul Scanlon, "The Force Behind George Lucas" *Rolling Stone* (25 August 1977) 43.

62. Dan Rubey, "Not So Far Away," *Jump Cut* (August 1978), 11.

63. Rubey 11.

64. James Luceno. *Star Wars: Revenge of the Sith: The Visual Dictionary* (New York: Dorling Kindersley, 2005) 18.

65. Patrick Brantlinger, *Dark Vanishings: Discourse on the Extinction of Primitive Races, 1800–1930* (Ithaca: Cornell UP, 2003) 189.

66. Brantlinger, *Dark Vanishings* 2.

67. Leif Furhammar and Folke Isaksson, *Politics and Film*, Trans. Kersti French (New York: Praeger, 1971) 216.

68. James S. Moy, *Marginal Sights: Staging the Chinese in America* (Iowa City: U Iowa P, 1993) 36–9.

69. Media Action Network for Asian Americans. "Restrictive Portrayals of Asians in the Media and How to Balance Them." <http://www.manaa.org/articles/stereo.html> 9 July 2003. All quotations are taken from the website.

70. Brent Staples, "Shuffling Through the Star Wars," *The New York Times* (20 June 1999) Sec. 4, 14.

71. Adair 5.

72. John Leo, "Menace Stereotypes," *Washington Times* (11 July 1999) B3.

73. Clarence Page, "Phantom Menace: War of the Stereotypes," *Washington Times* (4 June 1999) A16, Paul Craig Roberts, "Designer Face of Designated Demons," *Washington Times* (14 July 1999) A16, Christian Toto, "*Star Wars*: The Political Battlefield," *Washington Times* (19 February 2000) D2.

74. Roberts A16.

75. Page A16.

76. Reported in Jonathan Bing, "Lucasfilm Searches for Politically Correct Galaxy," *Variety* (February 14–20, 2000) 8. See also Jonathan Bing, "Inside Moves: Next 'Star Wars' Aims to Avoid Racial Stereotypes." *Daily Variety.* 9 February 2000. 3.

77. Grace Bradbury, "Next *Star Wars* Film to Feature Black, White and Greene," *Ottawa Citizen* (12 February 2000) A3.

78. Bing, "Lucasfilm Searches" 8.

79. Pollock 213.

80. Sardar 6.

81. Edward Said, *Orientalism* (New York: Vintage, 1979) 3.

Conclusion

1. Quoted in John Seabrook, "Why Is the Force Still with Us?" *New Yorker.* LXXII.41 (January 6, 1997) 46.
2. Bruce Handy, "The Force Is Back." *Time.* 10 February 1997.
3. John Seabrook, *Nobrow: The Culture of Marketing, the Marketing of Culture* (New York: Alfred A. Knopf, 2000) 146.
4. Christian Toto, "*Star Wars*: The Political Battlefield," *Washington Times* (19 February 2000) D2.

5. Handy 1997.
6. Patrick Brantlinger, *Rule of Darkness, British Literature and Imperialism, 1830–1914* (Ithaca: Cornell UP, 1988) 16.
7. Kenneth von Gunden, *Postmodern Auteurs: Coppola, Lucas, DePalma, Spielberg, and Scorsese* (Jefferson: McFarland, 1991) 78.
8. Sally Klein, "Introduction" in Sally Klein, ed., *George Lucas: Interviews* (Jackson: U Mississippi P, 1999) xiv.
9. Jonathan Rosenbaum, *Movie Wars: How Hollywood and the Media Conspire to Limit What Films We Can See* (Chicago: Acapella, 2000) 136.
10. Seabrook 160.

Filmography

Aliens. Dir. James Cameron. Screenplay by James Cameron. 1986.

Battle for the Planet of the Apes. Dir. J. Lee Thompson. Story by Paul Dehn. Screenplay by John William Corrington and Joyce Hooper Corrington. Twentieth Century Fox, 1973.

"Bread and Circuses." *Star Trek.* Dir. Ralph Senesky. Teleplay by Gene L. Coon and Gene Roddenberry. Story by John Keubuhl. Paramount. 15 March 1968.

The Bridge on the River Kwai. Dir. David Lean. Screenplay by Pierre Boulle. Columbia, 1957.

Chasing Amy. Dir. Kevin Smith. Screenplay by Kevin Smith. Miramax Films, 1997.

Conquest of the Planet of the Apes. Dir. J. Lee Thompson. Screenplay by Paul Dehn. Twentieth Century Fox, 1972.

"Devil in the Dark." *Star Trek.* Dir. Joseph Pevney. Teleplay by Gene L. Coon. Paramount, 9 March 1967.

The Empire Strikes Back. Dir. Irvin Kershner. Screenplay by Leigh Brackett and Lawrence Kasdan. Story by George Lucas. Twentieth Century Fox, 1980.

From Star Wars to Jedi: The Making of a Saga. Written and Produced by Richard Schickel. CBS Fox/Lucasfilm Limited, 1983.

The Hidden Fortress (Kukaushi Toride no San-Akunin). Dir. Kurosawa Akira. Screenplay by Kikushima Ryuzo, Oguni Hideo, Hashimoto Shinobu, and Kurosawa Akira. Toho, 1958.

One-Armed Swordsman (Dubi Dao). Dir. Zhang Che. Screenplay by Ni Kuang. Shaw Brothers, 1967.

Return of the Jedi. Dir. Richard Marquand. Screenplay by Lawrence Kasdan and George Lucas. Story by George Lucas. Twentieth Century Fox, 1983.

Seven Samurai (Shichinin no samurai). Dir. Kurosawa Akira. Screenplay by Kurosawa Akira, Hashimoto Shinobu, and Oguni Hideo. Toho, 1954.

Shaolin Master Killer (Shaolin san shi liu fang). Dir. Lau Kar Leung. Screenplay by Kuang Ni. Shaw Brothers, 1978.

Star Wars. Dir. George Lucas. Screenplay by George Lucas. Twentieth Century Fox, 1977.

Star Wars: Episode I: The Phantom Menace. Dir. George Lucas. Screenplay by George Lucas. Twentieth Century Fox, 1999.

Star Wars: Episode II: Attack of the Clones. Dir. George Lucas. Screenplay by George Lucas and Jonathan Hales. Twentieth Century Fox, 2002.

Star Wars: Episode III: Revenge of the Sith. Dir. George Lucas. Screenplay by George Lucas. Twentieth Century Fox, 2005.

Yojimbo. (Yojimbo) Dir. Kurosawa Akira. Screenplay by Kikushima Ryuzo, Oguni Hideo, and Kurosawa Akira. Toho, 1961.

Bibliography

Adair, Gilbert. "Cinema: It's Lucas Who's the Real Menace." *The Independent.* 18 July 1999. 5.

Alessandrini, Anthony C., ed. *Frantz Fanon: Critical Perspectives.* London: Routledge, 1999.

Allen, Harry. "Planet Rock: *Star Wars* and Hip Hop." *A Galaxy Not So Far Away.* Ed. Glenn Kenny. New York: Henry Holt and Company, 2002.

Allnut, Frank. *The Force of Star Wars.* Van Nuys: Bible Voice, 1977.

Arnold, Alan. *Once Upon a Galaxy: A Journal of the Making of the Empire Strikes Back.* New York: Del Rey, 1980.

Ashcroft, Bill, Gareth Griffith, and Helen Tiffin. *The Empire Writes Back.* London: Routledge, 1989.

Baker, Bob. "The Real First Family." *Los Angeles Times.* 16 February 2003. E1, E34.

Barbour, Ian. *Myths, Models and Paradigms: A Comparative Study in Silence and Religion.* New York: Harper, 1974.

Barthes, Roland. *Mythologies.* Trans. Annetta Lavers. New York: Hill and Wang, 1972.

Basinger, Jeanine. *The World War II Combat Film: Anatomy of a Genre.* New York: Columbia UP, 1986.

Baxter, John. *Mythmaker: The Life and Work of George Lucas.* New York: Avon, 1999.

Berger, Arthur Asa. *Manufacturing Desire: Media, Popular Culture and Everyday Life.* New Brunswick: Transaction, 1996.

Bernardi, Daniel Leonard. *Star Trek and History: Race-ing Toward a White Future.* New Brunswick: Rutgers UP, 1998.

Bettelheim, Bruno. "The Art of Moving Pictures." *Harpers* 263.1577 (October 1981): 80–83.

Bhabha, Homi. "Remembering Fanon: Self, Psyche, and the Colonial Condition." *Remaking History.* Eds. Barbara Kruger and Phil Mariani. Seattle: Bay Press, 1989. 131–148.

Bing, Jonathan. "Inside Moves: Next 'Star Wars' Aims to Avoid Racial Stereotypes." *Daily Variety.* 9 February 2000. 3.

_____. "Lucasfilm Searches for Politically Correct Galaxy." *Variety.* 14–28 February 2000. 8.

Biskind, Peter. *Easy Riders, Raging Bulls.* New York: Simon and Schuster, 1998.

Boehmer, Elleke. *Colonial and Postcolonial Literature.* Oxford: Oxford UP, 1995.

Bogle, Donald. *Toms, Coons, Mulattoes, Mammies, & Bucks: An Interpretive History of Blacks in American Film.* Fourth ed. New York: Continuum, 2002.

Boucher, Geoff. "Gone to the Dark Side." *Los Angeles Times* (10 May 2005): E1, E10.

Bouzereau, Laurent, ed. *Star Wars: The Annotated Screenplays.* New York: Del Rey, 1997.

_____, and Jody Duncan. *Star Wars: The Making of Episode I: The Phantom Menace.* New York: Del Rey, 1999.

Bradberry, Grace. "Next *Star Wars* Film to Feature Black, White, and Greene." *Ottowa Citizen.* 12 February 2000. A3.

Brandon, James. *Kabuki: Five Classic Plays.* Honolulu: U Hawaii P. 1992.

Brantlinger, Patrick. *Dark Vanishings: Discourse on the Extinction of Primitive Races, 1800–1930.* Ithaca: Cornell UP, 2003.

_____. *Rule of Darkness, British Literature and Imperialism, 1830–1914.* Ithaca: Cornell UP, 1988.

Brooker, Will. *Using the Force: Creativity, Community and Star Wars Fans.* New York: Continuum, 2002.

Buhler, James. "*Star Wars*, Music and Myth." *Music and Cinema.* Ed. James Buhler, Caryl Flinn, and David Neumeyer. Hanover: Weslyan UP, 2000.

Cameron, Kenneth M. *Africa on Film: Beyond Black and White.* New York: Continuum, 1994.

Campbell, Joseph. *The Masks of God: Creative Mythology.* New York: Arkana, 1968.

_____, with Bill Moyers. *The Power of Myth.* New York: Doubleday, 1988.

Carson, Tom. "Jedi Uber Alles." *A Galaxy Not So Far Away.* Ed. Glenn Kenny. New York: Henry Holt and Company, 2002.

Castaneda, Carlos. *Tales of Power.* New York: Simon and Schuster, 1974.

Champlin, Charles. *George Lucas: The Creative Impulse.* New York: Harry N. Abrams, 1992.

Chan, Jachinson. *Chinese American Masculinities: From Fu Manchu to Bruce Lee.* New York: Routledge, 2001.

Chen, Tina. "Dissecting the 'Devil Doctor': Stereotype and Sensationalism in Sax Rohmer's Fu Manchu." *Re/collecting Early Asian America: Essays in Cultural History.* Eds. Josephine Lee, Imogene L. Lim, and Yuko Matsukawa. Philadelphia: Temple UP, 2002. 218–237.

Chute, David, and Cheng-sim Lim, eds. *Heroic Grace: The Chinese Martial Arts Film.* Los Angeles: UCLA Film and Television Archive, 2003

Clooney, Nick. *The Movies That Changed Us.* New York: Atria, 2002.

Colebatch, Hal. *Return of the Heroes.* Perth: Australian Institute for Public Policy, 1990.

Crawford, Kryten. "The 'Star Wars' Blitzkrieg" CNN.com <http://money.cnn.com/2005/05/13/news/newsmakers/starwars/index.htm>. 13 May 2005.

Crow, Brian with Chris Banfield. *An Introduction to Postcolonial Theatre.* Cambridge: Cambridge UP, 1996.

Dante. *Inferno.* Trans. Allen Mandelbaum. New York: Bantam, 1980.

Davidson, Basil. *The African Genius.* Boston: Little, Brown and Company, 1969.

Derian, James Der. *Virtuous War.* Boulder: Westview, 2001.

Desser, David. "The Martial Arts Film in the 1990s." *Film Genre 2000.* Ed. Wheeler Winston Dixon. Albany: State U of New York P, 2000.

Dietrich, Matthew. "*Star Wars* Draws One Writer's Outrage." *State Journal-Register.* 6 June 1999. 52.

Dorfman, Ariel and Armand Mattelart. *How to Read Donald Duck: Ideology in the Disney Comic.* Rev. ed. Trans. David Kanzle. New York: International General. 1991.

Edwards, Ted. *The Unauthorized Star Wars Compendium.* Boston: Little, Brown and Company, 1999

Fanon, Frantz. *Black Skin White Masks.* Trans. Charles Lam Markmann. New York: Grove, 1967.

_____. *A Dying Colonialism.* Trans. H. Chevalier. New York: Grove, 1965.

_____. *Toward the African Revolution.* Trans. H. Chevalier. New York: Grove, 1988.

_____. *The Wretched of the Earth.* Trans. Constance Farrington. New York: Grove, 1963.

Farb, Peter. *Word Play: What Happens When People Talk.* New York: Vintage, 1973.

Ferlita, Ernest, and John R. May. *Film Odyssey: The Art of Film as Search for Meaning.* New York: Paulist Press, 1976.

Fischer-Schreiber, Ingrid. *The Shambhala Dictionary of Taoism.* Trans. Werner Wünsche. Boston: Shambhala, 1996.

Foster, Hal. *Recodings: Art, Spectacle, Culture and Politics.* Port Townsend: Bay Press, 1985.

Fu, Winnie, ed. *The Making of Martial Arts Films as Told by Filmmakers and Stars.* Hong Kong: Hong Kong Film Archive, 1999.

Furhammar, Leif, and Folke Isaksson. *Politics and Film.* Trans. Kersti French. New York: Praeger, 1971.

Galipeau, Steven A. *The Journey of Luke Skywalker.* Chicago: Open Court, 2001.

Germain, David. "Sci-fi Themes Hit Closer to Home." *Los Angeles Times* (16 May 2005): E5.

Giroux, Henry A. *Channel Surfing*. New York: St. Martins, 1997.

_____. *Living Dangerously*. New York: Peter Lang, 1996.

Gleiberman, Owen. "Vader to Black." *Entertainment Weekly*. No. 821/822 (27 May 2005): 116–117.

Goodwin, James. "Introduction." *Perspectives on Akira Kurosawa*. Ed. James Goodwin. New York: G.K. Hall, 1994. 3–23.

Gordon, Andrew. "*Star Wars*: A Myth for Our Time" *Screening the Sacred: Religion, Myth, and Ideology in Popular American Film*. Eds. Joel W. Martin and Conrad E. Ostwald, Jr. Boulder: Westview, 1995.

Gordon, L.R., T.D. Shipley-Whiting, and R.T. White, eds. *Fanon: A Critical Reader*. Cambridge: Blackwell, 1996.

Gotanda, Philip Kan. *Yankee Dawg You Die*. New York: Dramatists Play Service, 1991.

Graham, Elaine L. *Representations of the Post/Human: Monsters, Aliens and Others in Popular Culture*. New Brunswick: Rutgers UP, 2002.

Green, Martin. *Dreams of Adventure, Deeds of Empire*. New York: Basic, 1979.

Greene, Eric. *Planet of the Apes as American Myth: Race, Politics, and Popular Culture*. Hanover: University Press of New England, 1998.

Hall, Stuart. "The Whites of Their Eyes: Racist Ideology and the Media." *Silver Linings: Some Strategies for the Eighties*. Eds. George Bridges and Rosalind Brunt. London: Lawrence and Wisehart, 1981.

Handy, Bruce. "The Force Is Back." *Time* 10 February 1997.

Hart, Harold W. *Weapons and Armor: A Pictorial Archive of Woodcuts and Engravings*. New York: Dover, 1978.

Henderson, Mary. *Star Wars: The Magic of Myth*. New York: Bantam, 1997.

Hoberman, J. "All Droid Up" *The Village Voice*. 44.20 (May 25, 1999): 125.

Iaccino, James F. *Jungian Reflections Within the Cinema*. Westport: Praeger, 1998.

James, Edward. "Violent Revolution in Modern American Science Fiction." *Science Fiction, Social Conflict, and War*. Ed. Philip John Davies. Manchester: Manchester UP, 1990.

_____. "Yellow, Black, Metallic and Tentacled: The Race Question in American Science Fiction." *Science Fiction, Social Conflict and War*. Ed. Philip John Davies. Manchester: Manchester UP, 1990.

Jan-Mohamed, Abdul R. "The Economy of Manichean Allegory: The Function of Racial Difference in Colonialist Literature." *'Race,' Writing and Difference*. Ed. Henry Louis Gates. Chicago: U Chicago P, 1985. 78–106.

"Jedi 'Religion' Grows in Australia." *BBC News World Edition Online*. <http://news.bbc.co.uk/2/hi/entertainment/2218456.stm>. Posted 27 August 2002. Accessed 13 April 2004.

Jenkins, Garry. *Empire Building: The Remarkable, Real-Life Story of Star Wars*. Rev. Ed. Secaucus: Citadel, 1999.

Jenkins, Henry. *Textual Poachers: Television Fans and Participatory Culture*. New York: Routledge, 1992.

Jensen, Jeff. "What a Long, Strange Trip It's Been." *Entertainment Weekly*. No. 820 (May 20 2005): 22–30.

Jewett, Robert. *Saint Paul at the Movies: The Apostle's Dialogue with American Culture*. Louisville: Westminster/John Knox, 1993.

John, David, ed. *Star Wars: The Power of Myth*. New York: Dorling Kindersley, 1999.

Kenny, Glenn, ed. *A Galaxy Not So Far Away*. New York: Henry Holt and Company, 2002.

Klein, Sally, ed. *George Lucas: Interviews*. Jackson: U Mississippi P, 1999.

Knapp, Lawrence, ed. *The Page of Fu Manchu*. 25 July 1997 <http://www.njedge.net/~knapp/FuFrames.htm>. Accessed 17 July 2004.

Koo Siu-fung. "Philosophy and Tradition in the Swordplay Film." *A Study of the Hong Kong Swordplay Films (1945–1980)*. Program of the Fifth Hong Kong International Film Festival. Hong Kong: Urban Council of Hong Kong, 1981. 25–32.

Krämer, Peter. "*Star Wars*." *The Movies as History*. Ed. David Ellwood. Trowbridge: Sutton, 2000.

Krouse, Erika. "The Chrysanthemum and the Lightsaber." *A Galaxy Not So Far Away*. Ed. Glenn Kenny. New York: Henry Holt and Company, 2002.

Kuipers, Dean. "Darth Shadows." *Los Angeles Times.* 19 May 2005: E28–31.

Lao Tzu. *Tao Te Ching* Trans. D.C. Lau. New York: Penguin, 1963.

Lau, Shing-hon, ed. *A Study of the Hong Kong Martial Arts Film.* Hong Kong: 4th Hong Kong International Film Festival / Urban Council, 1980.

Lefkowitz, Mary. *Greek Gods, Human Lives: What We Can Learn from Myths.* New Haven: Yale UP, 2003.

Le Guin, Ursula K. *Dancing at the Edge of the World: Thoughts on Words, Women, Places.* New York: Grove, 1989.

_____. *The Dispossessed.* New York: Harper and Row, 1974.

_____. *The Word for World Is Forest.* New York: Berkeley, 1976.

_____, trans. *Tao Te Ching: A Book about the Way and the Power of the Way.* Boston: Shambala, 1998.

Leiter, Samuel L. *The New Kabuki Encyclopedia.* Westport: Greenwood, 1997.

Lemire, Christy. "At the Movies: 'Star Wars: Episode II — Attack of the Clones.'" *Associated Press.*

Leo, John. "'Menace' Stereotypes." *Washington Times.* 11 July 1999. B3.

Leong, Mo-ling, ed. *A Study of the Hong Kong Swordplay Film, 1945–1980.* Hong Kong: 5th Hong Kong International Film Festival / Urban Council, 1981.

Lev, Peter. *American Films of the 70s: Conflicting Visions.* Austin, U Texas P, 2000.

Lewis, Jon. "Perspective: *Return of the Jedi.*" *Jump Cut* 30 (1984): 3–6.

Liu, James J.Y. *The Chinese Knight Errant.* Chicago: U Chicago P, 1967.

Logan, Bey. *Hong Kong Action Cinema.* London: Titan Books, 1995.

Lucas, George. *Star Wars: Episode I The Phantom Menace Illustrated Screenplay.* New York: Del Rey, 1999.

"Lucas Blew It with Jar Jar" *Toronto Star.* 11 June 1999. E1.

Luceno, James. *Star Wars: Revenge of the Sith: The Visual Dictionary.* New York: Dorling Kindersley, 2005.

Makey-Kallis, Susan. *The Hero and the Perennial Journey Home in American Film.* Philadelphia: U Pennsylvania P, 2001.

Makino, Seiichi, and Michio Tsutsui. *A Dictionary of Basic Japanese Grammar.* Tokyo: Japan Times, 1989.

Maslin, Janet. "In the Beginning, the Future." *New York Times.* 19 May 1999. E1.

Maxford, Howard. *George Lucas Companion.* London: BT Batsford, 1999.

Maynard, Richard A., ed. *The Black Man on Film: Racial Stereotyping.* Rochelle Park: Hayden Book Company, 1974.

Media Action Network for Asian Americans. "Restrictive Portrayals of Asians in the Media and How to Balance Them." <http://www.manaa.org/articles/stereo. html> 9 July 2003.

Michalak, Laurence. *Cruel and Unusual: Negative Images of Arabs in American Popular Culture.* Washington, D.C.: American-Arab Anti-Discrimination Committee, 1983.

Miller, Walter James. "Afterword." *20,000 Leagues Under the Sea.* Jules Verne. Trans. Mendor T. Brunetti. New York: Signet, 2001.

Mills, Jeffrey H. "*Star Trek IV*: The Good, The Bad, and the Unquenched Thirst." *The Best of Trek #15.* Eds. Walter Irwin and G.B. Love. New York: ROC, 1990. 126–136.

Milton, John. *Paradise Lost and Paradise Regained.* Ed. Christopher Ricks. New York: Signet, 1968.

Mishra, Vijay, and Bob Hodge. "What Is Post-Colonialism?" *Colonial Discourse and Post-Colonial Theory: A Reader.* Patrick Williams and Laura Chrisman, eds. New York: Columbia UP, 1999.

Mitchell, Elvis. "Works Every Time." *A Galaxy Not So Far Away.* Ed. Glenn Kenny. New York: Henry Holt and Company, 2002.

Moy, James S. *Marginal Sights: Staging the Chinese in America.* Iowa City: Iowa UP, 1993.

Moyers, Bill. "Of Myth and Men: An Interview with George Lucas." *Time.* April 26, 1999. 90–94.

Okuda, Michael, Denise Okuda, and Debbie Mirek. *The Star Trek Encyclopedia.* New York: Pocket Books, 1994.

"Overview: 1985 — Hollywood's Banner Year for Martial Arts Movies" *Inside Kung Fu Presents the Best of Martial Arts Movies,* January 1985: 14–17.

Page, Clarence. "Phantom Menace: War of the Stereotypes." *Washington Times.* 4 June 1999. A16.

Pierce, John J. *Foundations of Science Fiction: A Study in Imagination and Evolution.* Westport: Greenwood, 1987.

Pollock, Dale. *Skywalking: The Life and Films of George Lucas.* Rev. ed. New York: DaCapo Press, 1999.

Prasro, Sheridan. *The Asian Mystique.* New York: Public Affairs, 2005.

Queenan, Joe. "Anakin Get Your Gun." *A Galaxy Not So Far Away.* Ed. Glenn Kenny. New York: Henry Holt and Company, 2002.

Read, Alan, ed. *The Fact of Blackness: Frantz Fanon and Visual Representation.* Seattle: Bay Press, 1996.

Reid, Howard, and Michael Croucher. *The Way of the Warrior.* New York: Simon and Schuster, 1987.

Reynolds, David West. *Star Wars Episode I: The Visual Dictionary.* New York: DK Publishing/LucasBooks, 1999.

Reynolds, Maura. "Senators Try for a Judicial Compromise." *Los Angeles Times.* 20 May 2005: A18.

Richie, Donald. *The Films of Akira Kurosawa.* 3rd ed. Berkeley: U California P, 1996.

Rinzler, J.W. *The Making of Star Wars Revenge of the Sith.* New York: Del Rey, 2005.

Roberts, Paul Craig. "Designer Face of Designated Demons." *Washington Times.* 14 July 1999. A16.

Robinson, Walter Ritoku. "The Far East of Star Wars." *Star Wars and Philosophy.* Eds. Kevin S. Decker and Jason T. Eberl. Chicago: Open Court, 2005. 29–38.

Rosenbaum, Jonathan. *Movie Wars: How Hollywood and the Media Conspire to Limit What Films We Can See.* Chicago: Acapella, 2000.

Roston, Tom. "Holy Sith!" *Premiere* 18.8 (May 2005): 52–60, 121–122.

Rubey, Dan. "*Star Wars*: Not So Far Away." *Jump Cut* 18 (1978): 8–14.

Rushing, Janice. "Evolution of 'The New Frontier' in *Alien* and *Aliens*: Patriarchal Co-optation of the Feminine Archetype." *Quarterly Journal of Speech.* 75 (1989): 1–24.

Ryan, Michael, and Douglas Kellner. *Camera Politica: The Politics and Ideology of Contemporary Hollywood Fiction.* Bloomington: Indiana UP, 1988.

Said, Edward. "Blind Imperial Arrogance." *Los Angeles Times.* 20 June 2003: M5.

_____. *Culture and Imperialism.* New York: Alfred A. Knopf, 1994.

_____. *Orientalism.* New York: Vintage, 1979.

Salewicz, Chris. *George Lucas Close Up.* New York: Thunder's Mouth Press, 1999.

Sardar, Ziauddin. "Introduction." *Aliens R Us: The Other in Science Fiction Cinema.* Eds. Ziauddin Sardar and Sean Cubitt. London: Pluto Press, 2002. 1–17.

Sasweet, Stephen J. *Star Wars Encyclopedia.* New York: Ballentine, 1998.

Scanlon, Paul. "The Force Behind George Lucas." *Rolling Stone.* 25 August 1977.

Scott, A.C. "The Performance of Classical Theatre." *Chinese Theatre from Its Origins to the Present Day.* Ed. Colin Mackerras. Honolulu: U Hawaii P, 1983.

Scott, A.O. "Kicking Up Cosmic Dust." *New York Times.* 10 May 2002. E1.

Seabrook, John. *Nobrow: The Culture of Marketing, The Marketing of Culture.* New York: Alfred A. Knopf, 2000.

_____. "Why Is the Force Still with Us?" *The New Yorker* LXXII.41 (6 January 1997): 40–53.

Seed, David. *American Science Fiction and the Cold War.* Chicago: Fitzroy Dearborn, 1999.

Seiler, Andy. "Something to Offend Everyone — Minority Groups Say Hit Films Fill Screens with Stereotypes." *USA Today.* 28 June 1999. 1D.

Shaheen, Jack G. *Reel Bad Arabs: How Hollywood Vilifies a People.* New York: Olive Branch, 2001.

Shakespeare, William. *The Riverside Shakespeare.* Ed. G. Blakemore Evans. Boston: Houghton Mifflin, 1974.

Sheehan, Neil. *A Bright Shining Lie: John Paul Vann and America in Vietnam.* London: Jonathan Cape, 1989.

Shohat, Ella. "Gender and Culture of Empire: Toward a Feminist Ethnography of the Cinema." *Visions of the East: Orientalism in Film.* Ed. Matthew Bernstein and Gaylyn Studler. New Brunswick: Rutgers UP, 1997.

Simon, Richard Keller. *Trash Culture: Popular Culture and the Great Tradition.* Berkeley: U California P, 1999.

Slavicsek, Bill. *A Guide to the Star Wars Universe.* Rev. ed. New York: Del Rey, 1994.

Smith, Kevin. *Clerks and Chasing Amy: Two Screenplays.* New York: Hyperion, 1997.
_____. "Married to the Force." *A Galaxy Not So Far Away.* Ed. Glenn Kenny. New York: Henry Holt and Company, 2002. 70–76.

Staples, Brent. "Shuffling Through the *Star Wars.*" *New York Times.* 20 June 1999. sec. 4, 14.

Stephens, William O. "Stoicism in the Stars: Yoda, the Emperor and the Force." *Star Wars and Philosophy.* Eds. Kevin S. Decker and Jason T. Eberl. Chicago: Open Court, 2005. 16–28.

Thornton, Mark. "*Star Wars* and Our Wars," 3 May 2002, Ludwig von Mises Institute, <http:www.mises.org/fullarticle.asp?control=948> 30 December 2002.
_____. "*Star Wars* Revisited," 7 August 1999, Ludwig von Mises Institute, <http:www.mises.org/fullarticle.asp?record=277&month11 > 25 February 2003.

Tiffin, Chris, and Alan Lawson, eds. *Describing Empire: Postcolonialism and Textuality.* London: Routledge, 1994.

Torgovnick, Marianne. *Gone Primitive: Savage Intellects, Modern Lives.* Chicago: U Chicago P, 1990.

Toto, Christian. "*Star Wars*: The Political Battlefield." *The Washington Times.* 19 February 2000. D2.

Turan, Kenneth. "It *Looks* Hot ..." *Los Angeles Times.* 16 May 2005. E1, E5.

Vebber, Dan, and Dana Gould. "Fifty Reasons Why *Jedi* Sucks." *The Unauthorized Star Wars Compendium.* Ted Edwards. Boston: Little, Brown and Company, 1999.

Verne, Jules. *The Mysterious Island.* Ed.

Arthur B. Evans. Trans. Sidney Kravitz. Middletown: Wesleyan UP, 2001.
_____. *20,000 Leagues Under the Sea.* Trans. Mendor T. Brunetti. New York: Signet, 2001.

Von Gunden, Kenneth. *Postmodern Auteurs: Coppola, Lucas, DePalma, Spielberg, and Scorsese.* Jefferson: McFarland, 1991.

Voytilla, Stuart. *Myth and the Movies.* Studio City: Michael Wiese, 1999.

Wetmore, Kevin J., Jr. "The Tao of *Star Wars*, or Orientalism in a Galaxy Far, Far Away." *Studies in Popular Culture.* 23.1 (October 2000): 91–106.

Windolf, Jim. "Star Wars: The Last Battle." *Vanity Fair*, no. 534, February 2005: 108–117, 166–167.

Winkler, Martin M. "*Star Wars* and the Roman Empire." *Classical Myth and Culture in the Cinema.* Ed. Martin M. Winkler. Oxford: Oxford UP, 2001.

Wittkower, Rudolf. "Marvels of the East: A Study in the History of Monsters." *Journal of the Warburg and Courtauld Institutes.* 5 (1942): 159–197.

Woll, Allen L., and Randall M. Miller. *Ethnic and Racial Images in American Film and Television.* New York: Garland Publishing 1987.

Wong, Eugene Franklin. *On Visual Media Racism: Asians in the American Motion Pictures.* New York: Arno Press, 1978.

Wood, Robin. *Hollywood from Vietnam to Reagan.* New York: Columbia UP 1986.

Woods, Bob, ed. *Star Wars: Episode I: The Official Souvenir Magazine.* New York. Topps, 1999.

Wyrick, Debra. *Fanon for Beginners.* New York: Writers and Readers, 1998.

Index